# From Voices to Results – Voice of Customer Questions, Tools, and Analysis

Proven techniques for understanding and engaging with your customers

**Robert Coppenhaver**

# From Voices to Results – Voice of Customer Questions, Tools, and Analysis

First published: April 2018

Production Reference: 2050718

Published by Impackt Publishing Ltd.
Livery Place
35 Livery Street
Birmingham B3 2PB, UK..

ISBN 978-1-78300-144-6

www.Impacktpub.com

# Credits

**Author**

Robert Coppenhaver

**Technical Editor**

Prajakta Mhatre

**Proofreader**

Safis Editing

**Production Coordinator**

Nilesh Mohite

**Copy Editor**

Safis Editing

**Cover Work**

Nilesh Mohite

# About the Author

 **Robert Coppenhaver** is a product management/marketing professional and is the founder of 5P Marketing, LLC. Currently he is a consultant to Denso Wave and is responsible for the sales and marketing activities for the OEM/ODM portion of their business. Prior to 5P Marketing, Robert was a director/VP in multiple companies with P&L responsibility for over $100 million. He has worked in the fields of industrial automation, energy management, real-time software, and safety technology during his tenure with Honeywell, Rockwell Automation, Wind River (Intel), and Draeger.

During Robert's career, he has trained marketing and product management professionals in organizations such as Honeywell, TDK-Lambda, ITT, Draeger, and was adjunct faculty for Marketing at Corporate College in Cleveland, OH. He is a proponent of using Voice of the Customer to create organizational value, and has personally been responsible for over $1 billion in incremental revenue in organizations deploying VoC best practices.

Robert enjoys training others on how to use VoC to create breakthrough products and champions continuous learning of new marketing and product management strategies and techniques.

# Contents

# > Preface

Early in my career, I was given a rather unique opportunity that would have a profound effect on not only my professional career, but my life. My employer at the time, Rockwell Automation, was trying to expand into other international markets where our market share was still very small. One such market, Japan, was in the middle of a manufacturing renaissance, as epitomized by the book The Machine That Changed the World, by James Womak. The book presented how Toyota and many other Japanese companies had embraced the teaching of Edward Deming to completely revamp their manufacturing processes. Where Japanese products and manufacturing were once regarded as junk, they were now manufacturing the highest quality and most efficient goods in the world.

My employer, Rockwell Automation, was a manufacturer of industrial automation and control equipment under the brand Allen-Bradley. Allen-Bradley had a very good reputation for quality in most of the world. Even the Allen-Bradley logo proudly exclaimed "Quality".

At Rockwell Automation, we prided ourselves on the quality of the products we produced and, recognizing the rapidly expanding market of Japan, we struggled to understand why our products did not enjoy more commercial success in the Land of the Rising Sun. During this same time period, we also entered into a partnering agreement with a company called Nippondenso.

Nippondenso was originally a part of Toyota but later became an independent company after World War II as the Supreme Command for the Allied Powers reshaped the Japanese automobile industry and Toyota was forced to spin off Nippondenso, although Toyota still maintained a sizeable minority share in the company. Nippondenso was, and still is, a large automobile parts supplier creating much of the components in a Toyota automobile. It would later expand to servicing the vast majority of automobile suppliers. While Nippondenso, now called simply Denso, was then largely an automobile parts supplier (with roughly 98% of their 2016 revenue of $40B coming from automobiles), they continued to explore other market opportunities and segments, creating divisions for robotics, data acquisition, and a division whose responsibility was to use expertise acquired from new technology in the automobile sector and apply it to OEM/ODM (Original Equipment Manufacturing/Original Design Manufacturing) markets.

It was a highly agreeable relationship between Rockwell Automation and Nippondenso. Nippondenso was looking for ways to expand their business by providing OEM/ODM design and manufacturing services and Rockwell Automation was trying to expand their product portfolio while setting up a sales channel for Japan. Rockwell Automation would contract Nippondenso to create products for the Japanese market based on the Rockwell Automation specifications, and Nippondenso would create a joint venture sales channel in Japan called AB-Denso to help sell both the newly designed products as well as the legacy Rockwell Automation products to the Japanese market. In particular, Toyota and Nippondenso's own manufacturing entities were seen as a significant opportunities.

After 3-4 years, Rockwell Automation had smaller, less expensive products produced by Nippondenso that were a better fit for the Japanese market, but still did not generate the volume of sales anticipated through the joint venture. Nippondenso explained that the new products were a great improvement over the original legacy products, but were still missing many of the features and the responsiveness exhibited by the Japanese competitors. Additionally, the quality was found to be substandard for the Japanese market. Rockwell Automation believed that they had more than enough of the key features to be successful and did not have a quality problem. They believed the issue had more to do with a lack of understanding how to apply the products in real-world applications than with any features or quality issues.

To resolve this issue, Rockwell Automation decided to send a member of their applications team to live in Japan and work with Nippondenso for three years to help train the Japanese staff and work with key customers such as Toyota on how best to use the Rockwell Automation technology in their applications. I was presented the opportunity and jumped at the chance to embark on this new adventure.

It took me very little time to realize that the Nippondenso view was the correct one. The Japanese engineers and staff, especially at Toyota and Nippondenso, were very well versed in applying automation technologies to solve real-world manufacturing challenges and they were every bit as good, if not better, than the engineers I had worked with in the USA. Rockwell Automation products were and still are considered world class with respect to quality, but were not at the same level of the Japanese competitors for the Japanese applications. Additionally, many of the features found on the Japanese-based automation products were missing from the offerings by Rockwell Automation, as they opted to focus on alternative feature sets required by other markets and customers.

My role changed multiple times during my stay in Japan as Rockwell began to realize that our products were not the global products we had believed them to be, but were really USA-centric and were designed and produced with the needs of the USA automobile market at their core.

Many in Rockwell Automation believed that the Japanese customers, and Toyota in particular, were the leading customers in the world and that if our products could satisfy their demands and applications, we could satisfy the vast majority of customer's wants and needs. Unfortunately, the will was not there to do a wholesale revamp of our products and offerings in order to be successful in Japan, so instead we offered incremental improvements, but never enough to capitalize on the larger market opportunity.

I did not realize it at the time, but I walked away with a number of methods and practices that would have a significant impact on the next phase of my career. I left Japan with an understanding of the Toyota manufacturing process, TQMS, Kaizen, competitive breakdowns, the five whys, and more. I learned how world-class customers think and make buying decisions and realized just how well customers can understand their applications and needs, but not have the ability to articulate these needs in a form that can be handed to an engineering team to develop. For that, a company needed a strong product management function to translate the customer wants and needs into product requirements that could be built.

As I rotated back to the United States, I was given the opportunity to join a team who was developing a next generation remote I/O system for Rockwell Automation. Then current remote I/O systems were either large and bulky with a lot of wasted space, or small and purpose built with little flexibility.

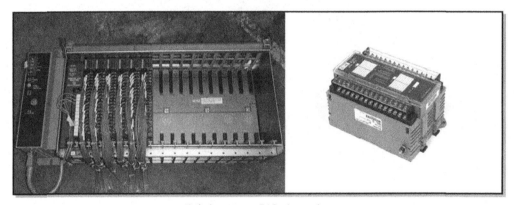

***Existing remote I/O alternatives***

With all the offerings in the market, the customers would need to install a large number of terminal blocks to accept every wire coming from the field devices the system was controlling/monitoring. The customer would then run wires from the terminal block through the panel to the automation device, whether it was a controller or a remote I/O system. This would require a large number of terminal blocks inside every panel. Additionally, there was a large amount of wire and space inside the panel allocated to running all the wires from the terminal block to the automation device, whether it was a controller or a remote I/O system as follows:

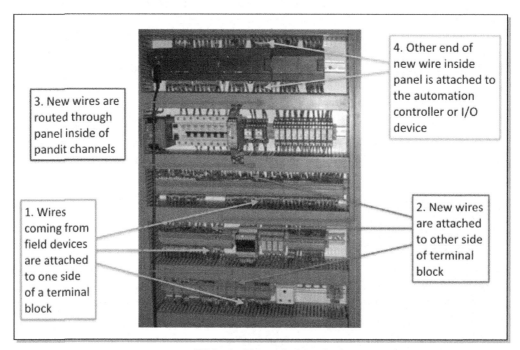

**Wiring inside a typical panel**

This system resulted in extraneous costs to the customer well beyond the price of the actual automation equipment. The customer needed to buy a large amount of terminal blocks and buy a larger panel to accommodate all of them. They also needed to run a large amount of wires from the terminal blocks to the automation equipment. This resulted in additional costs for the wire and channels to run the wire and even more space inside the panel. The larger cost was the manpower to label each side of every wire, run each wire inside the panel from the terminal block to the termination on the automation equipment, and then troubleshoot each wire to ensure they were run correctly. This system also resulted in hidden costs, as many times wires were misrun or mislabeled, resulting in start-up delays. Even after the system was started up there could be more hidden costs as each wire was a point of failure, and the more wires in a system, the higher the probability that a wire would vibrate loose or create an intermittent connection.

By the time I joined the team we already had a concept in place, which was derived through another joint venture we had with a Swedish company, Satt Controls. This next generation I/O system was very similar to another offering by the largest European automation supplier and my job was to go out and get market feedback to justify the large investment we had already spent on the technology licensing and tooling of this new product. I was given a list of questions to ask and a product mock-up to show the customers. Myself and a number of others from product management and engineering went out for our first round of interviews.

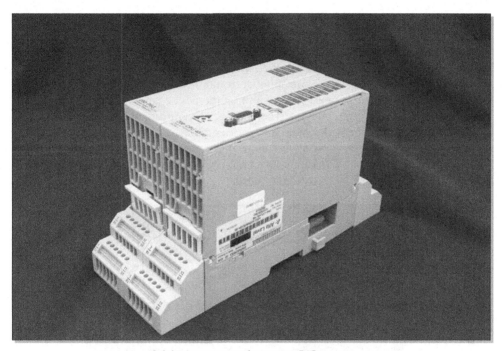

*Original next generation remote I/O concept*

Our first customer visits did not go especially well. After presenting the new remote I/O concept to the customers we met, most spent time offering criticism rather than providing feedback to the questions on our questionnaire. They explained that while the concept was somewhat different than what they were currently using, it did not offer significant advantages over the current offerings and would not have a compelling reason to change to this new product. They also shared with us that this concept was way too high and needed to be thin enough to fit in a standard 100mm deep panel.

Based on the first few visits' I began modifying our interview guide and started to ask more probing questions about what issues the users faced and what changes they would need to see with our current and future products to better meet their needs. I also asked them to help us understand how the perfect remote I/O system would look and operate. I slowly began to understand how the customers were focused on things like installation costs and total installed cost instead of simply the product price or some new feature. Many of the interview team derided me for moving too far from our original task, while others saw what I saw and realized the path we had already set for our next generation product was the wrong one and would result in a failed product if we attempted to bring it to market.

Due to other project demands, the team was streamlined to two people for the remaining customer interviews; my engineering project manager counterpart, Gregg, and myself. We continued interviewing numerous customers in both the United States and Europe in an effort to create a more global product. We continued to modify the interview guide as we went, continuing to learn more about customer needs and wishing to validate our findings with multiple customers. Soon, common themes began to emerge. The need for lower installation costs, the requirement for a reduced footprint inside the electrical panel, the flexibility to mount the I/O system in any orientation, and the reduction of waste and cost necessitated by "the ways we always did things" as opposed to how things should be. We took it upon ourselves to modify some of the original models into a system we believed would be closer to the customers' needs.

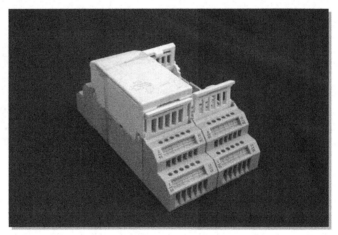

*Modified concept – reduced size and depth*

The customers we interviewed did feel like the modified models were better than the original concept, but still fell far short of what was required. They offered additional feedback that the product needed to have enough terminations for ALL the wires on the product and the need to have terminations on one side of the product instead of two sides. They also explained how space inside the panel was key to meeting their requirements and that they really wanted the same kind of flexibility in their I/O system that they had with their terminal blocks: buy only what they need today but add more capability later; flexibility to mount horizontally, vertically, or both; small footprint inside the panel; modularity for communications, I/O types and differing terminal block types; and ease of wiring.

We believed we had discovered the horrible mistake Rockwell Automation was making, and we believed that we had developed an understanding of what we needed to produce instead. We took our findings to our senior managers and our findings were flatly rejected. As was explained to us, Rockwell Automation had already invested over $3 million in this new concept and were not prepared to walk away from it. I was disappointed and dismayed, but asked senior management if we could continue gathering market input and they reluctantly agreed.

We continued our customer visits and research, paying particular attention to searching out the customers who were not necessarily the largest customers for Rockwell Automation, but were the ones pushing the envelope in creating more advanced manufacturing processes and systems. At that time, the US automotive companies represented the majority of Rockwell's business, but were not the ones pushing Rockwell Automation into new directions.

For this reason, we made the conscious decision not to interview them for this new development. They were already getting what they desired due to their buying power over Rockwell Automation and we did not consider them to be lead users, whose needs would help push us to creating innovative solutions to customer problems (although they have changed their approach considerably since that time).

In addition to continuing our customer interviews, we also took the approach of creating wooden models based on what we believed the customers were telling us they needed. These models, along with the models of the initial concept, were pulled out at the conclusion of each interview to gauge whether either concept met the needs of the customer.

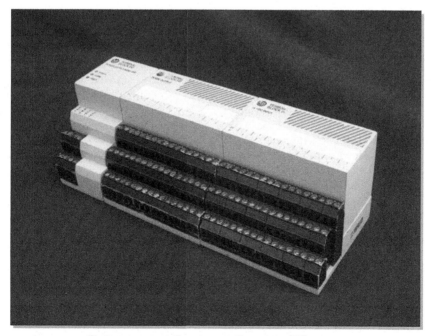

*Customer-generated next generation remote I/O concept*

This new customer-generated remote I/O concept appeared to meet many, if not all, of the requirements we had heard from our customers' including depth requirements, flexibility of communication modules and I/O types, and expandability without sacrificing space. Most importantly, by integrating the actual terminal block into the product design, we were able to eliminate the need for the customers to purchase and install terminal blocks in the cabinet (reducing space and costs) and run wires from the terminal blocks to the product (reducing expense and points of failure). We also discovered how installation costs would differ between the new customer-generated concept versus the current product and how much it cost to run wires inside the electrical panels. To help reduce the size and cost, we also determined what attributes were in the current product that the customer did not need, and most importantly, were not willing to pay for.

We went back to senior management, after meeting a multitude of customers representing multiple industries, segments, and applications, to share our findings. We had assembled the list of customers we had interviewed, our tabulated responses from those customer interviews, potential installation cost savings, and a series of direct quotations from the customers when reacting to the two potential concepts we were presenting at the close of the interviews.

We also explained the potential cost saving for the customer and how we could position this product. We explained that it would cost the customer approximately $1.00 to run each wire inside a panel based on labor alone. With the typical remote I/O system needing anywhere from 32-128 I/O points and each point needing 2-3 wires, we could save our customers $64-$384 using our system on labor alone. Then there were the benefits of more panel space, elimination of terminal blocks and wire channels, and reducing start-up time and costly failures once the system was running.

The overwhelming feedback we had showed that 95% of the customers greatly preferred the new concept versus the original concept, and we could save the customers a considerable amount of money in both materials and labor. From Rockwell's perspective, we could also extract a higher margin on this product versus our other products (and the alternative proposal) by charging a higher price. Our analysis showed we could charge a 10% premium over existing products and still have a compelling value proposition for our customers to save a large amount of money.

Presented with this feedback and analysis, the senior management team agreed with our findings and authorized us to proceed with the project, which was to be called Flex I/O.

Armed with the knowledge of the customer needs we had acquired during our extensive VoC research, we assembled a product team who shared our passion and spirit that was fueled by customer insight. Not only did we ultimately create a new category of product in the industrial automation space, but we did so at a much more rapid pace than the company had ever witnessed before. We went from wooden models to finished product in just over 2 years with 10 different catalog numbers at release...largely because we never had to revisit and re-write customer requirements, which many projects do, resulting in large time delays. As a result of the engineering project manager being so intrinsically involved in all the meetings and interviews, he also understood why we could not compromise on any of the attributes or size considerations we had heard from the customers. We knew what what the customer needed and what had to be done; we just needed to execute. When the engineering team believes as you do what needs to be done, you'll find there is no challenge that cannot be overcome. In the picture below, observe how the form factor of the wooden model and the final product are virtually identical. I can assure you that it was not an insignificant engineering challenge to fit the necessary functionality into a package this small, but as the engineering team believed we had to meet this size requirement the same way I did, they found creative solutions to every engineering challenge that was presented in following photo:

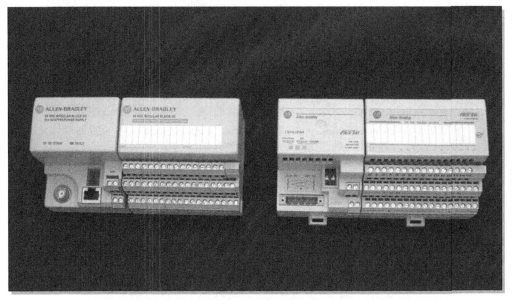

*Flex I/O wooden version 2 (left) and final released product (right)*

The feeling that we were doing something different and ground breaking was probably similar to how the first iPhone team felt. The freedom to do what is right as opposed to doing what we have always done resulted in innovations all through the development process, not only in the engineering function. This project alone helped to redefine the way Rockwell Automation did product development, documentation, packaging, marketing, and industrialization; and personally affected every member of the team.

The final Flex I/O next generation remote I/O concept resulted in a platform that not only met all the customer requirements, but did so in a package that was significantly smaller than the original next generation remote I/O concept. The following photo of the Flex I/O system (on the left) includes a power supply, communications adapter, an input card, an output card, and all the associated terminals for wiring from the cards to the field devices. In contrast, the original next generation remote I/O concept on the right included a power supply and communications only. You would still require an additional input card, output card, and terminal blocks to match the functionality of the Flex I/O system, resulting in a package size more than triple that of the Flex I/O system:

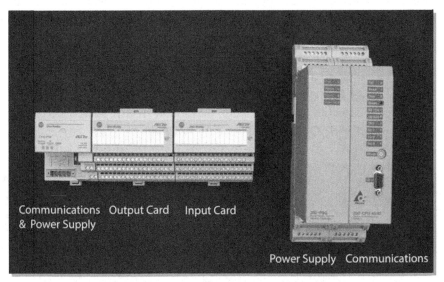

*Flex I/O - communications, power supply, output, and input (left) versus original concept – power supply and communications only (right)*

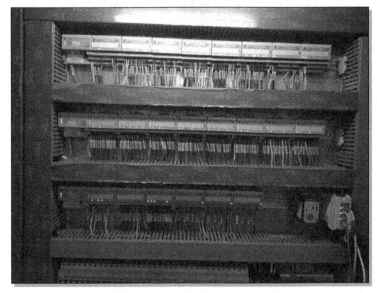

*Panel with 3 Flex I/O systems installed*

The results of our efforts speak for themselves. Flex I/O was an overwhelming success. The product was featured on the cover of Instrumentation and Control System Magazine. It also received an Editor's Choice Award from Control Engineering Magazine and a Product of the Year award from Plant Engineering.

The team was recognized internally for their achievements and was awarded the Rockwell Chairman's Team Award. The Chairman's Team Award was established to recognize the one team that best exemplifies outstanding performance of employee teams in its many businesses. The award emphasizes the importance of teamwork in customer responsiveness, quality improvement, enhanced productivity, and reduced lead times, and is presented personally by the Chairman of Rockwell.

Our results went far beyond the recognition the team and product received and also resulted in a large positive impact right to the core of Rockwell Automation. As envisioned, we were able to increase our profitability of this product line versus the other currently available products and used our customers' own analysis of cost saving as part of our marketing campaigns. Our initial estimate of $200M of sales in the first three years, which was considered unrealistic by management, was met and exceeded, much to their surprise. Since release, the product line has continued to proliferate with a plethora of new modules and derivations. The average sales of Flex I/O has been in excess of $100M/year, and total sales of Flex I/O and its permutations has exceeded $3B. Rockwell Automation, recognizing the impact the team had on internal processes and methods commissioned Boston Consulting Group to analyze what the team was able to accomplish and how we did it in an effort to try to develop new best practices for the rest of the organization.

That project has shaped my product management career and expertise exponentially and contributes significantly to this book. The following chapters attempt to summarize the things I learned during the Flex I/O project about VoC, and the knowledge and methods I have acquired since that first VoC project. It is my hope that you will be able to apply much of the learning I have gained to your product or initiative.

# What this book covers

*Chapter 1, Solving Problems and Driving Value with VoC,* We explore a short history of new product development and why many projects fail. We discuss why customer input is so important to the product development process and what it means to be customer focused. We also begin to define what is meant by VoC.

*Chapter 2, VoC in the Product Development Process,* We look at where VoC fits in the product development process and the major types of new products. We review the typical stage–gate process in new product development and how VoC can influence or drive each stage.

*Chapter 3, Laying the Groundwork,* We discuss some of the methods and tools to help understand your customers and markets. In this chapter, we review SWOT, Porter's five-force model, the BCG growth share matrix, customer segmentation, and competitive analysis.

*Chapter 4, Gathering the Customer Needs for Your Product,* We conduct a review of different methods and processes to gather customer feedback and insight. Methods discussed include surveys, interviews, focus groups, lead user analysis, and ethnography. In addition to an introduction of each method, we present the benefits and shortcomings of each approach.

*Chapter 5, The Interview Process – Preparation,* Here, we go through how to organize your VoC program, focusing on creating a plan, selecting your customers to interview, defining how many customers to interview, where to do the interviews, who will do the interviews, scheduling the interviews, and creating the interview guide.

*Chapter 6, The Interview Process – The Interview,* We discuss methods to collect customer information during the VoC interview, roles and responsibilities for each member of the interview team, practicing the interview before you meet the first customer, things to avoid in the interview, and ways to get the unspoken word through observational interviews.

*Chapter 7, Understanding the Customer's Voice,* We explore processing the customer data acquired during the VoC sessions to sort, prioritize, and translate the customer input into product requirements.

*Chapter 8, Validating the Customer's Voice,* We look at determining how the input received from the VoC can drive customer decisions in order to delight the customer, using tools such as Kano Analysis to help prioritize product features and finding out how to assign value to each of the perceived benefits the features bring.

*Chapter 9, Completing the Circle – Using the Customer's Voice in Your Organization,* We'll discover how to use the data generated from VoC to create actionable attributes and requirements for your product, and how to document these requirements into language the rest of the organization can use to create your new product using QFD. Once the product is defined, we discuss how to market it, assign value to its features, and price it so as to maximize profitability. Lastly, we create a value proposition for your product.

# Who this book is for

The audience for this book includes anyone who is interested in developing a better understanding of how customers can help influence product design and product success. Managers at every level as well and executives from every discipline will likely find tips and tools that can be deployed within their organizations to help drive informed product decisions. In particular, product managers, marketers, engineering managers, and business leaders who want to develop successful products and programs for their organizations that will solve a customers unarticulated needs will find this an indispensible reference document for their future VoC initiatives. While much of the book has a B2B orientation, the vast majority of the methods and practices are equally applicable to the B2C market.

# What you need for this book

The audience for this book does not need any particular knowledge or skill except for the ability to listen, and a basic understanding of their own products and customers.

# Conventions

In this book, you will find a number of styles of text that distinguish between different kinds of information. Here are some examples of these styles, and an explanation of their meaning.

**New terms** and **important words** are shown in bold. Words that you see on the screen, in menus or dialog boxes for example, appear in the text like this: "Clicking the **Next** button moves you to the next screen".

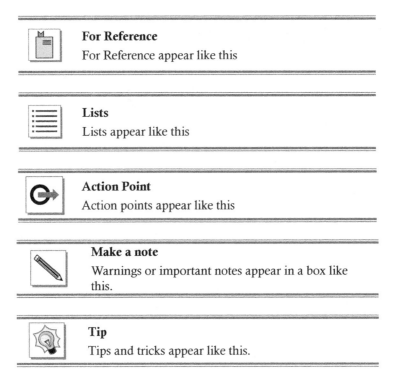

**For Reference**

For Reference appear like this

**Lists**

Lists appear like this

**Action Point**

Action points appear like this

**Make a note**

Warnings or important notes appear in a box like this.

**Tip**

Tips and tricks appear like this.

# Reader feedback

Feedback from our readers is always welcome. Let us know what you think about this book—what you liked or may have disliked. Reader feedback is important for us to develop titles that you really get the most out of.

To send us general feedback, simply send an e-mail to feedback@impacktpub.com, and mention the book title via the subject of your message.

If there is a book that you need and would like to see us publish, please send us a note via the **Submit Idea** form on https://www.impacktpub.com/#!/bookidea.

# Piracy

Piracy of copyright material on the internet is an ongoing problem across all media. At Packt, we take the protection of our copyright and licenses very seriously. If you come across any illegal copies of our works, in any form, on the internet, please provide us with the location address or website name immediately so that we can pursue a remedy.

Please contact us at copyright@impacktpub.com with a link to the suspected pirated material.

We appreciate your help in protecting our authors, and our ability to bring you valuable content.

# >1

# Solving Problems and Driving Value with VoC

*"The aim of marketing is to know and understand the customer so well that the product or service fits him and sells itself."*

*– Peter Drucker*

How is it that some companies seem to continually innovate and develop products that delight us? Why is it that they seem to know what it is that we need before even we do? How do they create products that we would never give up—even though they didn't even exist a mere five or ten years ago—so much so that some people would rather give up "intimate relations" than be without them?

The answer is grounded in a deep-rooted understanding of the customer and those customers' current and future needs. It's the ability to know your customers so well that you are aware of the problems they face and can anticipate their behavior in response to multiple situations. Successful companies develop a holistic view of the customer, and partnered with an understanding of technology to address their customer's problems develop new products or services that the customers gravitate to, and most importantly pay for. Understanding the **Voice of the Customer** (**VoC**) will not only let you understand how to build products that customers will buy, but will also let you create products and services that will delight your customers and solve their most pressing needs.

# Built to fail?

Innovation and new product development are, it can be argued, the lifeblood of a healthy organization. Without new products or markets, modern corporations face declining market share and ultimate death. Years ago, the concepts of **cost cutting** and **value engineering** drove many organizations to focus on driving out costs in current products at the expense of new product development. While this can yield some short-term advantages to the bottom line by way of cost savings, this will not help propel a company to growth and prosperity. One of the most impactful pillars of growth is a continual pipeline of new products and innovations. But even a pipeline of new products and innovations will not be enough to sustain a company unless those products can provide enough value for customers to buy them.

Until the 1980s, new product development was seen as the domain of scientists and engineers. It was these individuals, with their backgrounds in technology and science, who were seen as the stewards of seeing *what is next* and were given the responsibility of creating new and innovative products and technologies that would entice customers. Their new ideas would be developed into products and then *thrown over the wall* for marketing and sales. They would then be expected to create the demand and, ultimately, the orders for these new products which customers neither requested nor necessarily needed.

This philosophy of creating technological innovations driven by the engineering department instead of customer needs accounts for much of the reason so many products have been unsuccessful at launch. New products (products that have been on the market for three years or less) currently account for 25-30% of a healthy company's yearly sales, but many new products do not enjoy commercial success. According to a research study performed by the **American Productivity and Quality Center (APQC)**, just 53.2% of businesses' new product development projects achieve their financial objectives and only 44.4% are launched on time. Even more alarming, according to the **Product Development and Management Association (PDMA)**, only one out of nine new product concepts becomes a commercial success, 40% of new products fail at launch, 46% of the company's resources spent on **New Product Development (NPD)** go toward unsuccessful ventures, and 44% of a company's development projects fail to meet their internal profit objectives.

There are many reasons why products do not enjoy market success. Sometimes it is because the product has had technical difficulties, which compromised its success. Sometimes it is because the product is not positioned in the market correctly and the price is in conflict with the value proposition. Often, it is because the product does not meet the market window, and competitive products get to enjoy a first mover advantage.

There are a number of key things to avoid when developing new products to minimize the potential of failure:

> **Guessing**: Making the assumption that the company employees actually know more about what customers will buy than the customers themselves

> **Extrapolating**: Basing products and services on what current customers request rather than an understanding of unsolved needs that the larger market would gladly pay you money to address

> **Spinning**: Developing a product that does not really solve a customer need, but your organization attempts to create a need in the marketplace by investing in large upfront advertising budgets and armies of salespeople to deliver your message

Too many companies try to develop a product using information found solely within the walls of the organization. Either from the marketing expert who claims to know customers better than they do themselves, the executive who deems that we must create this new product because he/she knows best, or the product based on customer feedback that is delivered through the salesperson without a view of the entire market. The main reason new products are not successful *is because the companies did not have a clear view of who their customers were and/or what their customers want and need, as well as their willingness to pay for those wants and needs.*

There are a multitude of products introduced every year to the market that are *me too* products, or products that have simple incremental benefits to the customers. Some recognizable ones are the Microsoft Zune or the Blackberry 10, which were nothing more than incremental products versus the iPod and iPhone/Android phone. We also see examples of products that were obviously driven by engineers, developers, or the marketing department in the organization, such as many of the financial products offered by banks and brokerages, which are very confusing and customer unfriendly. Products can also be driven from the top down because management or the founder thought it would revolutionize the world, which was the vision for the Segway. Such products are destined to a niche or non-existent market. And too often, products are driven by one customer without any consideration to the larger market or non-customers who could provide much more revenue to the company offering the products. More often than not, these products are developed, launched, and go through their short life in search of a market.

New products that offer unique benefits and superior value to customers result in a *successful product* more than any other single factor. These products typically have four times the market share and four times the profitability of products that are undifferentiated from the rest of the market. As at least one study has shown, successful products have most, if not all, the following characteristics:

> ➤ A link to what the customer perceives as a *main* benefit
>
> ➤ Offers new and unique benefits over other products in the market
>
> ➤ Perceived to be a *better value* for the customer than other products
>
> ➤ Superior in meeting customer needs
>
> ➤ Superior quality as defined by the customer

All of these attributes of successful products share one key element in common. These are attributes as defined by the customer or the user, not by the engineering or RnD departments. A thorough understanding of the customer's needs and wants, as defined by the customer, with an eye toward the internal capabilities, competition, and nature of the market is what will define product success. Conversely, failing to understand the competitiveness of a market, your own development expertise, an unwillingness to understand the market, and, most critically, leaving the customer out of the product development process will spell certain failure. In more than 75% of product development projects, market studies are not performed at all, and the task that should be driving the future product definition, the marketing and customer analysis, account for less than 20% of the project, leading to multiple product failures.

# The fifth "P"

Everyone who has studied marketing in the last 50 years has been introduced to the **Four Ps of Marketing**. It was E. Jerome McCarthy who originally developed the mnemonic which acts as a functional and memorable classification system of the various elements of marketing. Originally, McCarthy defined the marketing mix as a *combination of controllable factors at a marketer's command to satisfy a target market*. Under the previous marketing model, we sold what we made or produced. Under the new model, we must sell what the customer wants. The old marketing mix looked at the 4Ps of marketing—product, price, place, and promotion. Whether you are thinking of setting up, starting, or expanding your business or selling any product or service, these four elements still need to be at the top of your mind all the time.

The first P is **Product**. This is what you are selling, whether it is an automobile, software program, diaper, or a service. But it is not just the product or service itself that is included in the product. It also includes the varieties of your product, the quality of your product, how it is designed, packaged, and branded. Anything that adds value to your product and any reason the customer may wish to buy your good or service is part of the product. This consideration must not be underestimated.

The next one is **Price**, exactly how much you are going to charge for your goods or service. You may believe this is merely the amount you charge customers to purchase it. While this is a key component, the price also includes the MSRP, wholesale price, volume discounts, special offers, incentives, payment plans, and credit terms. In short, it is anything remotely related to the money involved in this transaction.

The third one is **Promotion**. This is what most people think of when they think of marketing. Promotion includes advertising, the website and landing pages, direct mail and catalogs, e-mails and newsletters, selling, sales promotion, public relations, sponsorships, sales calls, brochures, inside sales, and many other aspects. All are parts of the promotion bucket.

The final P is **Place**. Place is also known as distribution. How do your clients find your product and where do you sell your product? Is it delivered to their door, is it in a retail store, or do they download it from your website? Place also includes the logistics for each of these things. If your product is sold in a retail store, how did it get there? How many of them are there? How soon do they need more inventory? Everything you need to consider in getting your product to your customer or to a place where your customer can find it is part of place.

It is not enough to define your product, place, price, and promotion unless you also understand whom you are selling to. Customer segmentation and defining your target market will be discussed in more detail in *Chapter 3, Laying the Groundwork*, but for now, it is enough to understand that the target customer is a critical part of any marketing mix. If my company were selling baby diapers, it would not matter how good my diapers were, how they were priced, where I sold them, or how much money I spent on promotion if my market was single people with no children.

And this is why the fifth P is so important. While many have suggested a fifth P in the past as a part of the marketing mix for such elements as **People** and **Process**, I believe a different P is required as so many products seem to ignore a key attribute for product success. *I believe the fifth P of marketing should be* **Problem***, and it refers to how well your goods or service can actually solve a target customer's problem or meet the need they have.* How many times have you seen a new product hit the market and wondered just who would buy this and why? Without an understanding of your customers, their problems, and how your product can address those problems, you will be rolling the dice with your company's money with each new product release.

And when I speak of customers' problems, I am not just referring to the problems they tell you about or the shortcomings they find with your products or your competitors' products. I am referring to the entire scope of potential problems the customer has and how your offering (which includes your goods or service, as well as distribution channel, website, method of promotion, sales process, customer support, and others) can help solve those spoken, as well as unspoken needs. The following are some obvious ways you can solve your customers' problems with your offering:

➤ Making their life easier

➤ Making them more efficient at their job

➤ Overcoming the issues they have in finding the products they need

➤ Resolving the difficulties they have in purchasing the products they need

➤ Reducing their total costs

➤ Giving them more free time

➤ Eliminating waste

➤ Providing them joy

It is through VoC that you will begin to understand the fifth P, the problems a customer faces and how you can create a meaningful solution to their needs. In a simple way, a well-executed VoC initiative will allow you to *provide a solution to the customer's needs (even if he doesn't know it yet) and allow him to buy it in the way he wishes.* And how well you can solve the customer's problems will be directly related to the value they will perceive as a result of buying your product or service.

# Customer input

Many may say that asking customers about product decisions is a waste of time and money, and argue that customers are not able to tell you what they want, or that they *don't know what they want until they see it.* They say that no customer would have told you they wanted a telephone, a microwave, or an iPad. Compounding the issue for development teams is that customers often do not know, or cannot communicate effectively, their actual needs and requirements. This is one of the major challenges facing businesses today. Because of this, businesses need to continue to find more creative methods of understanding customer requirements.

Part of the problem is that customers describe product attributes in **consumer speak** or **customer speak** while engineers and product developers talk in technical jargon which may be foreign to the consumer. If the customer says I want a *better computer,* are they asking for a computer with a faster processor, more memory, better memory management, a solid-state drive, increased bandwidth, or the ability to handle gaming as well as high-end business applications? If they ask for a more powerful car, do they want to go from 0 to 60 MPH in four seconds, or to have a top speed of 200 MPH, or do they just need the ability to tow a trailer?

Customers tend to talk in the language of needs, and it is our job, as product managers, engineers, or business owners, to develop the solutions to those needs. In the case of a microwave oven, customers were not asking for a microwave oven (the solution). Instead, they were saying they needed a way to heat up food quickly without drying it out and without taking the time or creating the mess to heat it on the range. As marketers, we need to get beyond the features or solutions or even specifications they ask for to understand the underlying needs they actually represent.

Ultimately, customers cannot always recognize or describe their needs in *solutions* or a specific set of attributes. As a result, customer needs often have to be *interpreted* from the *raw* data (but by using quotes whenever possible as they help to provide context). A customer might say they want a digital camera that is easy to use, with enough battery life to last all day, enough storage capacity to hold a full week's worth of picture shooting, the clarity to see the image on a large screen TV without being fuzzy, and the ability to do the occasional quick video. It is up to the marketing team, working with the engineering department, to define this product requirement into functional requirements, such as the number of megapixels, camera function and navigation, sensor size, battery life, composition, and so on.

While customers often cannot tell you the solution or the exact features or technical specifications they need in a new product, they are quite good at telling you their wants, needs, and the problems they are currently experiencing in their lives or work. What we need to do is to develop products inspired by customers, not designed by customers.

Sometimes, of course, there are innovations that address a customer need that customers had previously not known or been able to define, but such products end up being truly innovative and huge market successes. Twitter is one such example. However, if you uncover the thoughts behind products or services like these, you can see the customer voice loud and clear.

# Defining VoC

While all input from customers should be considered important to the business, I think it is an important exercise to describe what VoC is, and is not. VoC is not:

> ➤ A sales call
> ➤ An executive meeting with the customer
> ➤ A discussion at a tradeshow

➤ A random customer survey

➤ A customer satisfaction score

➤ Heresy from the sales team

➤ Golf meeting with the customer

The process of identifying customer needs and requirements must be a disciplined and repeatable one. This is where many companies go wrong. Organizations that go down this path with no tools or metrics, and a consistent philosophy for collecting, analyzing, and incorporating customer feedback into products, will ultimately waste their time and will abandon future VoC initiatives.

Wikipedia defines Voice of the Customer as a *market research technique that produces a set of customer wants and needs, organized into a hierarchical structure, and then prioritized in terms of relative importance and satisfaction with current alternatives.* While this is an acceptable definition, Gerald Katz, in *The PDMA Toolbook*, perhaps offers a more complete view of Voice. Mr. Katz writes that Voice of the Customer is:

➤ A complete set of customer wants and needs

➤ Expressed in the customer's own language

➤ Organized the way the customer thinks about, uses, and interacts with the product or service

➤ Prioritized by the customer in terms of both importance and performance

When we talk about a complete set of customer wants and needs, we are referring to any number of wants, needs, and desires, not just what the customer verbalizes. We are also referring to the way the customer uses and interacts with your product and competitive products, the benefits or lack of benefits your product brings, and the unarticulated set of problem solutions that could be had if only the customer had the right product.

There is a desire on the part of developers and even product managers to translate the **customer speak** into their own industry or company jargon. When doing this, the possibility of unintended manipulation or misrepresentation increases dramatically. The best alternative is to maintain the customers' vernacular as much as possible and preferably use direct quotes to illustrate the customer flavor and intent whenever and wherever possible.

When defining needs from customers, it is too easy to rank the ones you deem the most valuable higher based on your knowledge of the industry or your background. Don't fall into this trap. If you genuinely wish to understand the customer's voice, have them group the needs and rank those needs into primary, secondary, and tertiary buckets, and have *them* prioritize the needs statements you've developed by importance (or any other variable that resonates with the customer) so you can truly understand which ones the customer is most concerned about (and most willing to pay for).

# Being customer-focused

Much has been written about the customers being at the center of the business or the importance of being customer driven, and many companies have undertaken initiatives to become more customer focused. Many say that their most important job is satisfying the customer, but there is a large disconnect between the way senior managers think they are customer-centric versus the reality of how their customers actually rate them. Furthermore, the question remains that if you are only satisfying the customer, is this really enough to stop a customer from leaving for another product or company that could delight them?

Companies, whether it is through senior managers, product managers, or engineering managers, often think they know the markets and exactly what customers need. This can present a psychological barrier to unearthing the true customer needs, and often clouds the actual customer input they do receive. To become a true customer-centric organization, these barriers must be broken down and the organization must become a **learning organization** and invite the customer into the product development process.

The biggest factor in product launch failure to realize potential and meet the needs of the market is poor product definition. Although the best companies appear to spend more time with customers and conduct more in-depth market and customer analysis, the average time companies spend in the field is, on average, seven days. Seven days! While 70% of the product life cycle costs are determined during the product development phase, seven days is clearly not enough time to guarantee product launch success.

Companies can also fall into the converse trap of listening to their current customers and ignoring the larger market. These **customer-driven organizations** are actually current customer-driven organizations. Often, current customers represent a very small fraction of the total market. They tend to have different market problems than your non-customers and view the world through the eyes of your product, focusing only on incremental improvements to the way your current product performs.

Eventually, companies fall victim to taking small incremental steps to tweak features in the current offerings (because that's what the customers told them they needed) instead of taking the initiative to create new products and solutions that could solve the broader market's needs and frequently, the needs of their current customers as well. If you are only listening to the few, those that you currently do business with, you will end up creating a narrowly focused product to satisfy the needs of an ever shrinking market as the rest of the world is evolving. Eventually, you will lose many of these same customers as they migrate to the new and improved solutions offered by someone else.

Based on a number of studies, not only does a strong customer focus improve product success and profitability, it can also reduce the time to market. Market analysis and research does not add extra time, but rather it pays off with higher success rates and better time to market. Fully defining a product before engineering forces a company to commit their resources, which in turn helps the project stay on schedule, achieves better time utilization, and reduces the amount of scope creep and change of product specification. Most importantly, it is the best way to meet the needs of the market.

# Customer knowledge

An additional issue that can occur is a direct result of differing **pockets of knowledge**. Multiple organizations within the company tend to have a differing view of the needs of the customer. Senior managers, product managers, and engineering all have a view of the customer based on their interactions and history. Unfortunately, without direct customer input, they are nothing more than opinions and hyperbole.

Based on these customer understandings, someone or some group will suggest an idea for a product and infer it would be something customers would likely desire. The idea may have come from a sales meeting, a trade show, an executive meeting, as a reaction to a competitive offering, or it could be a technology-driven product from the company's own R&D group. The likelihood is that the product will have limited success with such a narrow view of the market.

There are, however, exceptions. It has been reported, but also contested, that much of Apple's success was solely due to the vision of Steve Jobs. Whether one accepts the premise that Steve Jobs was the innovative force behind most of Apple's innovations, or whether Apple has leveraged robust customer research and traditional VoC, one thing is certain. They understood the customer and were very tuned into the needs of the marketplace, both present and future. And while Steve Jobs may have been the driving force behind most of the successful products Apple has released in the last 20 years, I would argue that there are not many Steve Jobs in this world, and few have the insights into the mind of the customer that he had.

Although one would naturally think that doing market analysis and making the necessary product decisions before launching into full-scale product development would be almost second nature to companies both large and small, most products still fail to build into the product development process, the necessary steps that will ensure that customer needs are addressed before product development begins. In a recent study, fewer than half of the development teams thoroughly understood the user's needs at the start of a full-scale development, and the primary cause of major feature changes was reported to be the late discovery of customer requirements.

# Summary

So in conclusion, we have seen new product development evolve from the 1980s, where products were driven by the engineering organization, to an era where products are designed at the intersection of technology and customer need. However, many companies are still too internally focused and tend to organize around four main methods in taking products to market:

> ➤ Assuming company insiders know more than the buyers about what customers want to buy. Because you are an expert in the market or industry, you know more about your buyers and how a product can solve their problem or need.

> ➤ Basing products and services on what current customers request rather than an understanding of unsolved problems.

> ➤ Technology-focused products.

> ➤ Management "says so" products.

Many of these result in poorly defined products that miss the needs of the market, leading to many large expenses to the organization in not only lost opportunity, but also the necessity of creating a need in the marketplace by relying on expensive advertising or an army of salespeople, which results in more product failures than successes.

Companies that have taken the time to create a complete set of customer wants and needs, expressed these needs in the customers' own language, and have organized and prioritized this information consistent with the customers' thinking have been able to create goods and services that address their customers' needs before the customers even realize the need exists. These companies have enthusiastic customers, and have been wildly successful. Successful companies use VoC to get closer to their customers and understand their motivations, desires, needs, and problems.

Of course, it is not enough to collect this information from the customer. It is vitally important to take the customer's voice and inject it into your product development process so you too can create the next great breakthrough product, which is what we will be discussing in the next chapter.

# >2

# VoC in the Product Development Process

*"Your opinion, although interesting, is irrelevant..."*

*– "Tuned In"*

Most organizations have some sort of a process to develop products. Often, it is called a **new product development** (**NPD**) process or a **new product innovation** (**NPI**) process. Whatever your organization calls it, it is intended to guide the organization and development team from the beginnings of an idea through development, and ultimately, to the launch of the product and revenue generation. In some cases, there are very formalized approaches to this process, such as **stage gate**, **agile**, **iterative**, **waterfall**, and others. And in some cases, there is nothing more formalized than a spreadsheet or calendar system.

In organizations where VoC is used, most people would accept that VoC is a valuable input to the marketing requirements portion of the development. Far fewer people understand how VoC can be a key input to the product development process at every stage of the product's development, and how it allows an organization to better serve their market and be more responsive to changes in their marketplace. In this chapter, we will show you how to leverage VoC at every stage of the new product development, giving your product a much higher probability of success.

# Where does VoC fit in the product development process?

If you ask a typical product manager or business owner where VoC is used within their development process, they will typically highlight the following two key areas:

> **Idea generation**: Interacting with customers through interviews, as well as focus groups, to determine customer-generic needs and problems, and actively soliciting ideas from innovative and lead users during what is often referred to as the **fuzzy front end** (**FFE**) stage.

> ➤ **Design phase of the product**: Determining customer and user requirements with a user needs-and-wants study. Typically, this entails interviewing and listening to the customer or user to understand his/her problems and to determine both articulated and unarticulated needs, wants, and desires.

While this is not incorrect, customer input should not stop at the completion of the ideation or predevelopment market study phases of the project, but rather the customer input needs to be incorporated at all phases of the product development plan. While quality customer input is a critical piece of the upfront work, seeking customer input at critical stages of the development via concept tests, prototypes, beta trials, and other methods will also play a large role in the success in the new product innovation process.

Early customer input is critical to creating a successful product design. Multiple studies show the link between solid, up-front customer interaction and market analysis when creating a winning product. Successful firms tend to spend about twice as much time and money on the following critical up-front activities augmented by solid VoC:

> ➤ **Initial screening**: The first decision to enter into the project

> ➤ **Preliminary market assessment**: A first-pass market study

> ➤ **Preliminary technical assessment**: A first pass assessment of the technical complexity and the risk of undertaking the project

> ➤ **Detailed assessment**: A detailed market study including primary research with customers through VoC, as well as secondary research

> ➤ **Business case**: An analysis of the market potential, costs, and resource requirements needed to complete the development

As we have discussed earlier, a common complaint is that homework slows down the development process. Of course, the evidence points to a very different conclusion as studies have shown that if the homework is omitted, there is a much higher likelihood of product failure and the need to redesign the product. The additional time spent on project definition in this phase actually speeds up the development process by reducing the slippages caused by vague product requirements and unanticipated issues.

# Incremental, platform, and breakthrough products

There are typically three levels of new product development categories—**incremental**, **platform**, and **breakthrough** products.

Incremental products require few product modifications, and the customer experience is similar to that is generated by the current market offering. Incremental products often take the form of product extensions, cost reductions, value engineering, or minor product enhancements. Breakthrough products reflect significant product and/or customer experience changes. This often takes the form of significant performance enhancements, huge cost reductions, or totally new ways of performing a set function.

Many also see a third category of product in the field of product development, referred to as platform products. These products establish a base architecture for the next generation of products and require more money and resources than incremental products, but typically not as much as breakthrough products, although this is dependent on whether the platform product is multiproduct or multimarket. Good examples of platform products are evidenced in automobile manufacturers' usage of the same engine and slightly modified chassis to create differing automobile brands. The VQ35DE engine from Nissan is used in the Nissan Pathfinder, Altima, Maxima, Murano, Quest, 350Z, the Infiniti QX4, I35, G35, FX35, M35, JX35, QX60, as well as a number of vehicles from the Renault brand.

VoC can be a driver into your development whether you are creating an Incremental, Platform, or Breakthrough product; but the depth of the customer engagement and understanding will be significantly greater in the case of a platform or Breakthrough product than an Incremental product development.

# New product development

Regardless of which type of product you are developing, a systematic process for moving a new product from idea through development to launch is required for all but the most minor incremental products. A structured development process allows the information gathered from the customer in the early stages of the process to impact and drive the product decisions made throughout the development, resulting in the largest benefit for the organization. According to an early PDMA study of 383 firms, the top companies are more likely to use some form of formal NPD process, and 60 percent of firms use a **Stage-Gate** process. This value of a systematic approach to new product development been further confirmed by another PDMA study in 2012, where the best companies, as defined by those who had higher rates of product success, higher profits and more sales, were 30% to 50% more likely to have used a structured NPD process than those who did not. These organizations also initiated only four ideas for each successful market commercialization success, as opposed to the rest who initiated nine ideas to generate one commercial success. The conclusion is that the best do not realize more success simply from sheer number of projects, but by being more effective throughout the development process. The study also showed that for the best companies, more money was spent on the upfront activities that obtained information from the customer and market, including idea generation, idea screening, and business analysis, which allowed them to spend less on development, test and validation, and commercialization than other companies.

While the NPD process you use in your organization may be different than what I will use as an illustration, the concepts of how to use VoC in each area will apply whether you use fewer gates, more gates, or a different product approval process altogether. The key is to provide a consistent framework for new product development that also provides quantitative checkpoint criteria in line with the business strategy, a well-defined management decision process, and, most importantly, a method of linking the needs of the market and the customer with the development design and process optimization decisions during each stage of the development.

The following is a typical **Stage-Gate new product development process**, which I will use for the purposes of our discussion:

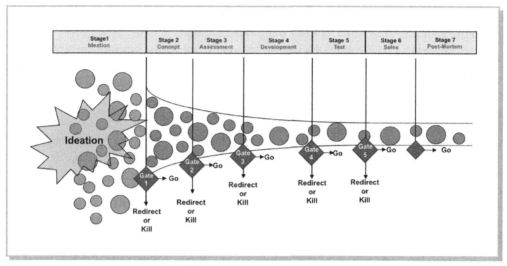

*Figure 2.1: Stage-gate process*

As you can see, a typical NPD process would include an **Ideation** stage, followed by **Concept**, **Assessment**, **Development**, and **Readiness,** followed by **Launch**. Throughout each stage, customer input through the VoC process is key to ensuring that the products you develop will actually serve the needs of the market (or, as a previous manager of mine would say, "This is where we'll see if the dogs eat the dog food"). After each stage, there is a decision gate where the organization must decide on whether to go or kill— that is, whether continue funding for this development or kill it and reallocate those resources to a better opportunity.

# Stage 1 – Ideation

The first stage is Ideation. Ideation is the creative process of generating, developing, and communicating new ideas, and is often associated with concepts such as brainstorming or problem solving. While there is never a shortage of new product extensions or line extensions, more and more of management is focused on creating the next breakthrough idea that will catapult the organization to success. In most instances, coming up with new ideas for products or services is not a problem for most entities. Even when businesses are declining or are being downsized, there is never a shortage of new ideas. The problem for businesses is selecting the right ideas to pursue that will be consistent with the brand, align with the business strategy, and generate the proper short-term and long-term revenue. Making the right product and service selections is critical to the future health and vitality of the business, and is one of the most important decisions a business can make. While one can assume there is never a shortage of new product ideas, the quality of these ideas is often lacking, resulting in mediocre projects and lackluster results.

New product ideas in the ideation stage can come from a multitude of sources. One such source is often a technology-driven idea from the research and development department of the organization, where a new technological discovery is looking for a customer problem to solve. You tend to see a fair amount of these product solutions in engineering-driven organizations. You will also often see ideas come about directly as an outgrowth of the organization's product strategy, where management has decided on a new market segment or customer target. Another main area for ideas, and potentially the most damaging for the organization, is from the sales force, whose ideas tend to focus on one customer's short-term need with neither an eye toward the technology nor the market as a whole.

While there are a number of good ideas that do come from within the organization, the best predictor of market success is whether the ideas are driven by customer need. A good starting point is to ask your customers about their market or industry to see if there are changes or new market dynamics. Understanding the industry where your customers are working or competing in and the changes that are occurring there is key in identifying the emerging needs in the market and where to focus your internal resources.

The concept of VoC in the discovery stage is often less structured than what we will see in the later stages of development. Some of the questions to ask your customers in the discovery stage could be the following:

➤ What changes are occurring in your market(s) and how does that affect your business?

➤ What new opportunities do you see from these new market dynamics?

➤ What new difficulties or roadblocks do you see from these new market dynamics?

➤ How will you react as a business to these trends, both positively and negatively?

➤ What other outside influences could affect these market dynamics both positively and negatively, and how?

What we are trying to do with this line of questioning is to identify your customer's problems, unmet needs, and unarticulated needs. While there is less structure than the later phases of the VoC research, the critical point is to listen to the customer's problems (both articulated and unarticulated) and understand their business and processes.

If you are close enough to the customer, and he is willing, it may also be a worthwhile exercise to work with the customer in applying Porter's five force model to their industry. In the Porter Five Force model, we work with the customer to understand the effects of the following market dynamics on their business:

➤ Barriers to entry

➤ Bargaining power of suppliers

➤ Bargaining power of buyers

➤ Threat of substitutes

➤ Competitors

An effective VoC methodology to deploy during the ideation stage, if you have the time and money, is *day in the life* research. With this research, you spend time observing and, if fortunate enough, participating in the customer's day. This gives the researcher an ability to observe nuances and innuendo, which may otherwise have gone unnoticed by the researcher or even the customer. This research can be as short as an hour, spent observing how a customer installs a new piece of equipment, or could take months of observation, where you are observing an operator or staff of employees. If you are in a B2B market, focus on the customer's workflow and how she uses your product to perform her daily tasks. Look for changes that could be made to make your customer more efficient and effective. Also make sure that you collect any information about your product during the observation, both what the customer likes as well as what they do not like when interacting with your product. This research technique, also called **anthropological research**, will be covered in more detail in *Chapter 3, Laying the Groundwork.*

---

**Make a note**

An interesting side note worth sharing is the additional benefit from anthropological research in the area of unintended consequences that many do not see. By observing your customer and how they use your product, you will often find that the customer uses your product in a way that it was neither intended nor designed for, but the customer had a need that was not fulfilled and had to resort to a solution that you were not even aware existed.

---

If you are fortunate enough to be in an industry where there are obvious *leaders* or *innovators* and you have the good fortune to have a good relationship with one or more of them, I would highly encourage you to use them as part of your VoC research in the Ideation stage. Often, the leaders and innovators are where they are because they have led the market in their own products or solutions. As such, they often have needs and problems that are well ahead and beyond the needs and problems of the larger market. By addressing the needs, problems, and unarticulated needs of this customer segment, you are able to get a jump on the future needs of the larger market. One-on-one interviews with this group will often lead to significant product breakthrough, but if you are in a position to host a workshop with multiple lead users and your key in-house marketing and engineering teams to define their problems and future product concepts, I think you will find it can be worth the incremental time and expense.

The Concept stage of a new product development will take the ideas you have gathered in the Ideation stage and sort and prioritize those ideas into a list of the ones that are most worthwhile investing in. The purpose behind the first gate between the Ideation stage and the Concept stage is to take a first pass at the long list of ideas and determine which ones should be considered for additional investment. As we pass through this gate we decide whether this idea is worthy of going to the Concept stage of development, where we will invest additional time and resources getting a preliminary view of this product, from both the business side of the organization to begin to define the product and opportunity and from the technical side of the organization, where we begin to define the technical feasibility and risk.

# Gate 1

Gate 1 is considered a *preliminary* commitment to the project. It often has a handful of key deliverables the project should or must meet before moving through the gate, often including strategic alignment, opportunity size, market attractiveness, competitive differentiation, technical feasibility, and fit to the organization's capabilities. The gate deliverables are tenuous at best, and further research is required to flush these out in more detail in a later stage.

Just as the Ideation stage has a gate allowing the project to pass to the Concept stage, each later stage will have an accompanying gate allowing the project to pass to the next stage of the process. In the interest of brevity, for each of the following stages, I will also describe the information required to exit and pass through the gate as the project goes to the next stage in the development process as part of the stage description.

# Stage 2 – Concept

The concept stage is the first time we allocate resources to the project with the intention of determining the project's business and technical worth. This is not meant to be a time-consuming nor expensive stage, and often, the stage is bound by organizational direction to spend no more than $x$ days or $x$ hours on doing the preliminary assessments. In this stage, we typically have three key deliverables.

The first two are a **preliminary technical assessment** and a **preliminary financial assessment**. In the preliminary technical assessment, we perform a limited technical feasibility study and highlight possible technical risks, which should be done with the development team. The financial assessment is a "back of the envelope" financial analysis looking at estimates of expected sales, costs, and investments. It is designed to be a reality check as to whether this investment has any possibility of providing a return to the organization.

The third is a **preliminary market assessment**. The market assessment provides a limited view into the market dynamics in an attempt to determine if the proposed product has the possibility of commercial success. The preliminary market assessment typically will attempt to define market attractiveness and potential market segments, target markets, and growth opportunity.

While much of the Concept stage is done with minimal costs and mostly desk and internet research, there is an opportunity, and I would recommend that you consider this option, to inject some limited VoC into the development at this point. It is worthwhile to expose this early concept to a handful of key customers who understand the market this product will play in and can provide some early feedback on the concept. These customers can also provide some insight into the overall market and attempt to solidify some of your assumptions of market attractiveness, segments, and growth rates. This will be less structured than later VoC initiatives and is only meant to be exploratory, but there is nothing like direct customer feedback when looking to move a project through the various gates and stages within an organization.

# Gate 2

Exiting the concept stage and going through gate 2 is much like going through gate 1, except that the expectations are that you will have more robust information than you had for the initial screening process. While you will not have detailed information, it is also expected that you will have a preliminary idea of the likelihood of product success, which could include input from the sales team and/or customers, a high-level financial analysis that shows potential impact to the organization's bottom line, and input from the development team as to the risk and probability of success from a technical/development perspective.

# Stage 3 – Detailed assessment

The Detailed assessment is where the bulk of the VoC takes place, as well as the remaining up-front work before development resources are committed. As we have discussed, this is the area where many projects fail in the rush to move on to development and get something launched. Often, organizations are so excited to commence development after the Ideation and Concept stages that many of the Detailed assessment deliverables are short-changed or product managers merely *check the box* in an effort to get through the gate.

The Detailed assessment stage, if done correctly, is the largest, most difficult, and expensive part of the predevelopment stages. Typically, the Detailed assessment stage will have a number of deliverables from three different parts of the product organization, the marketing team, the engineering/project management team, and the operations or manufacturing team. These deliverables will build the business case and justification, product deliverables, capital requirements, costs, resource requirements, and plan. In the following figure, you can see at a high level the various inputs required to create these deliverables and move into the development stage, as well as the typical part of the organization responsible for each. You will also notice that a high percentage of these deliverables also require some form of customer input or VoC to provide a complete picture of the market, competition, product requirements, sales assessment, and financial justification:

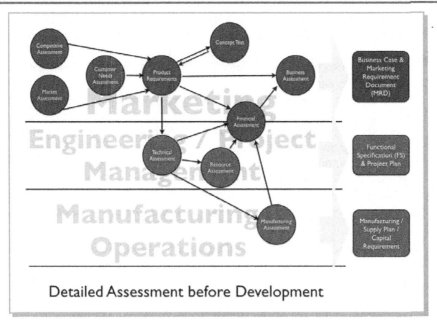

Detailed Assessment before Development

*Figure 2.2: Assessment*

Let's look at each of the deliverables in this stage and how customer input and VoC can help drive product success:

> **Competitive assessment**: This entails a detailed look at the competition, and could include a SWOT (a list of each competitor's **strengths, weaknesses, opportunities**, and **threats**), as well as your competitor's product features, pricing, and channel to market. By leveraging your customers' input, not only can you help to provide the details for a detailed look at your competition, but you can also learn what it is in the competitor's offerings that they truly value and how much they are willing to pay for these features. Customers can tell you the things you should emulate that your competition is doing, as well as things you should discard and how best to attack them in the market.

> **Market assessment**: This looks at general market dynamics, including market size, segmentation and segment size, buyer behavior, and trends in the marketplace. While much of this information would likely be gathered from secondary sources, who better to talk about buyer behavior than the buyers themselves? Insight into the target market and the market dynamics that could affect profitability and competitive response can be invaluable. Also, if you are fortunate to have innovative and lead customers, oftentimes they can share their view of market trends and the future direction of the marketplace well before the mass market makes the move.

➤ **Customer needs assessment**: When one thinks about VoC, this is one of the areas one tends to think about. This area includes VoC research to determine customer needs, wants, and preferences. This typically happens through face-to-face interviews and/or spending a *day in the life* with the customer. The engagement results in an understanding of the customer's likes, dislikes, and trade-offs when choosing a product design and functionality. It seeks to quantify what the customer's value drivers are and what the potential benefits are that your new product offers, as well as what they are willing to pay for these new-found benefits. This knowledge also helps in understanding future positioning and pricing for your product. Details of how to use various tools and technologies for capturing the VoC will be explained in *Chapter 4, Gathering Customer Needs for Your Product*, while preparing and conducting the customer interview will be explained in *Chapter 5, The Interview Process – Preparation* and *Chapter 6, The Interview Process – The Interview*.

➤ **Product requirements**: This is the other area one thinks about when describing how VoC fits into the new product development process. The product requirements definition will largely be an extrapolation and combination of the information gleaned in the customer needs assessment with an eye toward the competition and market dynamics gathered in those sections. Some would say this is where the magic begins as successful product managers and business people are able to bring together the needs of the customer with an eye toward the current competition, technical possibilities, and market dynamics. More information about understanding the needs of the customer and market and turning it into winning products will be covered in *Chapter 7, Understanding the Customer's Voice*.

➤ **Concept test:** This is the last, but very important part of the market testing section of the Detailed assessment gate. Before we move ahead with full-blown development, you must be certain that the new product will meet the target market's needs and wants better than the competition and will achieve your sales goals. Here, we test the product as we have envisioned it from the previous analysis and get direct feedback before committing large development resources by using wood block models, stereo lithography, and now 3D printers to help test the physical attributes and design of products in the market. 3D CAD drawings can also be helpful to show more complex products. In the case of software products, it is typically relatively easy to create virtual mock-ups and show UI design well before large development resources are committed. Oftentimes, no matter how good the market research and VoC done by the organization, the product will not be quite what the customer wants, or it might lack those key differentiators that would lead a customer to buy it over the competition. Most of the time, this is no fault of the marketer, as it is very difficult to understand the needs of the market when the customer does not always understand their own needs, or cannot verbalize them in a way we can understand. By doing a concept test, we hopefully reduce the likelihood of a failed product and also address what so many customers have told us in the past, "*show me the product and I will tell you whether I like it or not*".

As you can see in *Figure 2.2*, this is often an iterative process as the feedback gathered in this stage can be fed directly back into the product requirement deliverable to iterate to the next concept. We will also talk about concept testing in more detail in *Chapter 4, Gathering the Customer Needs for Your Product*.

> **Financial assessment**: Here, we will use the customer needs assessment to understand the customer value of your new offering and what they are willing to pay in conjunction with the market assessment and competitive assessment to determine the initial pass at a market price for your new products. We will also look at the technical and resource requirements to understand the costs to the business. Putting everything together, we can generate a detailed financial analysis and determine NPV, IRR, and others.

> **Business assessment**: In this area, we will look at the strategic fit of the new product we have identified and how well it aligns with the future goals and direction of the company. While the business/marketing side of the organization is conducting these assessments, the other parts of the organization must weigh the costs of developing the technology, deploying the capital equipment, and coordinating the deployment of resources. The business rationale for the product is conducted by reviewing the customer input we received in the earlier sections, weighing the potential market acceptance and profitability against the investment required by the business to create our new product or service. This must also be considered with an eye toward the question of making this product versus making another product, or making this product versus making nothing at all.

The typical deliverables for this stage in the development process is a marketing/business document outlining the customer needs, market trends, competition, product specification, alignment with company strategy, suggested pricing and profitability, investment, and market window. Oftentimes, this is referred to as the **marketing requirements document** (**MRD**). In addition, the engineering/project management organization delivers the technical assessment and resource requirements and plan while the operations manufacturing team delivers the capital requirements and manufacturing or supply plan.

Assuming the needs are robust, the payback is favorable, and the product is feasible, the product will likely pass on to the next stage unless there are competing projects that are a better investment for the organization.

# Stage 4 – Development

You've conducted all of the customer interviews, organized the data, and put it into your company's MRD or business plan template. You've passed through all of the gates leading into development, so you can stop focusing on the *customer* and start focusing on development. Right? Wrong!

Now is the time we find out just how well you have integrated your customer's voice into your development and how well you have paid attention to the message of your customers and the market. We will see if you have internalized the spirit of your customers, or if you simply went through the exercise of "checking the box" during the interview and MRD development.

In this phase, your development team is allocating resources and starting to spend a lot of money. Invariably, there will be areas of discovery and unforeseen roadblocks during this stage, which would have been hard to foresee in the initial assessments made by the marketing and engineering teams. Conversely, they will constantly be pushed by the organization (and you) to accelerate the time to market and reduce the total spend on the project to meet the original budget. And here is where the "perfect product" you had researched and documented begins to unravel.

A popular approach by the project managers who are running the development team goes something like this: "*to have a successful product, you need to have three things—the feature set as defined by the marketing team, the timeline committed to meet the market window, and the original planned costs and resource...but you can only have two*". More often than not, the organization is not likely to want to commit more resources to your project, so you will be stuck with having to decide which product features and attributes you can live without or change, or whether you can wait for the product and potentially miss the market window.

And so, this is where the customer's voice is just as important than it was in the assessment stage, but you will likely not have a customer as part of your development team (although it is not a bad idea to consider having a customer advisory council who could act as your product "board of directors"), and you must act as a proxy to the customer, making the daily decisions and tradeoffs to ensure the customer's voice is ever present in all of your team meetings. It is important not to fall into the trap of "what I think", but rather, "what would the customer think" as you are confronted with decisions about product features, interoperability, product look and feel, user interface, navigation, and so on.

And while the product is of paramount importance in this phase of the development, one must also remember that it is not the product alone that defines the customer experience. There are a multitude of other decisions that must be made with an eye to the customer, including product packaging, product documentation, channel strategy, and so on, ensuring that the total customer experience is a delightful one. The customer product is not the only thing that is developed in this stage. You will also need to develop the market message, promotion strategy, and value proposition based on the previous customer VoC that you've done so that you will be able to take your shiny new product out to the market and have the potential customers recognize the value it will bring into their lives and company. In *Chapter 9, Completing the Circle – Using the Customers Voice in Your Organization,* we will talk in more detail about how to wrap the customer input into your promotional process and market message.

The end of the development stage is a functioning product and market message that hopefully has met the needs of the market and will delight your customers, but you are not done yet, and neither is your customer's input into the development process, as we will see in the next section.

# Stage 5 – Test (and Readiness)

Now, we have our shiny new product and desperately want to go show it to everyone and start collecting those massive revenues as a result of all of the hard work we have done, but there is still one more step and one more area of vital customer input.

In the testing phase, the development team will take the results of all their efforts through a battery of internal tests. Even if you have been performing test processes during development, if you are making a complex piece of hardware or a pharmaceutical drug, this can still be a long process to reach final approval to ship.

While the internal tests are necessary and critical to ensure the product will meet the original specification, there is another test to get one last and critical piece of customer input before launch. This is through a customer test or beta evaluation. In this stage, a set of customers are given a fully functioning product to deploy in their application or to use as part of their day. Most of the time, we will give the customer the final product for free or give him a reduced purchase price for his willingness to commit time and resources to review our product. Ideally, giving this product to some of the customers you interviewed in the Detailed assessment stage would provide a closed-loop feedback process, and you could measure how well your new product met the original customer VoC.

Whether or not you have the luxury of going back to some of the original customers, it is just as important to collect and measure feedback from the customer at this stage as the previous ones. As part of the Beta evaluation, it is recommended that the customer be assigned to review specific features and functions in their application as well as record their impression and feedback as to how well the product performed. A customer test plan should be constructed and agreed to by you and the customer before engaging a beta evaluation.

And much like the Development stage of the process, this would also be a good time to get additional customer feedback on such things as the packaging, the documentation, the market message, and other aspects of the product.

I know many organizations will try to circumvent this stage in an effort to get the product to market faster. Don't do it! It is far better to take a little extra time making sure the product is everything you believe it to be before launching the product into the general market. Nothing can do more to damage a new product introduction than a product malfunction or product recall because you rushed the product to market. Even if the product does perform as well as you imagined, sometimes, the market will change during development, and this is your last chance to get feedback before committing a considerable amount of resources supporting the marketing and sales functions. It is still better to cancel a product that is complete rather than take a product to market that the market does not need and will not buy.

Assuming you have passed all the internal tests and the beta customers are as delighted as you imaged, it is time to pass through the final development gate and launch your new product!

# Stage 6 – Sales

Finally! All the efforts in collecting the market data and customer VoC, all the horse trading in getting the product through the development process, all the checking and double checking to make sure the product will meet the original needs of the customer and the market hasn't changed.

While we may be in the sales stage, customer input must not stop. We'll need to verify that the product is meeting the needs of the larger market, not just the limited set of customers we engaged in the testing stage. Continual customer feedback will tell us if "the dogs are truly eating the dog food" and make us aware of incremental improvements we can make to the product for the next iteration or release, ensuring that the product will evolve to meet the ever-changing market.

I would recommend you do not just go out on "sales calls" and try and push the new product you've just released, but also go out in the same spirit that drove you in the Ideation and Concept stage. Try and truly understand what the customers like, dislike, would change, or how they are using the product in ways you never imagined. Most of the time, this section of customer VoC can provide real breakthrough opportunities as the customers actually have something in their hands and are much better equipped to provide feedback than they were in the early esoteric stages.

Of course, the data collection process must be as rigid and repeatable as it was in the Concept stage, and we will discuss ways to make these customers' VoC engagement more meaningful in *Chapter 7, Understanding the Customer's Voice.*

# Stage 7 – Post-Mortem

This is the feedback loop stage of a new product's development, and in my experience, one that is rarely done. All too often, the marketing team is consumed with generating sales for the new product and the development team is off to the next project.

The post-mortem stage is designed as a way for the product team to look back on the project and determine how well they executed it. Which things went well and which went poorly? Which methods or processes worked well and should be incorporated into the organization's DNA, and which things must we shed or change to make the next product development better?

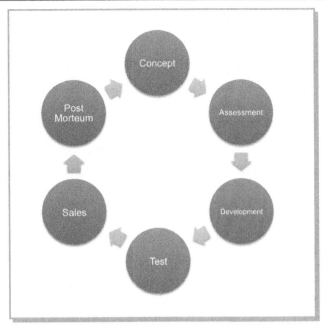

**Figure 2.3: NPD Continual Process**

While we talked about the NPD process earlier and how it is a series of stages and gates, world class organizations view it more as a continual process that feeds into itself even after the project is complete, as shown in the preceding diagram. As we can see here, the additional data collected in the sales part of the process should be reviewed and codified in the post-mortem stage so we can see what worked and did not work in our development. This is key both for our internal learning, but also so that the rest of the organization can learn from our successes and failures.

# Who's responsible?

According to some practitioners of VoC, they will tell you that the entire product development team is responsible for VoC, that it takes a cross-functional team to sustain the integrity of VoC for the duration of the product cycle. They will put the responsibility on a cross-functional *core team*, *tiger team*, or *VoC steering committee* of 5–7 individuals from marketing, engineering, manufacturing, service and repair, and finance to ensure that the VoC is obtained, processed, and included in your new product.

While I applaud their desire to make sure that VoC is everyone's responsibility, what I have found in most organizations is that when something is "everyone's responsibility", no one ends up being "responsible".

I believe the responsibility of VoC falls squarely on whoever is responsible for product management. That could be a product manager, it could be a product marketing manager, or it could be a marketing manager. It could also be the owner of the business, depending on how big the organization is. The point is, when you are responsible for the product, you are responsible for the product research that includes VoC.

But that does not mean that the rest of the organization can ignore VoC, nor does it mean that only the product manager can play a role in the VoC. What it means is that the product manager is the quarterback in ensuring that the VoC is obtained and included into the product. He/she must organize the activities within the organization to ensure that VoC is being collected and incorporated into the product decisions. He/she must be the one to "sell" the validity of the VoC to the senior staff and the engineering team. He/she must also be the one to bring in other people from other disciplines and make them experience the customer input, which will greatly speed the development process, and make it more likely that a successful product is created. I will talk about this more in *Chapter 6, The Interview Process – The Interview*, but a huge discovery for me was how much better a development team could perform if you made the engineering team participate in each and every one of the interviews in the interview process. Ultimately, the product manager must be the customer "champion" throughout the development!

# Summary

While many believe that customer VoC in a new product development process is a specific event that occurs as part of the business case or marketing analysis, the promise and impact of VoC in a new product's development can be so much more. Many organizations use a stage-gate or similar process for their new developments as a way to provide structure to the new development process. Regardless of which stage of predevelopment you are in—Ideation, Concept, or the Detailed assessment—Customer VoC plays a pivotal role in shaping your product deliverables. If you are in the Development stage of your project, Customer VoC provides the input to make the intelligent choices and tradeoffs that inevitably occur during a development. If you are in the test or the Sales stage, VoC helps you ensure that your assumptions were correct and provides the foundation to articulate the market value to the customer segments. If you are in the post-mortem stage, VoC is critical to evaluate how well you've met the needs of the market and also share your lessons learned with the rest of the organization.

Hopefully you now have a better appreciation of not only how powerful VoC can be in new product development, but how to use it in every stage of the NPD. This helps to ensure that your product is always in tune with the needs of your customer and marketplace, and will ultimately lead to your product success.

In *Chapter 4, Gathering the Customer Needs for Your Product*, we will start to discuss some of the tools available to us to begin to gather customer VoC, but before we do that, it is worthwhile to discuss some of the other marketing tools and techniques that have a close relationship with VoC and can help to augment a successful VoC initiative in the next chapter, *Chapter 3, Laying the Groundwork*.

# >3
# Laying the Groundwork

*"Failing to focus leads to a state of mediocrity"*

*– Treacy and Wiersem, Discipline of Market Leaders*

In the previous chapter, we discussed ways of incorporating your VoC into your organization's **New Product Development** process and touched on some of the process and tools to bring the customers' voice to life, helping to ensure that the process does not just result in a 'check the box' exercise which will not ultimately meet the needs of the market. In this chapter, we will go even deeper into some of the basic tools, processes, and strategies that should be undertaken prior to embarking on a customer VoC, and when used in conjunction with VoC, provide a much more complete view of the customer, market, and opportunity.

This chapter is meant as a high-level primer on these other marketing methods and how they provide more value to VoC research. In this chapter, we will discuss performing the following types of analysis:

- SWOT
- Porter Five Force Diagram
- Growth-Share Matrix
- Segmentation
- Competitive Analysis

We will only present an overview of each of these tools and encourage the reader to leverage the plethora of information available online and in many marketing books if there is an interest in learning more.

It is very likely your organization has already undertaken some of the methods presented in this section. An understanding and incorporation into your business model of these tactics will make your VoC efforts more robust and meaningful. While it may not be necessary to perform all of these tactics before you start a customer VoC, I highly recommend that you perform a SWOT, a segmentation analysis, and a competitive analysis at a minimum to derive a base level understanding of the market and your organizations capabilities to get the value out of your VoC initiative.

We will also dive deeper into other, more specific VoC tools in the next chapter.

**Tip**

While all of the tools presented in this chapter and the next are not mandatory, my intent is to provide you with the necessary arsenal to conduct effective VoC research, and be able to take the information you gather to create an effective business case for your new development.

# The SWOT process

While we briefly discussed the concept of SWOT in *Chapter 2, VoC in the Product Development Process*, it is important to note that this is one of the most fundamental building blocks in understanding your market and your position within that market. It provides a basic model that yields direction and serves as a basis for the organizations marketing plans.

The word SWOT derives from the initial letters of the words Strengths, Weaknesses, Opportunities, and Threats. Factors internal to the organization are considered either strengths or weaknesses. External factors are classified as either opportunities or threats. The SWOT analysis assesses the organizations strengths (what the organization can do), weaknesses (what an organization cannot do), opportunities (external influences which are favorable to an organization), and threats (external influences which are potentially unfavorable to an organization). The SWOT process should ideally be a multi-disciplined view of the organization and/or the product. To this end, if you are performing a SWOT for an organization, it is best to get all factions of the organization to share their view. If you are responsible for marketing, you may not have a good view into supply-chain issues or opportunities. Likewise, if you are doing a product SWOT, at a minimum you need to have input from sales, marketing, and engineering, but even here, you can see where something like supply-chain could have a large impact on a products' viability. Consider the first iPhone. While many would consider the iPhone a product breakthrough in both engineering and marketing, it was through the sourcing of Gorilla Glass that was one of the pillars of its success. Would it have been as successful if it had a plastic cover (as per the original design) or a glass that scratched easily? I seriously doubt it.

To briefly summarize, the main purpose of a SWOT is to determine which things will be or could be a benefit to the organization, and which things must be addressed or overcome to achieve the desired result. This is a key consideration as you prepare for your VoC. Not only will it give you a better understanding of your organizations internal capabilities and shortcomings as well as the outside opportunities and challenges, it will also give you a better foundation and insight to new product opportunities as they present themselves during your VoC.

When performing an organizational or a product SWOT, it is necessary to examine the things *inside* your organization that contribute to your position in the market, as well as those things *external* to your company or your control. The things of an *internal origin* are those contributing factors inside your organization you, or your organization, have a high amount of control over and you can take steps to modify or change (even if it is not immediate). Conversely, the contributing factors of an *external origin* your company may not have any or limited direct control over. The internal origin factors can best be thought as contributing to an organizations or a products Strengths and Weaknesses, while things of an external origin are often thought more as Opportunities and Threats, as they often become contributing factors to the company's future success or demise.

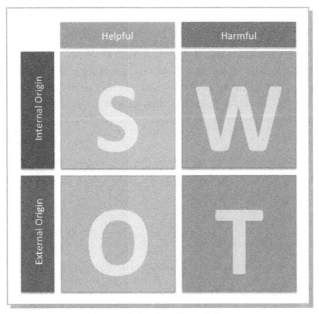

*Figure 3.1 – SWOT analysis*

**Strengths** of an organization are its internal capabilities and resources that it can put to bear to develop a competitive advantage over others in the marketplace. A well-developed list of strengths articulates the firm's advantages and what it does well. Examples of strengths include:

➤ Customer intimacy

➤ Good reputation among customers

➤ Strong brands

➤ Patents and other intellectual property

➤ Product or technology superiority

➤ Distribution channels

➤ Cost advantages

➤ Supply chain advantages (the ability to source the parts and components you need, when you need them, at a cost which will allow product success)

**Weaknesses** may be viewed as the absence of key strengths in an organization. A robust list of weaknesses will help an organization to understand what is done poorly and what can be improved. As an example, the following are examples of weaknesses:

➤ Poor customer intimacy

➤ Poor reputation

➤ Weak or unknown brand

➤ No competitive differentiator

➤ Poor channels to market

➤ High price

➤ Lack of access to key components

Sometimes, an organization's weakness is the flip side of its strength. As an example, large multinational companies often have larger engineering and product development resources allowing them to allocate a lot of resources to a new development or product. While this is true, many times these same companies have difficulty in reacting quickly to changing market dynamics due to their sheer size and consensus required in creating a new product or offering.

**Opportunities** is an evaluation on those things that are outside the four walls of an organization that can yield new opportunities for profit and market expansion. Some examples include:

➤ Unfulfilled customer needs

➤ Changing marketplace desires

➤ New technologies which can be deployed in an organization's product

➤ Loosening or removal of regulations

➤ Loosening or removal of trade barriers

➤ Market confusion from consolidation

Some may not see an opportunity from market consolidation, but this may actually be one of the rare times when an industry follower has the chance to overtake the incumbent in a market without a large expenditure for a new product line or marketing program. How many times have we seen a large company acquire the assets of a successful market leader, only to have them change the offering or business model of the company that was acquired? In the last few years, we have seen companies like Honeywell acquiring the assets of safety technology companies like Sperion and RAE gas detection.

If I am a customer, in particular, a small customer of those companies, I may be asking if a company like Honeywell will service me the same way that the smaller company did, or is this an opportune time to leave? Or take the case of Google, who acquires companies at the rate of one per week since 2010. They have acquired such companies like Picassa (photo storage and sharing), Bump (contact management and sharing), and Feedburner (RSS syndication). After buying Bump in September, 2013, it was gone a scant six months later. It is also reported that Feedburner may be next to be jettisoned after the demise of Google Reader. Certainly, you could see if you had a competing technology or product to Bump or Feedburner, and given the market turmoil from these acquisitions, you may end up in a much more favorable spot largely through no action on your behalf.

**Threats**, as external factors can provide new opportunities for growth, they can also provide new threats to the profitability and ongoing vitality of the organization such as:

> ➤ Shift in consumers taste away from the organizations offering
> ➤ New technologies making current organization's product obsolete
> ➤ New regulations
> ➤ Increasing trade barriers
> ➤ Substitute products displacing the organization's product

Often times, the drive to substitute products in driven by cost and availability. Consider how the effect of rising electric prices affects the adoption of gas in a neighborhood. The higher the prices rise, the more pronounced the migration to the new fuel. Many utilities even plan for this by creating power plants that can use multiple sources of fuel based on price and availability.

To illustrate how technology and consumer tastes can affect your market, consider if you were producing recorded music on cassette tapes. Unless you were savvy enough to see the future of CD's coming along and able to make that switch to this new medium, you were likely out of business. And even if you did make the switch to CD's, if you are not cloud based at this point with the ability to stream your music to your listeners, you probably have a very small market indeed.

As we look around, we can see how the threats and opportunities from yesterday are yielding the new reality of today. Consider banking (in-person tellers to ATM's), Computers (desktops to tablets to phablets), Computer storage medium (floppy disks to hard disks to USB to the Cloud), Researching (Libraries to Google), and a multitude of things all around us.

To better understand the market dynamics embodied in a SWOT, a matrix is often used to exemplify those variables and develop strategies to address them. You should fill out this matrix like the one presented documenting the internal variables, which are helpful and harmful (strengths and weaknesses), as well as the external variables which are helpful and harmful (opportunities and threats).

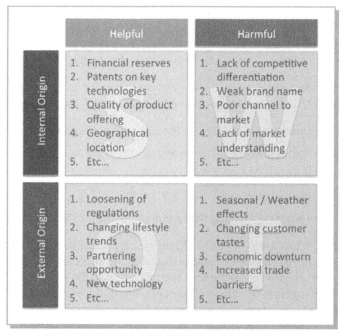

*Figure 3.2: Completed SWOT Matrix with example data*

As we discussed in *Chapter 2, VoC in the Product Development Process,* when performing a SWOT, it is far preferable to perform not only an internally focused SWOT, one which is done by the people in your organization based on their experiences and understanding of the market, but also a customer-focused SWOT (preferably with the assistance of your customers) that seeks to present your strengths and weaknesses from your customers perspective to ensure that the customers' voice is being presented in your analysis. As we know, a company or products strength is only a strength when it is useful in satisfying the needs of a willing customer.

Strategies should be developed to analyze an organization's weaknesses and how to turn them into strengths, and understand threats and how to turn them into opportunities. It is also a worthwhile exercise to review multiple dimensions together to develop an Organizations strategy such as:

➤ **S-O strategies**: Pursue opportunities that leverage the organization's strengths

➤ **W-O strategies**: Analyze changes that could be made to address the organization's weakness which would provide new opportunities

➤ **S-T strategies**: Review how an organization can use its strengths to address and overcome any vulnerability to outside threats

➤ **W-T strategies**: Establish defensive tactics to minimize the disruption to the organization due to its internal weaknesses

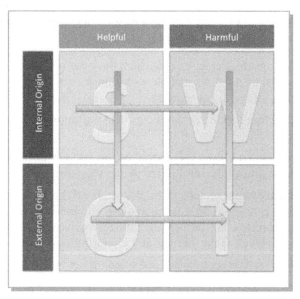

*Figure 3.3: SWOT strategies*

You can modify your SWOT sheet to also both view the company or product SWOT and also develop key strategies to address each factor by developing and documenting your strategies in the outer boxes:

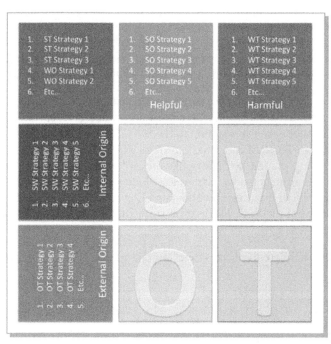

*Figure 3.4: Completed SWOT Strategy Matrix*

Some readers may also be familiar with the term **PEST** or **PESTLE** analysis that is also used by some organizations. PEST stands for Political, Economic, Social, and Technology. Expanding the analysis to PESTLE adds Legal and Environmental factors. I following briefly summarizes each, but most would consider this as a part of the opportunities and threats section of a SWOT analysis:

> ➤ **Political factors** are the degrees to which the government influences or acts in the market. Political factors include such things as tax policy, trade restrictions, import tariffs, and political stability.

> ➤ **Economic factors** include economic growth, inflation rates, labor rates, and exchange rates.

> ➤ **Social factors** include cultural aspects, norms and attitudes; population growth rates, demographics, education, lifestyle, and age distribution.

> ➤ **Technological factors** include technological breakthroughs and the rate of technological change, as well as automation and innovation. Technological shifts can also have a key influence on the Strengths and Weaknesses of an organization as well as the Threats and Opportunities.

> ➤ **Legal factors** include regulations and standards as well as employment law

> ➤ **Environmental factors** encompass weather, green and ethical issues and include pollution, waste, and recycling.

# Porter's five-forces

In business, your ability to make a good profit is dependent on your position within the market. As an example, do you have competitors offering similar products; is it easy for people to enter a market when they see you are making a profit? Can customers bully you into lowering your prices? If you don't think about your position in the market, it is very easy to spend a great amount of time and yet still struggle to stay ahead.

This is where a tool like **Porters Five forces** can be used in your business. The tool was created to help us understand who has the most power in a market situation and was developed by Michael Porter in reaction to the SWOT analysis, which he considered un-rigorous and ad hoc. The tool can also illuminate whether a product or service is likely to be profitable in a given market. Much like the SWOT analysis presented previously, this tool helps to illuminate market dynamics which provide a robust foundation to your organizations VoC initiative. By understanding these forces, you will be in a better position to understand the VoC information you gather as well as how to leverage it to a more successful product.

The tool assumes there are five forces determining market power. Porter defined the five forces as:

> ➤ Supplier power
> ➤ Buyer power
> ➤ Competitive rivalry

➤ Threat of substitution

➤ Threat of new entry

Any of these forces can work for you or against you in the market. To use Porters Five forces tool, you should look at each of the variables individually and then weigh the relative advantage/disadvantage of entering this market with your product or service. We will explain how to use Porter's five forces as part of the market requirements document we present in *Chapter 9, Completing the Circle – Using the Customers Voice in Your Organization.*

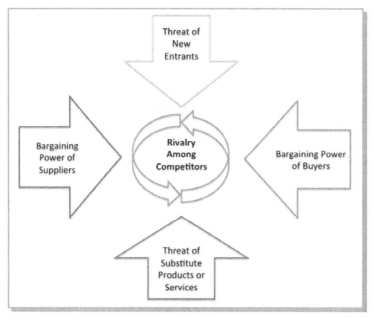

*Figure 3.5: Five-force diagram*

**Supplier Power**—this is a basic assessment on how easy it is for suppliers to drive up prices on the goods and services you need for your product, or reduce quantity supplied. Suppliers of raw materials, services, and labor can have power over a firm when there are is lack of alternative suppliers or substitutes, or when the cost of switching from one supplier to another is high. The fewer the supplier choices you have and the more you need the suppliers, the more powerful they are.

Factors contributing to supplier power:

➤ **Differentiation**: How specialized are the products the supplier is providing you

➤ **Sources**: The amount and variety of sources for the products or raw materials required to make your product

➤ **Substitute Products**: How easy is it to use an alternative product or raw material in your design

➤ **Supplier Channel**: How strong is the suppliers own channel and how much control do they have over the channel

**Buyer Power**—Conversely, this is an evaluation of how easy it is for buyers to drive the prices down (and reduce your margins). Buyer power grows when they become more concentrated or organized, when the product is undifferentiated, or when switching costs are low. If you deal with a few, powerful buyers who also have access to alternatives, they are often able to dictate terms to you.

Factors contributing to buyer power:

> **Substitute Products**: How easy is it for the consumer to buy a different product that meets the same customer goal

> **Buyer information**: How available is information about your product, capabilities, competition, and so on.

> **Switching Costs**: Ease of the customer to use a competitive product without severely impacting their costs

> **Buyer volume**: If there are few buyers for your product, they will have more control over your ability to control the market

> **Commoditization**: How plentiful and alike are the competitive products where it is extremely easy to switch out one product for another at little or no cost

**Competitive rivalry**—this is an evaluation of the number and capabilities of your competition. For most industries, the intensity of competitive rivalry is the major determinant of the competiveness of the market. If you have many competitors and they offer equally functional products and services, you will likely have little power as the suppliers and customers will go elsewhere if they do not get a good deal from you. It is even more unattractive if the market is stable or declining, exit barriers are high, or competitors have high stakes in staying in the segment. Conversely, if no one else can do what you do or offer the products you offer, then you can have much higher power.

Factors contributing to competitive rivalry:

> **Competitor pipelines**: Does the competition have a robust pipeline of new products continually being released to the market?

> **Innovation**: What is the innovation process at your competitors and how quickly are they able to adapt new processes and technologies to create new and unique products?

> **Customer understanding**: Do they have a developed VoC process to understand the customers current and future needs?

> **Engineering and manufacturing capabilities**: How good is the technological staff at developing products the customers need in a way that is timely and cost effective?

> **Strategic plans**: The ability of an organization to chart a future course and put together the plans necessary to get them there

> **Budget and organization size**: How many resources and money can the organization draw upon to make new products?

**Threat of substitutions**—This is affected by the capabilities of your buyers to find a different way to achieve their goal without using a product like yours. Substitutes impart limits on prices and profitability. If technology advances, prices and profits in these industries are likely to fall. As an example, if you were a low priced camera manufacturer or a handheld calculator vendor, you have probably seen your market evaporate as more and more customers use their phones for basic picture taking and calculations. If substitution is easy and viable, then this weakens your power.

Factors contributing to threat of substitution:

> **Quantity and availability**: Volume of possible substitute products in the market

> **Functionality of substitutes**: How well can they perform the duties and meet the requirements of the customer?

> **Price of substitutes**: What is their purchase price and total cost relative to yours?

> **Buyer propensity to substitute**: Is the customer willing to switch from one supplier to another with no qualms?

> **Buyer switching costs**: What is the actual cost for the buyer to switch to a substitute product?

> **Perceived level of differentiation**: Does your product have unique characteristics or functions versus the competition, and most importantly, does the customer have that perception?

> **Ease of substitution**: How much of a *drop-in* replacement is the substitute product for yours? If it is a resistor, it is very easy. If it is a CRM system, not so much.

**Threat of new entry**—Profitable markets with attractive yields will attract new players. Power is also affected by the ability of new competitors to enter your market as more entrants typically reduce profitability for incumbent firms in the industry. If it costs little in time or money to enter the market, if there are few economies of scale or if you have little intellectual property protection, then new competitors can enter your market and weaken your position. If there are strong barriers to entry, your position can be upheld.

Factors contributing to threat of substitution:

> **Intellectual property**: How many patents and trade secrets do you have that the competition cannot copy?

> **Capital requirements**: Is there a high cost to enter a market? This is a large benefit for the incumbent. What is the cost to exit?

> **Distribution channel**: Will your distributors easily carry a competitive product, or is their investment into your product and technology such that they would not want to do that?

> **Government policy**: Are there rules or regulations that define who can play in the market?

> **Economies of scale**: If you have the ability to ramp up or down based on buyer demand, you will have an advantage in the market.

➤ **Brand equity**: How much *value* do the customers put into working with you, your company, your brand, and everything that represents to them?

➤ **Switching costs**: The actual costs a customer must make, both in terms of money and time to switch to an alternative product.

➤ **Customer loyalty**: Will the customers stick with you, even if there are occasional problems or things do not go as planned and just as importantly, how much of an evangelist will they become for you?

➤ **Industry profitability**: If there are a lot of profits to be had in a market space, you will find a lot of new competitors, unless some of the other variables (capital requirements, intellectual property safeguards, government policies, brand loyalty, and others) come into play.

These forces can be put into a diagram like the following one to analyze your situation. Use this as a template to evaluate and brainstorm the relevant factors for your market or product. It is also recommended that you summarize the scale and force on the diagram in the accompanying circle using:

➤ +: A force moderately in your favor

➤ ++: A force strongly in your favor

➤ -: A force moderately against you

➤ - -: A force strongly against you

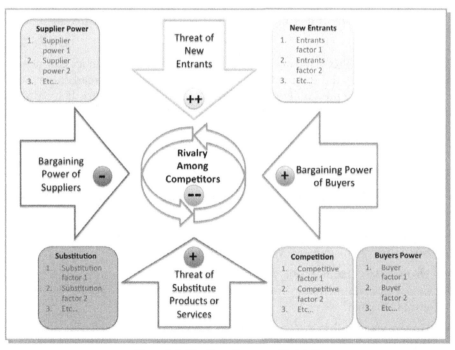

*Figure 3.6: Five-force diagram with detail*

The five forces framework has been challenged by some and adaptations and modifications have been suggested by others by adding forces such as innovation, complementary products and services, and government. However, it can be argued that these other factors only serve to influence the original five and this should be adequate for most analysis.

Once you've completed a five forces analysis, you will see clearly where you are at risk so you can take steps to overcome those risks and if you are looking to enter a new market, you can see at a glance how potentially attractive it will be for your organization.

# Growth-share matrix

Many organizations use additional analysis to evaluate their products and portfolios. A popular methodology was developed by the Boston Consulting group in the 1970s, and is also known as the **BCG model**. This model helps companies analyze their businesses and product lines and ranks their products on the basis of relative market share and growth rates using a 2x2 matrix as shown in the following diagram. The analysis group's products into four different categories (**Cash Cows**, **Dogs**, **Questions Marks/Problem Children**, and **Stars**) based on these variables:

*Figure 3.7: Growth share matrix*

**Cash Cows** are where a company has a high market share in a low or slow growing industry. These products typically are in a mature market and require little investment, resulting in cash generation well in excess of the amount of investment required to maintain the products. The term is derived from the concept of "milking" these products as they require little investment and yield good returns, if not great, returns.

**Dogs** are products with low market share in a mature, slow growing market. These products typically do little better than "break-even" and are often identified as potentials for divesture through selling off the product family, or killing the product altogether. Occasionally, these products do serve as a benefit to the organization as they provide a future migration path for current customers who can be moved to better performing products.

**Question Marks** (or **Problem Children**) are products operating in high growth markets, but have low market share. Question Marks have the potential to increase market share and become Stars, or if the market slows, can very easily turn into Dogs. Often times, these are the starting points for new businesses and must be monitored carefully to gauge whether they have the potential to become Stars and deserve additional funding to grow their market share, or whether they will ultimately become Dogs depleting the organizations limited resources from where they could be used more effectively.

**Stars** are products that enjoy high market-share in a rapidly growing industry. These are often innovative, new products that require higher funding to fight evolving competition and maintain their growth rate. The iPod and iPhone are examples of products that were Stars when they were released. As the industry growth rate slows, Stars who have been able to maintain their market leadership develop into Cash Cows. Those that cannot ultimately become Dogs due to low market share in a slow growth market.

The natural cycle for new products is they start their lives as a Question Mark. If they are able to capitalize on a rapidly growing market they turn into Stars, and if not they turn into Dogs. Stars ultimately become Cash Cows and over time also become Dogs.

As BCG stated,

> *"To be successful, a company should have a portfolio of products with different growth rates and different market shares. The portfolio composition is a function of the balance between cash flows. High growth products require cash inputs to grow. Low growth products should generate excess cash. Both kinds are needed simultaneously. They went on to say that a balanced portfolio has Stars whose high share and high growth assure the future; Cash Cows that supply funds for that future growth; and Question Marks to be converted into Stars with the added funds."*

The BCG matrix helps managers and product leaders make resource allocation decisions once different products are classified. Depending on the product, an organization might decide on a number of different strategies for it. One strategy is to build market share for a business or product, especially a product that might become a Star. Many companies invest in Question Marks because market share is available for them to capture. This process is often used as a means to help Question Marks become Stars by taking money from Cash Cows and diverting the investment into Question Marks in hopes of them ultimately becoming Stars.

# Customer segmentation

The concept of segmentation has its roots in companies like Proctor & Gamble where consumer-marketing companies recognized the value of dividing customers into groups or segments. These packaged goods companies could effectively focus resources promoting specific products into specific customer groups where they would produce the highest possible revenue, at the lowest possible costs.

Initially, simple demographic segmentation was used as packaged goods companies promoted products such as perfumed soaps to women, while to men, they would promote a more sharp and spicy fragranced soap, smelling much like an aftershave. It was eventually discovered that not all men and women wanted the fragranced soaps. Some because they did not care for the smells the soaps imparted, and others for the simple fact that some needed to avoid the scented soaps so as to avoid an allergic reaction. These types of discoveries illustrate the value of segmentation to help provide a means to divide (and conquer) a market.

We experience segmentation today in virtually every facet of our lives, whether it is the commercials we see on TV, the advertisements we see in magazines and the customized ads we see online, the targeted mailings we get both online and offline, the packages that are offered from our phone and cable providers, and others. Virtually everywhere we turn we are being segmented and served advertisements and products that have been tailored to meet the needs of the segment we are a part of, sometimes, even if the segment is very, very small.

Simply defined, market segmentation is the division of customers into groups we can target for future products, research, or market messaging. According to Philp Kotler:

> *"Market segmentation is sub-dividing a market into distinct and homogeneous subgroups of customers, where any group can conceivably be selected as a target market to be met with distinct marketing mix."*

What we are really trying to accomplish with segmentation is relatively simple and straightforward. We are working to divide a broad target market into subsets of customers, who have common needs and priorities, and then work to design and implement strategies and products to target them.

Segmentation is a key marketing tactic/strategy that has a large bearing on the organization both before a VoC analysis is undertaken, as well as after. Before we conduct a customer VoC initiative, we need to step back and figure out just who are our future and current customers? If I were an automobile manufacturer with a range of automobiles from an entry-level fuel efficient two-seater to a $100K luxury car, would it make sense to do a customer VoC for the high-end $100K luxury car with a middle-class recent graduate? Probably not. It is unlikely he will be in the market for this particular automobile so his *wants and needs* (and ability to pay) are not consistent with the target market. On the flip side, after a customer VoC is deployed, we may learn specific attributes or needs for a target segment that we can put into our new products, or deploy as part of our marketing campaign.

Organizations have a number of reasons to look at segmenting their markets. The main reason, as discussed earlier, is to develop a target market. Once this is accomplished, it is much easier for the marketing team to develop more in-depth understanding of customers within that segment, as it is a smaller group. By the same token, it also becomes easier to understand the competitive landscape within a more narrowly defined segment, it becomes more effective at developing marketing campaigns in a more defined segment, and opportunities for differentiation are more likely discovered in a narrower band. As we know, it is very difficult to have mass-market appeal for the majority of products in the market today, so segmentation allows companies to focus their resources where they will derive the most value.

This division into groups can be based on a number of factors, but usually, we like to see one or more of the selection criteria to be an important characteristic relevant to their purchase or usage behaviors. Some of the typical ways to segment a consumer market are as follows:

> **Geographic segmentation**: Marketers can segment a market according to country, region, states, locales, cities, neighborhoods, or postal codes. With respect to region, marketers would find willing customers for such things as snow blowers, gloves, and thick warm coats in the Northern part of the United States but would not find as much success or demand in the South and some Western states of the US.

> **Demographic segmentation**: Using such variables as age, gender, religion, ethnicity, income, family size, occupation, and social class marketers can divide a market to best target their likely customers. The US census bureau uses demographic segmentation when it conducts its census every ten years. This information is also available for the public and can be used to aid in your own demographic research.

> **Psychographic segmentation**: In this type of segmentation, buyers are divided into different groups based on lifestyle, personality, or personal values. Whether someone is outdoors oriented, sport oriented, or entertainment oriented are examples of psychographic segmentation.

> **Behavioral segmentation**: In this case, buyers are segmented on the basis of their knowledge of, attitude toward, use of, or response to a particular product. These can be classified as to whether a customer is a user of a product or not, what drives when the user needs a particular product, the benefits they achieve in using a product, the frequency of product use, user brand loyalty, attitudes toward the product, and how ready the user is to purchase the product.

Like consumer markets, business markets can also be segmented using similar variables like geography, benefits sought, and usage. The variables defining the segments vary somewhat from the consumer markets, but are very similar in concept and execution as the consumer segmentation. Some business segment variables could be considered as follows:

> **Demographic**: What geographical locations do they serve? How many locations do they have?

> **Business**: Which industries do the companies operate in? What is the company size and finances? What products do they sell and who do they sell to? Is the company private or public?

> **Operating variables**: What types of users should we target and what serves/ functions do they require? What customer technologies are required?

> **Purchasing approaches**: Do we target companies that are quality oriented, price oriented, or service oriented? Should we target companies with centralized or decentralized purchasing and will we target companies who prefer to lease or buy? Do we target companies where we already have a strong relationship, or go after the most desirable companies?

> **Situational factors**: Should we focus on companies with large order requirements or smaller ones? Do we focus on companies requiring fast turn-around or long-lead times? Do we focus on certain applications of our product or the full suite of our offering?

> **Personal characteristics**: Do we focus on companies that show high amounts of loyalty to suppliers or focus on transaction-oriented companies? Do we serve risk-takers, or more cautious customers?

Once the preliminary market segmentation is complete, it is necessary to evaluate the segments against a set of criteria to insure the segments are properly defined. The following set of evaluation criteria should be followed to guarantee the segments are useable and businesses should only target the segments if it is:

> **Homogeneous**: Each of the customers/companies in the segment must be related to each other in some way and similar in terms of needs and/or characteristics.

> **Heterogeneous**: Each segment of consumers/companies should be relatively unique as compared to the other segments. This results in different customers grouped by differing need.

> **Measurable**: There should be some form of measurement available as to the size of the segment so the overall number of customers and attractiveness of the segment can be considered.

> **Substantial**: The segment should be large enough to warrant the organizations attention to return a benefit to the organization by investing in the segment. Often, organizations may conclude that a segment is desirable, but not large enough to invest into.

> **Accessible**: The organization must have the ability to reach the segment through distribution and communication.

> **Practical**: The organization must have the capabilities to develop products and services to address the needs of the segment.

The following is an example segment analysis done for a hypothetical automobile manufacturer:

| | |
|---|---|
| **First timer**: Young person recently passed drivers license test with nominal income. Looking for low-priced transportation solution with excellent gas mileage. | **All about Luxury**: Customers focused on having the best, most luxurious automobile with all the latest bells and whistles while taking a Sunday drive in the country. |
| **Family First**: Family with two or more children needing safe effective transport for children to school and activities. | **Getting it Done**: Consumers who use their automobile in the work environment and need to haul equipment to and from a job site. |

In this example, you see that each segment has been grouped according to a shared need, each segment is significantly different in what their purpose is for the vehicle, using demographic data we should be able to measure each segment, each of the segments are substantial enough to be targeted, the company likely has dealers that can address the needs of each segment, and we would assume the manufacturer has the capabilities to develop the vehicle to meet the needs of the various segments.

# How to segment a market

A step-by-step process for segmenting your market is mentioned as follows. Depending on your segmentation goals you may only need to complete the first three steps, or may need to complete all six:

1. **Define the market**: The first step is to define the market of interest. It is unlikely your market is the entire world, so as a first step, you must define who that would be. Looking at our previous example, we may define the market as the US automobile market.

2. **Create market segments**: Now that we have defined the overall market, we need to determine which types of different consumers form that overall market. To do this, we need to review the list of segmentation variable we discussed previously (demographic, geographic, or others) and choose the ones that we think are influencing the purchasing behaviors of the market. As a starting point in segmentation, it is preferable to try and split the market using the largest criteria at first to divide the market, and then continue to further divide the market based on the other criteria. In the case of the consumer market, this would often be based on age, gender, or income as the first step. An approach which helps marketers to visualize and explain market segmentation is through a segmentation tree, as shown as follows:

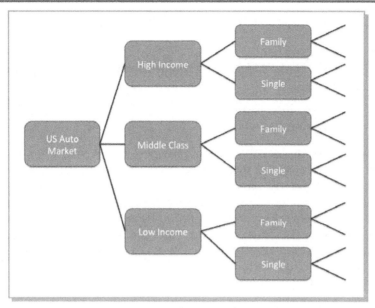

*Figure 3.8: Market segmentation for US auto market*

3. **Evaluate the market segments**: Assess each of the market segments based on the evaluation criteria discussed previously in terms of Homogeneous, Heterogeneous, Measurable, Substantial, Accessible, and Practical. If, for some reason, your market segments do not meet one of more of the evaluation criteria, revisit this step to and change the segment variables you have selected.

4. **Construct segment profiles**: In this step, we want to take a deeper dive into the segments to try and understand them a little more. A segment profile is a detailed description of the market segment across a range of factors and is designed to provide the organization with a good understanding of customers within each segment for comparison and strategy purposes. A segment profile would likely outline important aspects of demographic and psychographic descriptions; segment size, share, and growth rate; segment needs; customer behavior; brand preferences, usage rates, price sensitivity, and others.

5. **Evaluate the attractiveness of each segment**: Next, we will evaluate the relative attractiveness of each segment in comparison to the organizations goals and resources. We also evaluate whether this particular segment fits with our strategic direction, whether it is the best use of our resources, and to whether or not we are able to compete in this segment:

   The following factors should be considered as part of this step:

   ➢ **Financial**: Is the segment the correct size for us, is the growth rate attractive, and what are the profit margins?

   ➢ **Attractiveness**: What is the competitive landscape and do we have the right channels to market? Consider incorporating variables uncovered during the Porter Five forces exercise and use this for additional consideration.

> ➢ **Strategic**: Does this segment fit with our organizations strategy and goals?

> ➢ **Expertise**: Do we have the right resources, technology, and capabilities to serve this market? Do we have, or can we develop, a brand in the segment?

> ➢ **Opportunity costs**: What is the range of other opportunities for the organization and is this the best use of available resources?

**Entry and exit barriers**: When entry barriers are high and exit barriers are low, few new firms can enter the industry and poor performing ones can easily exit. When both entry and exit barriers are high, profit potential is high but firms face more risk competition because incumbent firms stay in and fight it out, even when performing poorly. When both entry and exit barriers are low, entrants enter and leave the industry and the returns are stable, but low. The worst situation is where entry barriers are low but exit barriers are high. In this case, firms enter during good times, but find it hard to leave in lean times resulting in overcapacity and reduced profitability.

6. **Select target markets**: Using the analysis you just completed, you can select the most appropriate target, or targets, for the organization. While you may not be able to address each point in step 5, at a minimum, you should consider the organizational strategy, the attractiveness of the segment, the competitive landscape in the segment, and the organization's ability to compete.

It should be noted that often, organizations that are performing segmentation analysis will give a descriptive nickname to the market segments. The purpose of the nickname is to create a moniker to quickly identify and understand the segment inside the organization during meetings and presentations. Ideally, these nicknames should be memorable and descriptive of the needs of the segment they are identifying. We have all seen examples of segment nicknames with the description of a generation of people born between the years of 1946 and 1964 as *Baby Boomers*, those born from the early 1960s to the early 1980s as *Generation X*, and the generation to follow, from the early 1980s to the early 2000s as the *Millennial Generation*.

Segmentation is typically part of the **Segmentation**, **Targeting**, and **Positioning (STP)** process within a company. After the segmentation is complete, this information can be leveraged to develop new products to meet the needs of the target segments, target those segments with this new product by position the company for success by managing the customer's perception, and understanding of key benefits of your new product. More details of the STP process and how to use it to position your product in the market will be discussed in *Chapter 9, Completing the Circle – Using the Customers Voice in Your Organization*.

# Competitive analysis

We have already discussed competition when we spoke of the Porter Five forces model, but before embarking on a customer VoC, I would encourage you to dive deeper into your competitive landscape and truly understand who your competitors are, how they are positioned, and what their relative strengths and weaknesses are. Like all the tools presented in this chapter, understanding your competitors positioning, capabilities, strengths, and weaknesses will allow you to assimilate and process more information more rapidly from the VoC's you undertake.

Does this sound familiar? Hopefully it does, as the one of the first steps in performing a competitive analysis is to do a SWOT or each of your major competitors, but before we can do that, we need to understand who our competitors really are. It would seem a simple task for a company to identify its competitors. GM knows that Toyota is a major competitor, Apple knows that Samsung is its major competitor, and Coke executives go to bed every night thinking about their major competitor, Pepsi. However, the range of a company's actual and potential competitors is in reality significantly larger. A company is more likely to be hurt by emerging competitors, new entrants, or substitute products as defined in the Five forces exercise, than by its current competitors. Let's consider the traditional book-sellers market as an example.

Not that long ago, Borders Bookstores & Barnes and Noble were racing each other to see who could build the most megastores with comfortable couches and easy access to premium coffee. While they were deciding which products to stock and coffee to serve, Jeff Bezos was building the online behemoth Amazon.com. Of course, Amazon.com had the advantage of offering an almost limitless supply of books at very low prices due to no stocking inventory costs. Additionally, customers no longer needed to leave their office or home to get the next Bestseller delivered to their door free and with no tax fees.

Barnes & Noble and Borders spent years trying to catch up, but the effect on traditional bookstores was devastating. While the number of Barnes & Noble bookstores were growing by leaps and bounds in the early 2000s, the number of Barnes & Noble stores peaked at 726 in 2008 and has been declining to where they currently operate only 696 stores and plan on closing a third of these remaining stores over the next decade.

In 2003 Borders had 1,249 stores under the Borders or Waldenbooks brand. By 2011, Borders applied for Chapter 11 bankruptcy protection and began liquidating 226 of its stores in the USA. By July, Borders starting closing its remaining 339 stores and by September of that year, Borders shuttered their online operations, transferring their trademarks and mailing list to Barnes & Noble, which is the only national bookstore in existence today. The message is clear: do not look only at your current competitors when evaluating a market, but keep a keen eye toward future competitors, wherever they may come from.

When analyzing current and future competitors, you must try to ascertain their strategic profile; specifically, you must try to put yourself in the shoes of your competitor to understand their strategy, objectives, strengths, weaknesses, and reaction patterns. Often times, a company will telegraph its strategic orientation by the actions it takes in the market. If a particular company is starting to acquire companies who supply materials the company uses in their product, you know they are focused on vertical integration to drive out their costs. If they begin to acquire companies with complementary channels to theirs, you know they are focusing on expanding their market reach. You should also try to understand the objectives of a company by understanding a little more about their behavior. Many variables affect competitor's objectives including size, history, current management, and financial situation. Are they going for market-share maximization and will invest today for future returns, or do they need to maximize profits as they need to hit a certain return to satisfy the parent company?

As mentioned previously, after you have defined who you're current and likely future competitors are, an effective tactic in doing a competitive analysis is to perform a SWOT on each of them. Just as a SWOT will help you to understand your own company's internal strengths and weaknesses, so can it provide the same illumination for each of your major competitors.

Just as we have done with our own internal SWOT, you should review each of your competitors using the following strength and weaknesses guidelines:

- **Products**: Standing and strength of products from a user's point of view in each segment. Breadth and depth of product line(s).

- **Marketing and Sales**: Capabilities in each area of the marketing mix, strength of channel and ability to manage and serve those channels.

- **Channels**: Dealer/Distributor coverage and quality. Strength of channel relationships and ability to serve the customers.

- **Engineering**: Strength and capabilities of engineering organization to develop new technology, creativity, R&D, and others. Patents, copyrights, and intellectual property. Access to outside resources.

- **Operations**: Manufacturing capabilities and cost position. Sophistication and flexibility of facilities and equipment. Proprietary manufacturing technologies. Location and labor pool. Supply chain strength and access to and cost of raw materials.

- **Costs**: Overall relative costs. Ability to scale and leverage other developments or business units.

- **Financial strength**: Cash flow. Access to capital. Credit and accounts receivables.

- **Organization**: Consistency of organization direction and clarity.

- **Management**: Leadership qualities of senior staff. Ability to motivate and adaptability of team. Depth of experience. Personnel turnover.

In addition to a detailed SWOT for each competitor, it is also best practices to analyze each one on the following variables if they are not included as part of the competitive SWOT:

> **Share of market**: The competitors share of the target market

> **Share of Mind**: The percentage of customers who named this competitor in responding to the statement: *name the first company that comes to mind in the industry*

> **Share of Heart**: The percentage of customers who named this competitor in response to the question: *name the company you would most prefer to do business with*

You should also try to get your customers to provide input on your competitors by focusing on their perceived value in the marketplace. It is commonly understood that customers will tend to choose competitive brand offerings on the basis of which delivers the most value to their enterprise. Customer value is defined articulated as:

*Customer Value = Customer Benefits – Customer Costs*

You can conduct your own customer value analysis by having your customers help you understand your own strengths and weaknesses relative to various competitors:

1.  Identify the major attributes customers' value. Customers are asked what specific attributes and benefits they seek when choosing a product or vendor. Often times, these are identified as **Key Performance Indicators (KPIs)**.

2.  Rate the importance of each value in step one.

3.  Assess the company and competitors performance for each value identified in step one.

4.  Analyze how differing customers from differing segments answer the preceding questions. If there are key differences between the segments, there could be an opportunity to position your product differently in different markets.

5.  Continue to monitor the customer values over time as economy, technology, and competitive responses change.

Lastly, if you have the internal capabilities and resources, few things will beat performing a competitive teardown on your competitor's most successful products. Performing a competitive teardown will provide ammunition to the marketing and sales team in understanding potential product deficiencies and capabilities, but can also be a treasure-trove of information to the produce development teams.

Competitive teardowns are very common-place in high-tech industries, like automobiles and electronics, where teams can learn design choices made by the competition, emerging component suppliers, cost drivers, competitive strengths and capabilities, packaging trends, and others. It is not unusual for automobile companies to purchase fully-loaded competitive products costing $50,000 and more, only to have them completely disemboweled within a week.

# Summary

In this chapter, we have discussed various tools and methods to gather market, product, and organizational data to provide a more holistic view of your market and opportunity, which are as follows:

> ➤ **SWOT**: An articulation of the organizations internal and external forces which aid in understanding your strengths and weaknesses in the marketplace, as well as the opportunities and potential threats you face

> ➤ **Porter's Five forces**: A more focused and detailed view of the forces within a market which will have an effect on your ability to be successful

> ➤ **Growth-Share Matrix**: A more detailed look at your own product portfolio and allowing you to understand those products that should be invested in, those products you should "milk", and those products you should jettison

> ➤ **Segmentation**: A deeper look at your customers market with an understanding of how to identify which segments you should target for your products and research

> ➤ **Competitive Analysis**: A more detailed understanding of your competition and the value they bring to the market

While you may not see the immediate application to our VoC research, it is through an understanding of these key elements that you will be able to both understand the feedback you receive from your VoC, but also how to present your finding in the context of your current market when presenting to your senior leadership by taking the analysis detailed in this chapter and the next to building your internal business case in *Chapter 9, Completing the Circle – Using the Customers Voice in Your Organization.*

In the next chapter, *Gathering the Customer Needs for Your Product*, we will build upon the foundation we created within this chapter, but will dive deeper into quantitative and qualitative tools that are more specific to VoC research. We will explore basic concepts like measuring customer satisfaction and surveys through and including more complex VoC concepts like conjoint analysis, lead user analysis, and ethnography.

# 4

# Gathering the Customer Needs for Your Product

*"You can observe a lot just by watching."*

*- Yogi Berra*

In the previous chapter, we outlined the various tools and processes one should undertake before embarking on a **Voice of the Customer** (**VoC**) journey. In this chapter, we will focus on the various additional strategies and tools available to the marketer to do effective VoC. While I find that there are certain tools I would not do a VoC without, I am presenting a variety of VoC tools in this chapter to allow the reader to decide which method(s) would work best for his or her particular situation. I recommend that you consider using multiple tools to conduct your research, as often differing tools give differing views of the customer. As Abbie Griffin, an NPD practitioner who also did early VoC research, has stated in the past, "the best do not succeed by using just one NPD practice more extensively or better, but by using a number of them more effectively simultaneously."

# Evolutionary versus revolutionary

In the previous chapter, we discussed how VoC could be used throughout the development process. At a high level, we can consider VoC being deployed during three main phases of product development—the **Discovery** phase, the **Definition** phase, and the **Evaluation** phase. When we are dealing with the "fuzzy front end" of a customer problem, we don't really have the new product concept or solution imagined quite yet. We are conducting research in the market to understand what types of problems our customers face and how we might be able to develop a product to satisfy their needs. This is when we would use a Discovery phase project. When we have already developed a product concept, but we are still fleshing out specific details and functions to add to our product or solution to best satisfy the customer needs, we would undertake a Definition phase project. If we have already fully developed our product and have defined the detailed design, and we are trying to understand the best way to launch our product and which marketing strategies and tactics we should use, we would deploy an Evaluation phase project.

To provide a little more context, I'd like to delve a little deeper into each of these phases and discuss typical VoC methods deployed in each of the three phases. Keep in mind, these are recommendations for which VoC tools typically work best in each phase, but the list is not absolute, and you may find a need to use a tool in a different phase than that which is listed.

# Discovery phase

During the discovery phase, the marketer is conducting high-level, open-ended exploratory research in an effort to learn about the customer's methods, culture, and unarticulated needs. This is the type of research that typically generates breakthrough or innovative products as there is not as much of a preconceived product concept, or if there is, it is still possible for existing product concepts to morph considerably as there is minimal capital investment in the new product or service you are researching. Typical VoC collection methods deployed in this phase include:

- ➤ Focus groups
- ➤ Customer visit interviews (open-ended)
- ➤ Ethnographical research
- ➤ Lead-user analysis

Interaction through interviews, focus groups, and ethnological research are the main tools the researcher has for the first, and I would argue the most important, phase of a customer VoC as part of the discovery research. If your budget or time do not allow you to use multiple methods in this phase, it is well advised that the researcher should use a combination of interviews in conjunction with some degree of ethnographical research as this will likely yield the deepest insights to your customer needs.

# Definition phase

When we already have a product concept, but we need to make the necessary tradeoffs about which functions the product will perform and at what cost to the organization, we will do definitional research. In this phase, we focus on the specific uses and features of the product to meet the goals of the customer. We begin to understand the value of the functions and features we are putting into our product in an effort to determine which are *must have* functions that the customer will ultimately pay for and which are the *nice-to-have* functions that do not impact the buying decision nearly as much. Typical VoC research methods deployed in this phase include:

- ➤ Interviews (more structured than in the Discovery phase)
- ➤ Ethnography
- ➤ Lead user analysis
- ➤ Customer advisory board
- ➤ Conjoint analysis

# Evaluation phase

In the case where you already have a working prototype or product, and you wish to understand how well the product features meet the customer's needs, the usability of the product from the customer's perspective, or how best to launch the product or create the marketing strategy around a product launch, you will want to deploy evaluation research. Quite often, this is carried out at the end of the product development just before launch. Some of the VoC tools available to you in the Evaluation phase include:

> ➤ Focus groups
> ➤ Surveys
> ➤ Feedback interviews, including usability testing

To better understand each of the tools that we have outlined earlier in each phase, the bulk of this chapter will provide a description of each method, the value gained from each method, potential downsides of each method, and some thoughts about how best to use each one. In later chapters, we will spend considerable time putting many of these key VoC methods into practical use.

# Idea management and VoC

As we have discussed previously, the impact of new products is the single largest contributor to the future revenue growth of an organization. While market intelligence, product development processes, strategic planning, and technology and resource management all have an impact on the sales of new products, the number one attribute responsible for new revenue growth is idea management.

While many would agree this is true, a major benchmarking study found that only 19% of businesses have an ideation system proficient enough to feed the development process. Furthermore, only 31% of firms have an effective method to select which ideas to actually invest in, and the best performing companies are four times more likely to have an effective ideation process than the poorest performing companies.

The research shows us that the best companies take the time and make the investments to generate the best ideas. But what are the best ways to generate these ideas, and where do they come from?

Robert Cooper and Angelika Dreher published a paper researching the sources of new product ideas in a survey of 150 firms. Their goal was to identify which sources were the most popular and, more importantly, the most effective in generating robust new product ideas. They analyzed 18 different sources of new product ideas to understand which methodology provided the most consistent results across all the firms.

The research identified eight VoC methods, six methods that fall under the category of **Open Innovation**, and four other methods that were neither VoC nor Open Innovation.

The concept of Open Innovation has become very popular as of late. The concept states that the firm should *open* their doors and minds to those thousands of people outside your organization who may have the next great product for your organization.

The researchers then mapped out the 18 methods in a graph that showed the percentage of times that companies used the various methodologies versus the effectiveness of each method. The popularity of each method was measured as a percentage of each of the firms that extensively used each method, and was measured on the horizontal axis. The effectiveness of each method was shown on the vertical axis, but only for users of that method. Some VoC methods were extensively used, including customer visits and focus groups, as shown in the upper right quadrant. Other newer methods, such as ethnography, were shown to be less popular. While many of the VoC methods were not used as often as the other nonVoC methods, the VoC methods were rated consistently more effective than the other methods by the 150 firms analyzed, and constituted the top five of all the methods researched. The following chart is a sample of the research conducted by Cooper and Dreher:

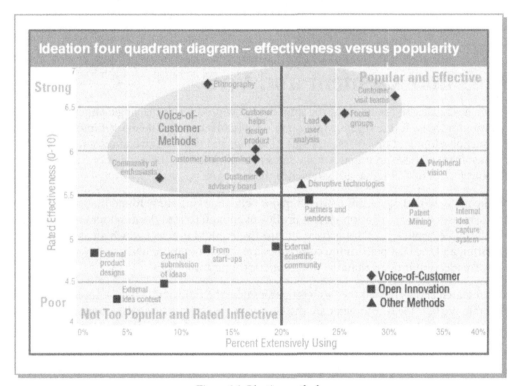

*Figure 4.1: Ideation methods*

# Customer visit interviews

I've always felt that the heart of a good VoC is driven by face-to-face customer interviews. As we discussed earlier, these interviews can take the form of open-ended interviews that help a marketer define the needs of a next-generation product, or they can be a more structured interview that will help derive which specific functions and features need to go into a product. A feedback or user- experience interview where the customer can provide insight into product usability can also be used to help define the best launch strategies to deploy. Customer interviews are ranked very high (along with ethnography) in terms of their effectiveness, as shown in the Cooper and Dreher research, and are ranked number one in terms of popularity versus the other VoC research methods.

With this method, the product development teams visits current customers/users as well as potential customers/users to get a total view of the product requirement. In-depth interviews are conducted, driven by a pre-crafted interview guide to uncover user wants, needs, and problems with regard to the new potential product. This guide lays out the questions and topics and guarantees a level of consistency across the interviews, and is a repeatable method of recording customer responses.

Customers and customer sites are identified for potential interviews and an agreement is made to interview a small group of customer representatives, typically the key purchase influencers and users. The teams performing the interviews are typically two–three people with representatives from marketing and engineering (and occasionally sales). I find it is imperative that the engineering side of the organization is involved in this initiative as this greatly reduces the potential misinformation and lost information from second-hand discussions. The interviews are conducted using the interview guide, with a special emphasis on open-ended questions that address user needs, functions, and benefits with respect to their job or position and not just product features.

As the interview process is so critical for customer VoC, and there are so many ways to help ensure you have a successful customer visit interview, I have devoted the next two chapters, *Chapter 5, The Interview Process – Preparation* and *Chapter 6, The Interview Process – the Interview*, to outline the construction and execution of the interview process with a special focus on the Discovery phase.

# Surveys

Although customer surveys were not specifically referenced in the research by Cooper and Dreher, I believe customer surveys offer a very easy method to get feedback, from as little as 30 customers to as many as 100,000.

Customer surveys can be used to collect customer feedback about a new product or product concept, but can also be used to get feedback shortly before product launch regarding product features and functionality, as well as marketing launch plans and campaigns, before the final product is released to the market. Customer surveys are very versatile tools, and in addition to these typical survey uses, surveys have been used for getting feedback on adjusting new features, for mid-production research, manufacturing quality research, usability testing, new market analysis, and pricing.

There are a number of ways customer surveys can be administered. Certainly, a survey is part and parcel of the customer visit as it will provide the interview structure, but there are other ways we can also gather customer feedback using surveys. We can deploy mail surveys, in-person surveys, phone surveys, online surveys, and mobile surveys.

# Mail surveys

A mail survey involves mailing out a printed questionnaire to a group of preselected respondents. These respondents could be from your customer list, your dealers, or a magazine list. Respondents are asked to fill out the survey and return it to the researchers. The advantages of the mail survey are:

- **Cost**: Only requires printing and postage, and no training is required for company personnel
- **Privacy**: Respondents can choose to leave any personal information blank, thereby ensuring their privacy is maintained
- **Convenience**: The respondents can take their time to fill out the survey when it best suits them

The disadvantages of the mail survey are:

- **Low response rate**: Typically, response rates are poor, with many surveys only getting a low, single-digit number of returns.
- **Speed**: The response time from survey creation to final respondent tally can take weeks or months.
- **Self-selection**: The survey researcher only receives the surveys of those who choose to return the questionnaires. Quite often, this sample does not accurately represent the sample of the respondents the researcher intended.

# In-person surveys

Some researchers choose to use in-person interviews with an interviewer talking directly to respondents to get the information they require. While the team visit interview would also fall into this loose definition, the survey I am referring to here is a much shorter survey that does not require a preplanned visit or a lengthy customer meeting, but is rather a very short survey that you may find conducted door-to-door or at a mall.

While the sample size of a survey can be considerably larger than what you may be able to achieve with a team visit interview, you may find the feedback you get is not as detailed or valuable. As most surveys are intentionally designed to be short and simple to generate the highest response rates, it is often not possible to probe in real-time as to what the respondent was thinking, or to ask clarifying questions; the result of a survey may just be the realization that you require additional VoC programs to get the detailed information you need.

The advantages of the in-person survey are:

> **Response rate**: Typically, the response rate of an in-person survey is significantly higher than you would find from a mail or email survey

> **Depth**: You are often able to probe much deeper in an in-person interview, and much more complex questions can be asked and answered

> **Speed**: Most in-person surveys are very quick, and it takes the respondents much less time to answer questions versus a mail or email survey

> **Reach**: Using in-person interviews, you are able to target specific geographical locations very precisely, and you can reach people you may not have been able to reach using a mail or telephone survey.

As you can see, there are a number of advantages to the in-person interview, but of course there are a couple of disadvantages as well:

> **Cost**: An in-person interview can be very costly because of the necessity of training the interviewer, the expenses for the actual interviews, and costs associated with the salaries or contracting for the interviewers

> **Accuracy**: While the in-person interview is not necessarily inaccurate, there exists the potential for the interviewer to inject his or her own bias into the questions or responses, which could affect the impartiality of the survey

# Phone surveys

While many might believe that phone surveys were a thing of the past with the advent of "do not call" lists, there is still a very large place for telephone surveys for those instances where you have a preexisting relationship with a customer. In this case, telephone surveys have a number of key advantages:

> **Speed**: Telephone interviews are typically the fastest method to query a customer base, and get results much quicker than in-person or mail-in surveys

> **Cost**: Telephone surveys are usually more economical than an in-person interview, and are not considerably different than a mail survey in terms of cost

As expected, there are some downsides to telephone surveys too:

> **Control**: The interviewer is not able to gauge visual clues from the respondents so as to guide the interview appropriately. Also, it is very easy for the respondent to disengage by hanging up the phone, and many respondents feel their personal or work lives are disrupted or violated when receiving a survey over the phone

> **Visual**: As the entire survey is given orally over the phone, it is impossible to share visual aids such as mock-ups or pictures to explain the survey questions

# Email/mobile surveys

In the last 10 years or so, the internet has changed the way many surveys are conducted. It has become very easy and inexpensive to use internet technology to reach a large number of users, as well as a particular segment of your target audience. With an email or mobile survey, respondents are typically given an embedded hyperlink to a web-based survey. This methodology of customer surveys has many considerable advantages over the other survey methods, which helps to explain its explosive growth and popularity:

> **Speed**: A survey can be written and distributed in less than a day. Respondents can be given a time frame to reply that can be very short. Survey analysis is near instantaneous as the respondents are feeding the answers directly into the survey database, allowing real-time reporting and analysis.

> **Cost**: The administration of the survey is very economical. The user can choose to use free survey tools if their target group is small (such as `surveymonkey. com`, `zoomerang.com`, `surveygizmo.com`, and many others) or can pay for a premium package if their needs are greater. Even the premium packages are very economical compared with the other survey methods. It is very easy to send out surveys to thousands of people for very little cost.

> **Customization**: As the surveys are online and are being hosted, it is very easy to customize the surveys based on factors related to the respondent, such as geographical location, gender, family income, or other demographic information. Using branching technology, it is also possible to instantly change the question being asked depending on how earlier questions were answered by the respondents.

Of course, no survey method is perfect, and there are still a few negatives when using an online survey:

> **Response rate**: Typically, the response rate is very low with online surveys because of the sheer volume of emails many of us get each day

> **Self-selection**: Much like a mail-in survey, the survey researcher only receives the surveys of those who choose to fill out the online survey, and quite often this sample does not accurately represent the sample of the respondents the researcher intended or needed to reach

You must decide which method is best for you and your research, but given the high degree of customization and the relatively low cost, most people will opt for an online survey when given the choice.

# Constructing your survey

While it is far more preferable to do a customer visit interview, customer surveys offer an opportunity to poll your users and potential customers on questions that might otherwise go unanswered. But to be effective, it is necessary for you to have a plan as to how to get the best out of your surveys. The following are some of the suggestions I have found to be effective at developing robust and meaningful customer surveys.

**Think about your target audience**—Who are they and where/when/how will they respond to your survey? Is your ideal survey respondent an executive concerned about the bottom line of his/her manufacturing plant, or is it someone who is interested in making his or her life easier or more enjoyable? Will they respond to your survey on a PC or on a phone? Grid questions work well on a PC, and you are better able to present a slightly longer survey. Mobile phones, on the other hand, do not support grid questions very well, and the expectation is for a much shorter survey.

**Choose your preferred survey method, and how best to distribute your surveys**—As discussed previously, a computer-based survey may be better for surveys requiring a more detailed response, but what about respondents who are not digital natives or computer savvy? In that case, a paper, mail-in survey may be preferable. If you are targeting existing users, an online survey on your website may suffice, but if you need to reach new consumers, a paid ad targeting specific customer demographics and allowing you to target specific people may be a better option:

> **KISS (keep it simple and short)**: Find the shortest way to ask the question without losing its intent. There is a direct correlation between survey length and rate of abandonment. Research has shown you can expect a steep drop in responses if your survey takes more than 5 to 10 minutes—if you want people to finish your survey, be respectful of their time.

> **Have a plan for every question you ask**: Every question you ask must have a well-defined purpose and a strong reason for being asked. Make sure you also fully understand how a customer's response will drive changes in your research. If it doesn't matter how they answer it, why are you asking it?

> **Get buy-in from other parts of the organization**: Discuss the survey with other departments, such as marketing, product management, sales, engineering, and so on. Managers from other departments may have insights you haven't considered. Nothing is more painful than doing customer survey research when you are missing that one vital piece of information because you neglected to ask a specific question.

> **Construct smart, open-ended questions**: While it is easy to ask yes/no questions or multiple choice questions, by far the most enlightening responses will come from survey questions that allow customers to describe, in their own words, their responses. However, the survey structure must also be a consideration as nothing is quite so intimidating as receiving a survey with a large text block connected to the first question.

> **Make use of yes/no questions**: While the open-ended text questions will give you richer data, most of the time a yes/no response is all you need. It has also been shown that closed-ended questions make for great starter questions because they are typically easier to evaluate and complete. A good rule of thumb is to put demographic questions first and make them mandatory. Then, transition from general to more specific questions. Open-ended questions work best at the end of the survey, allowing respondents to provide comments or express opinions.

> **Ask one question at a time**: Do not group questions into the same query. Don't ask questions such as *How did you find our product? What did you like best and least about it? Why or why not?* Multiple point questions greatly limit your probability of getting answers to any of the questions.

> **Make rating scales consistent**: If you ask one question and the directions are for the respondent to choose between 1–5, with 1=Strongly Agree and 5=Strongly Disagree, don't ask another question later in the survey with scales in the opposite orientation like 1=Least Important and 5=Most Important.

> **Avoid leading questions**: Questions that point respondents to answer a certain way may make you feel better about your product, but won't give you the data you need. You should avoid phrasing the question as *We have recently upgraded our capabilities to be the most powerful widget you can buy in the world. What are your thoughts on our new features?*. Instead, you should ask *What do you think of the new widget features?*.

> **Avoid acronyms and jargon**: Unless your surveys are extremely targeted and customers are very knowledgeable about your industry, you are likely to run into problems as the customer may answer untruthfully or incorrectly if he/she does not understand what you are asking.

> **Consider reporting back to the customer**: Quite often, a customer will be interested in understanding their perceptions versus those of their peers. By offering the chance to see how they answered the questions compared with other respondents, you will increase the participant's engagement level and thoughtfulness of response.

> **Test your survey**: Once you have gone through the process of creating your questions and planning your survey, conduct one last check to make sure everything is working as it should by doing a pretest with your coworkers or a few members of your target audience to make sure there are no glitches or unexpected question interpretations.

Once you have collected all the data, it will be necessary to analyze the results. This is where online surveys really shine as most have built-in analysis capabilities, including tables, charts, graphs, cross-tabulations, and more advanced functionality. With most of the tools available on the market, you can also export it into Excel to build bar charts or pivot tables that help you draw more meaningful insights.

# Focus groups

A focus group is a form of qualitative research in which a group of respondents are asked about their feeling, opinions, perceptions, and attitudes toward a new product, concept, or service. This is used typically in the discovery phase when organizations wish to create an overall direction for a new product concept. They can also be used in the evaluation phase as a last check before launching the new product, to test market the new product, name the new product, explore packaging alternatives, or to gain feedback regarding market launch strategies.

Typically, a focus group is an interview conducted by a trained moderator with a small group of respondents. The respondents are recruited on the basis of a predefined criterion, and could include demographics, attitudes, buying behavior, or other behavior signals. Quite often, the interviews are held in a specially designed room with two-way mirrors, allowing the organization the ability to monitor the interactions via two-way mirrors. Ideally, the interactions are informal and conversational, allowing the respondents to give views that may or may not be applicable to the research. An advantage of the focus group is the relatively low cost compared to customer visits, although the costs can ramp up dramatically if the research is to be done on a nationwide basis and it is necessary to gather responses from multiple locals throughout the country.

In the case of focus groups, often the *group discussions* produce data and insights that would be less likely to appear during other VoC methods, such as surveys or one-on-one interviews. As participants listen to others comments and experiences, quite often this will stimulate memories, ideas, and experiences in other participants' minds. This is sometimes called the **group effect**, where group members engage in a cascading result where one comment leads to another and to another and to another.

A popular form of focus group is the customer brainstorming session. This type of program is often deployed at customer events in the form of B2B markets. In this case, we gather a group of users and deploy formal brainstorming methods to come up with new product ideas. It is recommended that you kick off these focus groups in an *inverse brainstorming* exercise to uncover user wants, needs, points of pain, product shortcomings, and deficiencies. This is sometimes called PAIN storming and uncovers the fundamental drivers of new opportunities. This helps to focus your innovation process on the specific needs of the customers.

Here are the steps and the things you must identify before you engage in a PAIN storming process:

> ➤ **Person**: Who is the specific person or customer?

> ➤ **Activities**: What are the everyday things they do in their work or life and why?

> ➤ **Insights**: What are the methods or processes they use to get their work done and what ways have they invented to reach their desired goal?

> ➤ **Needs**: What are the biggest pain points that are the root causes of the customers' problems or unmet desires? What are the workarounds they have created and what is responsible for the stress, pain, or dissatisfaction in their life or work?

Once these "pains" are identified, the group is then led into possible solutions to address the identified deficiencies.

While focus groups may provide great customer insights if they are executed properly, my own personal observation is that there are many things that can go wrong in a focus group if the moderator is not very well versed in his craft, and in this case, the negatives can greatly outweigh the positives. A potential issue with focus group research can manifest itself because of the actual process itself. If the focus groups are held in a special room with two-way glass or in a laboratory setting with recording instruments, the participants may hold back or attempt to answer the questions the way that they think the moderator wishes them to. A secondary issue with focus groups arises from the potential of *observer dependency*. The researcher's own analysis of the data collected from the session can influence the results obtained.

But the largest downside I have observed when using focus groups is "groupthink" or "peer pressure", which is similar to things that have been known to happen in a court of law in the case of juries. Sometimes a particularly outspoken or knowledgeable individual will voice his or her opinion, and based on the way they present their information, it is construed as fact, and opposing viewpoints could be perceived as being wrong-headed or uninformed. Here, the skills of a trained moderator cannot be underestimated and the moderator must ensure that this does not happen.

Douglas Rushkoff, in his piece *Get Back in the Box: Innovation from the Inside Out*, has found that focus groups are often useless, and frequently cause more trouble than they meant to solve, with focus groups often aiming to please rather than offering their own opinions or evaluations, and with data often cherry picked to support a forgone conclusion. An excellent example of this was the disastrous introduction of New Coke in the 1980s.

In the 1940s and 1950s, the Coca-Cola company owned the beverage market with 60% market share. By 1983, it declined to 24% and Pepsi was outselling Coke. The research showed that young drinkers preferred the sweetness of Pepsi, which was attributed to its gains. Coca-Cola commissioned a secret effort, *Project Kansas*, to test and perfect a new, sweeter flavor for Coke.

The Coca-Cola marketing group conducted taste tests on focus groups. While the results of the focus groups were strong, with the majority favoring the new formula over the old formula or Pepsi, there was a noticeable and distinct segment who felt angry and alienated at the very thought of Coke changing their formula.

Regardless of this, the Coca-Cola management decided to move forward with the new formulation, and in April 1985, New Coke was introduced and production of the original formulation ended the same week. The new formulation was a direct contradiction to the advertisements that had been running for years. Spokesman Bill Cosby would tout the less-sweet taste as a reason to prefer Coke over Pepsi and Coke had long been marketed as "The Real Thing", constant and unchanging, which had, apparently, now changed.

After its introduction, Coke recognized an 8% gain versus sales from the previous year. Despite New Coke's acceptance with a large number of customers, a vocal minority resented the change in the formula and were very vocal about sharing their views—just as had happened in the focus groups. Company headquarters received a 300% increase in call volume with over 400,000 calls and letters expressing dismay and disgust at the decision. According to a psychiatrist that Coke had hired to listen in on the calls, some people sounded as if they were discussing the death of a family member when lamenting the loss of the original Coke.

Talk show host and comedians mocked the switch. Ads for New Coke were booed when they appeared during a baseball game in Houston. Fidel Castro called the New Coke "a sign of American decadence" and the "Old Cola Drinkers of America" organization was formed to try and persuade Coke to reintroduce the old formula or sell it to someone else. Finally, due to pressures from the bottlers who had also received their share of negativity from their customers and friends, and who were hinting *boycott*, Coke moved the discussion from *whether* to reintroduce the old formula to *when*. Coca-Cola announced the return of the original formula in July, less than 3 months after it was retired, and renamed it Coca-Cola Classic.

There are a number of lessons to be learned from the Coke experience. First and foremost is the cautionary tale of how to interpret data from focus groups. The messages were clear from the focus groups that there would be a small but vocal minority who would find great dissatisfaction with changing from Coke to New Coke, but the company ignored the feedback as it only represented a small percentage of the focus group participants. Another interesting note is the flawed way these focus groups and taste tests were held. In these tests, drinkers were given small samples to try out. Had the marketing team conducted ethnographic research and conducted home-use tests instead of taste testing via focus groups, they would have understood that although many consumers react positively to the sweeter taste when drinking a Pepsi or New Coke in small quantities, it may become unattractively sweet when drunk in quantity, while Coke may be more attractive for drinking in volume precisely because it is less sweet.

# Lead user analysis

As we've discussed, the best companies often work very closely with their customers to uncover wants, needs, and desires that can be translated into new features, improved products, or new service offerings. Companies typically reach out to their current and potential customers to understand what matters most to the people who will ultimately choose whether or not to purchase their products. The lead user research methodology goes a step further, looking not only at the current and potential typical customers, but to those customers and users whose needs and wants lead, and ultimately drive, the market.

These *lead users* will often have needs the rest of the market does not yet have, and will modify existing products or use your products in unforeseen ways to meet the needs they've identified.

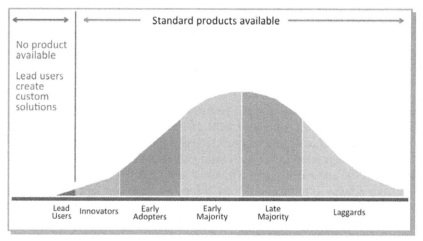

*Figure 4.2: Lead user adoption versus the rest of the market*

When dealing with the masses, the feedback one often receives is a reticence to change. "This doesn't taste like cola", the focus group proclaimed when evaluating Red Bull. "Only secretaries have keyboards on their desk," they said about PCs. All kinds of great ideas, from the Walkman to nacho chips, originally died in research with average consumers. As Malcolm Gladwell explained to us in his epic book *Blink*, that's because regular people don't like change very much.

What Malcolm Gladwell didn't tell us is that there are people out there that will gravitate toward a new idea and, sometimes, they even have the new idea for you. Sometimes it is because they are ahead of the curve and sometimes it is because their needs are different. Red Bull didn't taste like a cola, but clubbers loved Red Bull as it helped them rave all night.

The lead-user research method was developed by Eric von Hippel in 1986 as a systematic way to delve into the insights and innovations of these lead users. Von Hippel developed the term, **lead user** and his definition is:

➤ Lead users have new product or service needs that will be general in a marketplace, but they face them months or years before the bulk of the market encounters them.

➤ Lead users expect to benefit significantly by finding a solution to their needs. As a result, they often develop new products or services themselves because they can't find a solution to their problem in the marketplace.

As Eric von Hippel remarked, "This is not traditional market research—asking customers what they want. This is identifying what your most advanced users are already doing and understanding what their innovations mean for the future of your business". Von Hippel went on to say that a lead user is motivated to innovate in order to solve his or her own problems rather than to sell a product or service. What was truly remarkable about von Hippel's research is the observation that, in certain industrial fields, innovations most often come from users. As an example, 100% of "first of type" innovations in scientific instruments and semiconductor process equipment during the research period came from users. Of course, in this context a user could be an individual, a group, or a company. But lead users do not just come from technology markets. We all know of many examples such as Robert Weinreb, founder and president of the Tenba Bag Company, who developed breakthrough innovations in ergonomic camera bags. He had been a photographer who desperately needed a flexible, special-purpose, and lightweight, protective equipment bag to take on photoshoots. There was no bag that fit the needs Mr. Weinreb had on the market, so he designed and manufactured his own, and has since become a major seller of camera equipment bags.

Very few people are aware of this, but lead users can have profound affects on us all. The following is an excerpt from *Technology Review* in July 1996

> *"Berners-Lee did not set out to invent a contemporary cultural phenomenon; rather, he says, "It was something I needed in my work." He wanted to simply solve a problem that was hindering his efforts as a consulting software engineer at CERN.*

> *"Berners-Lee's innovation was to apply hypertext to the growing reality of networked computers. He expanded the idea he had developed at CERN and made it available on the Internet in the summer of 1991."*

> *– Technology Review, July 1996, p.34*

You may or may not know the name Tim Berners-Lee, but it was because of Tim Berners Lee's need for a more robust way to share information with his colleagues over a network that resulted in the World Wide Web, or what we refer to simply as *the internet.*

As you can see, lead user analysis does have the potential to create some highly innovative and impactful products, but it can also have a significant affect on a company's bottom line. In a recent study, it was found that projects based on the lead user method resulted in eight times higher sales than projects with traditional methods at 3M, a proponent of lead user research. 3M executives went on to say that lead user analysis resulted in "the highest rate of new product line generation in 50 years for the 5 divisions tested".

There are four key differences between lead user research projects and standard market research efforts.

Lead-user research projects:

> ➤ Focus on the needs of leading-edge users, not typical or average users

> ➤ Seek not only needs but innovations—user-developed solutions to leading-edge needs from users

> ➤ Seek needs and solutions in adjacent markets and nonobvious adjacent markets in addition to the target market

> ➤ Employ a cross-disciplinary team bringing in perspectives from various parts of the organization

In addition to the excellent research Eric von Hippel did, he continued to develop more resources for lead user practitioners. The following is a high-level roadmap you can use to deploy a lead user program in your company. If you need additional reading, Dr. von Hippel also has an excellent lead user project handbook published through MIT at `http://web.mit.edu/people/evhippel/Lead%20User%20Project%20 Handbook%20(Full%20Version).pdf`.

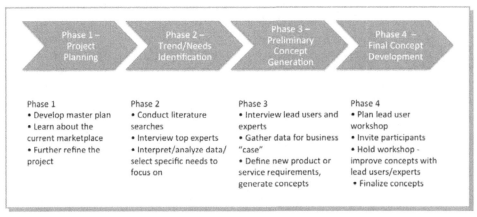

*Figure 4.3: Lead user project*

> ➤ **Phase One, preparing to launch the lead-user project**: The team plans the project schedule, learns about the current marketplace, and shapes the project focus.

> ➤ **Phase Two, identifying key trends and customer needs**: The team seeks out lead users and lead use experts in order to understand trends that impact the area of study and glean deeper insight into the needs of leading edge users by observing how they are innovating solutions to address gaps in the market. This phase culminates in framing the needs that will be the focus of the next phase.

> **Phase Three, exploring lead-user needs and solutions and creating preliminary concepts**: The project team continues to find lead users through networking and interviews. The team may make site visits to observe lead users and uncover tacit information. (A lead user may not be aware of the uniqueness or innovative quality of his or her work, and the project team, in observing the user, may glean additional insights.) At the same time, the team generates preliminary solution concepts by putting together insights gleaned from various lead-user innovations and outcomes from team synthesis activities. These solution concepts will be refined further in a workshop with some lead users.

> **Phase Four, final concept development and improving solution concepts with lead users and experts**: The team invites a select group of lead users and lead use experts to attend a two-and-a half day workshop focused on improving or adding to promising preliminary concepts. The project team takes the concepts generated from the workshop, ties them into the other pieces of the solution, creates a business case, and delivers recommendations to management.

While a lead user project can have significant upsides to the organization for new and innovative product and services, it must be mentioned that a lead user project is a significant investment of an organization's time and financial resources. Typical lead user projects run from 6 to 8 months with a cross-functional team of four to six people all working part time with senior leadership buy-in and support. There should also be one or two additional coaches as part of the team, who are knowledgeable about the lead user process.

# Ethnography

Ethnography is the study of human behavior. Researchers and scientists who want to understand other cultures have long used ethnographic methods. It really isn't possible to ask people details about their culture and how it is different to other cultures because culture is such an ingrained construct. Sometimes the best way to understand a culture is to experience it by living in it, much the way researchers have done in the past by living with remote tribes in Africa or the Amazon.

As the need to understand customers at a deeper level grows, it becomes more and more apparent that at times, the traditional customer research methods are incomplete in creating breakthrough innovations. To help deal with this shortcoming, many practitioners are resorting to methods based on anthropology, and their approach to VoC is commonly referred to as ethnography. You may also know of these methods as immersion or observational research.

In the past, surveys have been one of the primary tools that marketers have used to gather this type of customer data, but ethnography has the ability to provide a much deeper and richer view into the customer than any survey could achieve.

Today's corporations are deluged with data and research revolving around customer behavior and needs. While there are often numerous data points about customers, what is often missing is how to understand customer behavior in context.

*Observing your customers, how they interact with your products, and how they perform their daily tasks will help you to understand your true customer needs, which may be vastly different than the perception of those needs.*

Marketers and product developers who are not, and cannot, become customers may be able to observe and question those customers as they perform their work duties or attempt to solve a problem over the course of their day. This research technique is called **shadowing**. An example of shadowing might be a researcher spending a day with a user of an accounting program to see their daily usage and patterns when using the software.

When it is difficult or impossible to access a customer in their own place or work, such as a secure government facility, or in their personal life, such as in their home, it is possible to use *Self-Observations/Diaries* where you request that your customers provide self-observations about their activities in using your product and document their observations in a diary or report. While this is preferable to not having any ethnographical research, it is not nearly as accurate or robust as performing in-person research.

While it is far preferable to use the shadowing method of ethnographical research, whichever method is used, it is imperative that the researcher imposes a minimum of his or her own bias on the results of the analysis.

In either case, it has been shown that if a product developer or market researcher relies only on methods that are based on what customers say, and ignores what they actually do and how they use their product, then this can interject significant errors between their perception of the customer's need and the true voice of the customer.

As an example, in one focus study conducted by Microsoft, customers were asked whether they liked the product and whether there were any features they did not like or wished to add. The respondents claimed they did like the product and there were no features they did not like or wished to add. However, when the Microsoft developers began videotaping these customers and recording their keystrokes, a much different picture emerged. The developers could see the difficulty users had in using the product, the hesitation when not knowing what to do next, and the facial expressions, which told the developers that the customers did not really embrace the product.

All too often, developers and marketers simply ask; *What do you think about my product?* instead of understanding the actual customer wants and needs, and as we know, what a customer says is not always the complete truth. This happens for a number of reasons:

➤ The customers are not technical experts. Often customers have difficulty expressing exactly what they are having trouble with or what kind of product would solve their needs.

➤ In a related example, some customers are not willing to admit that they have problems with your product for fear they will appear ignorant or not smart enough to use it.

➤ A customer's ability to describe a product's problem requires a certain amount of familiarity. If they are not familiar enough with a product, they will not be able to elaborate on its shortcomings.

➤ Conversely, if a customer is too familiar with a product, then he or she has learned how to get around it and may have found ways to make up for its shortcomings by modifying their own processes. In this case, the customer may have a hard time remembering the details of the pain he or she initially experienced or just chalked it up to not understanding how to use it.

➤ When a customer is asked about their past problems with a product, much of the response has to do with the way the question has been asked. Unfortunately, a developer or marketer who is not always completely objective can author many of the survey questions a customer is asked.

➤ Customers have their own agendas. While this may not be conscious, this greatly effects how a customer will answer questions in a survey or in an interview. Often they will have preconceived notions about what a marketer wants to hear or who is in the room when the question is being asked, which results in inaccurate, and sometimes diametrically opposed, responses.

It is important that any researcher using ethnographical methods does so with the proper frame of mind. While it is very easy to make assumptions about why a customer is behaving in a particular fashion or why he/she is using your product in a certain way, it is much better to simply observe and record as much fine detail as possible during the fieldwork. You are trying to understand the customer's view and point of reference and not trying to fit your preconceived judgments or assumptions. Leave the analysis piece for when the observation is complete or as part of a follow-up discussion.

As one would expect, part of the process in an ethnological interview is selecting the right customers to conduct this research. As most of the time we will conduct ethnological research in conjunction with the interview process, I will discuss how to select customers in more detail for both the ethnological research as well as the customer interview in *Chapter 5, The Interview Process—Preparation.* We will also talk about integrating ethnographic research as part of the customer interview in *Chapter 6, The Interview Process—The Interview.*

# Other VoC methods

There are a number of other VoC methods that are used, but that are not as effective or as widespread as the preceding examples, although that may be changing in the field of customer or user designs. A brief summary of each follows:

> - **Customer advisory board**: This VoC approach has been around for many years and is comprised of your best and most vocal proponents, and sometimes detractors, of your product to advise the firm of what problems they are having and what new products might be needed. This can be mutually beneficial if they are done correctly, allowing the firm to send a key signal to these targeted customers that we value their input, and further allowing the firm to also uncover some new opportunities to satisfy this often demanding set of customers. While this has a long history, it is not found to be especially effective. This may be due to the nature of customer advisory boards, or more likely, due to the way the customer advisory board meetings are structured. Most of the time, these meetings are very loosely structured, with no real agenda or defined outcome. If you are going to deploy a customer advisory board, make sure you have a structured session with clear discussion points and exercises to gain the most benefit from everyone's time.

> - **Community of enthusiasts**: This is not dissimilar to the customer advisory board. The organization forms a community of enthusiasts who discuss the product problems and ideas for new features/concepts. Typically, this is done on the internet and is relatively easy to set up with the various wiki and chatting software that is available at little or no cost. The advantages are much like the customer advisory board, as many of the best ideas for products will come from those who know the product the best and push the product boundaries. It is very easy to monitor the activity in the chat room to gain insights into what is actually going on in the community and to attempt to develop new product solutions or concepts. The downside of this approach is that it takes considerable time to make sure you are actively participating in the group discussions, or the community will likely die. The second challenge is the skill it takes to ferret out the information necessary for good product decisions from the other noise that often occurs in these types of forums. Certainly, this method is not useful for all product categories, and is best suited for product categories where there is already an enthusiastic community. Samples would include sports equipment, automobiles, some software, and mobile phones.

> - **The customer or user designs**: This is a relatively new VoC process and has largely been made possible through the advent of information technology and the internet. As part of **Open Innovation,** the concept of *customer designs* often falls under the area of *crowdsourcing*. While the Cooper and Dreher research considered Open Innovation a separate methodology, I believe this is an area where the lines are much more blurred and I consider this both an Open Innovation concept as well as a VoC methodology. In the concept of crowdsourcing, customers or users are invited to help the product designer design the next product. The benefits can be substantial, as you are potentially tapping into the needs and wants of thousands of customers.

Crowdsourcing got its start in the early 2000s. Companies such as Starbucks and Dell released their *My Starbuck Idea* and *Dell IdeaStorm*. If one looks at My Starbucks Idea, you will see comments about bringing back a certain coffee or cake, but you will also see ideas on how to make Starbucks a better retailer (emailing a reminder before rewards expire, notifying baristas on-screen of card reward, freezing gold card status for military while deployed) as well as new product offerings and ways to conduct business (short-sized fraps for kids, bicycle-friendly service, and dairy alternatives).

You may believe that crowdsourcing is a very niche play and that more complex businesses could not benefit from it. Fiat, the number one car manufacturer in Italy, would vehemently disagree. In 2009, they sought a design for a new concept vehicle. Rather than turning inward to their team of designers and engineers, the company took an unusual tack and turned outward, to their customers. With the aid of a viral marketing campaign, Fiat crowd-sourced the design of their new concept car, the Mio, and let the world decide how the car would look, feel, and drive. The company set up a crowdsourcing platform on its website that elicited over 10,000 different suggestions from 160 different counties for the new vehicle. The Fiat Mio became the world's first crowd-sourced car, with Fiat implementing many of the suggestions they received during the campaign. The Fiat Mio was unveiled at the San Paulo International Automobile show to rave reviews and has garnered numerous design awards:

*Figure 4.4: Crowdsourcing automobiles*

Crowdsourcing is becoming more and more common as companies are looking for new ideas, and new ways to cut costs. Crowdsourcing continues to grow. Nokia has launched the *Invent with Nokia* scheme, where Nokia will pay would-be inventors for their ideas if they like them enough to prototype them.

Whole new business models have evolved as a result of crowdsourcing through sites such as Quirky (www.quirky.com), and at least one new crowd-sourced car company, Local Motors, is selling crowd-sourced cars to the public, as well as a very unique buying experience where you become part of the assembly team, at a considerable premium over an off-the-line automobile:

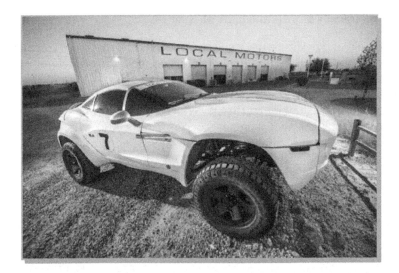

Additional VoC analytical tools, such as conjoint analysis and QFD, also use the same methods that we have described here to collect customer data. Tools like these will be very helpful in parsing the customer data we collect, and will be discussed in more detail in *Chapter 7, Understanding the Customer's Voice*, where we will review how to take VoC and create successful products.

# Summary

Every company wants to get closer to their customers and understand their unarticulated wants, needs, and desires. Unfortunately, there is not a silver bullet that will give you all the answers you need to make the next great breakthrough product, but rather you likely need to deploy multiple methods to get the result you desire. In this chapter, we discussed the various types of ways you can choose to conduct VoC research, from interviews, to ethnographical research, to crowdsourcing. Ultimately, you must decide which method, or combination of methods, will work best for your organization. Many of us are well aware of survey research and how that has changed over time with the introduction of the internet and email. While it has been around for a long time, it is still a very economical way to get feedback from 30 to 30,000 customers. Some organizations have used focus groups for their customer research and some have found great success, but perhaps too many have had mixed results. Ethnographical research and lead user research both have the ability to drive true innovation, but both require a considerable time and financial commitment.

In the research conducted by Cooper and Dreher, customer interviews were the most popular VoC method used and are very close to being the most effective of all the VoC methods analyzed. In the next chapter, we will begin to put together the framework on how to construct a customer interview, and in *Chapter 6, The Interview Process—The Interview*, we will talk about the execution of the customer visit and interview.

# 5

# The Interview Process – Preparation

*"If you don't know where you're going, any road will take you there".*

> —*Exchange between Alice and the Cheshire Cat in Alice in Wonderland by Lewis Carroll*

In the previous chapter, we talked about the various tools and methods available to reach out to customers to get their feedback. We reviewed how to construct and administer surveys, developing focus groups and the benefits and shortcomings of them, focusing on your power users through lead user analysis, discussed incorporating ethnography into your interview process, as well as a number of other VoC methods. While all these methods do have their place in customer research, none are as complete or provide as rich of a view of the market as actual face-to-face interviews that you have with your customers. Customer interviews, if they are done correctly, can provide the insight into the customer's unarticulated needs that few other research techniques can duplicate.

But before you start scheduling interviews with customers, you need to develop a plan. You need to understand which markets you wish to focus on, which customers you wish to interview and what job titles they have, who will do the interviews, what questions you will ask, and how you will schedule the meetings. In this chapter, we will answer all these questions about preparing for the customer interview, and in *Chapter 6, The Interview Process – The Interview*, we will take the next step and talk about how to actually conduct the customer interview.

## The plan

In many organizations, customer visits are not planned to elicit feedback, but are rather a reaction to an event (typically a negative one) or are part of the sales process. As a result, there is no consistent quantifiable data that comes out of these visits, but they are rather a necessity of running the day-to-day business.

For those organizations that do plan customer visits as part of exploratory research, quite often these visits remain unstructured and are typically opportunistic. For most businesses, customer visits are also very expensive as there are many costs involved, including travel, expenses, and most importantly, time.

To successfully embark on a customer visit initiative, it is necessary to develop and quantify the goals you are hoping to achieve and formulate a plan to achieve the goals, thereby justifying the expenditure of time and resources that the company will be investing. A plan for customer visits that are designed to elicit customer feedback outside of the day-to-day sales or addressing customer complaints or issues will typically have the following elements:

> A clearly defined, written objective of what questions the customer visit program will help answer

> A team who is assigned to plan and execute the customer visits (and who is given the necessary time and budget)

> A method of choosing the correct customers to interview and getting their buy-in

> A discussion guide that helps the team accomplish the written objective through a consistent methodology of investigative inquiry

> A process for conducting the customer interviews

> A process for analyzing, reporting, and internalizing the results

We will address the first four points in this chapter. The fifth point will be covered in *Chapter 6, The Interview Process – The Interview,,* and the sixth will be covered in *Chapter 7, Understanding the Customer's Voice,* and *Chapter 8, Validating the Customer's Voice,* where we will discuss the ways of analyzing and presenting the data you collect in the interview.

# Visit purpose

A necessary first step in any customer visit process is to understand why you are conducting the market research in the first place. As alluded to in the preceding quote from *Alice in Wonderland,* unless you have clearly defined objectives for the VoC initiative you are undertaking, how will you use the information you learn, how will you know when you have gotten there?

To define the task at hand, the best thing you can do is to write it down! While it is often beneficial to visit customers, even when there is no clear goal, you will not end up where you need to be. And though it is often difficult to fully articulate what it is you hope to accomplish, by writing it down you reap a number of benefits.

First, it forces you to decide between various paths and make a commitment, both to yourself and the organization. All too often, product and marketing managers are pulled in multiple directions with multiple priorities, all of which need to be done. When analyzing a potential new offering for the business, there will be a host of avenues to explore and areas of ignorance you wish to learn more about. Writing your objectives down will likely help to reduce the scale of the actual task as it will allow you to become more focused on devising a plan to meet the ultimate goal and not get pulled in too many adjacent areas with less intrinsic value to the organization or the task at hand.

While difficult for many, the goal is to develop a statement of intent for the VoC interviews from which to develop a plan. This statement of intent needs to be concise enough so that it is clear in your own mind exactly what will be executed and accomplished. If it is too vague or ambiguous, it will be very difficult for you to explain to others in the organization and it will leave you with questionable results.

The following are some guidelines you may wish to adhere to when developing your own statement of intent for your customer visits:

> **Your statement of intent should be no more than two sentences, 25 words max (ideally somewhere between 10–20)**: If you end up with a longer statement of intent than this, chances are you are either biting off more than you can chew or you don't have a clear, concise idea of what it is that you are trying to accomplish.

> **The statement of intent should be achievable**: While it is noble to try and solve all the problems of your company with your VoC initiative, the statement of intent must be doable while still being framed so as to provide a benefit to the organization that will need to fund and resource your program.

> **The statement of intent must be framed as being consistent with the goals of the organization**: Only by articulating and showing value will you get the organizational buy-in you require.

> **The statement of intent should provide a clear direction for the VoC process**: While your actual plan for the VoC interview process may differ from everyone else's expectations, your statement of intent should be such that it will not be a significant difference.

> **Look to key action verbs when defining your statement of intent**: Consider verbs such as identify, describe, define, create, understand, generate, explore, investigate, and ascertain when formulating your statement of intent. It is also beneficial to identify whether you will be studying/interviewing all your customers or a particular sub-segment. A good rule of thumb is to create a statement of intent with the following formula:

*To [action verb]…[market segment]…resulting in [objective]*

The following are some B2B examples to help illustrate the preceding points:

> ➤ To understand small manufacturers' buying considerations for conveyor systems resulting in our next generation conveyor rollers

> ➤ To identify new market opportunities in the ethanol chemical processing market resulting in new distilling equipment

> ➤ To investigate how customers in the food processing industry measure raw material purity resulting in enhancements to our vision system

> ➤ To describe key processes in the automobile painting application industry resulting in identification of key product features for industrial painting robots

> ➤ To define key interface requirements for embedded software stacks for the telematics market resulting in a prioritized list of required product attributes

When creating your statement of intent, do be careful not to use verbs that would be more clearly associated with other mass-market research techniques such as surveys. Some of the words you should avoid when constructing your statement of intent would include evaluate, test, measure, project, and forecast.

While a statement of intent will help you, the program manager, greatly, it will also have additional benefits to your organization regarding two key constituents:

> ➤ Your management

> ➤ Your associates in other departments whose support you will need to conduct an effective VoC program

Your management is likely paying for this program and has a vested interest in the results and success you generate. If your statement of intent is ambiguous or lacks clarity, it is likely your management will walk away with a different set of expectations than what you will be able to deliver. If your statement is clear, but management does not concur with the direction you have outlined in your statement of intent, there is still the opportunity for the following:

> ➤ Educate management why the direction you have set out is the correct one

> ➤ Refine the statement to more closely align with the direction management is setting for the organization

> ➤ Get additional resources (if required) to meet the new direction if management changes the scope of the program

It is far, far better to be aligned with management before you start a VoC program than trying to justify the program and results after the fact.

Almost as important as getting buy-in from management is the need to get buy-in from associates in other parts of the organization who will be affected by, may need to help resource, or will ultimately use the results you generate. As anyone who has worked in a corporate environment will tell you, if you don't get buy-in from your associates at the beginning of an initiative, there is very little chance you will get buy-in at the end.

If the other departments in the organization are able to offer their input, advice, and criticism, then not only will you end up with a better program, you will also likely end up with wide support across the organization.

Once you have completed your statement of intent, you should also put some structure around the next level of detail outlining the *objectives* of the visit. Specifically, the objectives will clearly enumerate the number of visits you intend to pursue, a timeline with the critical dates, an articulation of the types of customers you will visit, and a defined resultant report to be sent out to the organization.

By way of some illustrative examples:

*Complete a total of 16 customer interviews in eight companies with software engineers in the embedded software telematics market. Output will be delivered to the organization via presentation to upper management and findings will be incorporated into software release 3.4.*

*By the end of December, we will have interviewed a total of 20 people in the automobile assembly market with 50% in engineering and 50% in production design. The resultant findings will be incorporated into our Excelsior Project MRD and presented to the directors by January 31.*

# Segmenting the market

The task of selecting customers to visit as part of your VoC initiative is one of the most critical and difficult parts of the entire process. No matter how excellent your execution in all other aspects of the VoC program, if you select the wrong customers for your interviews, your time and money will have been wasted, but worse, you will end up with a distorted view of the market and will likely take a path that will not yield the success you expect.

The first step in the selection process is to review the segmentation we discussed in *Chapter 3, Laying the Groundwork*. In that chapter, we saw that the goal of any segmentation exercise was to define your target market. If you have already heeded the advice given within that chapter, you may have already classified your customer according to a multitude of criteria such as geography, demographic, psychographic and behavioral attributes, purchasing approaches, volume, industry classification, business type, and so on. During the segmentation exercise, you should have also evaluated each market segment, constructed segment profiles for each, evaluated the attractiveness of each segment, and lastly, selected your target markets. It is these target markets or segments that we wish to use and expand upon to identify potential customers to interview.

If all we had to do was identify our target markets, our task would be difficult enough. Unfortunately for us, target segments are but one dimension in choosing customers to interview.

# Who is the customer and selecting the right customers to visit

After we have a good handle on the market segments we wish to analyze, we need to answer three key questions:

> **Who are you going to interview?**
>
> You will need to identify which of the market segments you need to focus your attention on for this program. Will you look to interviewing small, medium, or large customers? Will you focus on North America, Europe, or Asia, or do you need to interview customers in each geographical region? If you serve more than a few market segments, which ones will you pick to participate in this study? Once you have completed this, you must also decide which functions and job titles are the most important for you to talk to.

> **How many customers will you interview?**
>
> Once you have decided on segments, geography, size of company, and job titles, you must decide how many people of each job title in each segment/category you must speak to in order to meet your objectives.

> **Where will I conduct the interviews?**
>
> Will you send teams to each of the identified target customer locations, or would the process be better served by having the customer visit your location?

# Who are you going to interview?

As we stated in the preceding section, the first step in customer sample selection is to review our segmentation and pick out the ones that are the most valuable for our VoC initiative. This task is best done in a group setting with all the stakeholders present and engaged. There should be a robust discussion with senior management in the organization to make sure your VoC program aligns with the strategic direction of the organization. As you can imagine, if you or your team selects interviewees and builds your next generation product based on the needs of a segment that is *not* a target segment, the likelihood of your VoC program meeting the needs of the company management will be greatly diminished.

When deciding whom you wish to interview, you will need to come up with a sample selection process to decide what would be the best use of your time and resources. This process is meant to be a way to identify the most representative profile of your target customers that are true to the objectives you have set, but it is critical that you try and keep your target selection process as simple as possible. It is best to try and devise one or more two-dimensional tables showing the most critical aspects of customer selection on the axis.

You can have any number of attributes for the customer selection axis, including the types of customers (lead users, satisfied customers, dissatisfied customers, former customers, noncustomers), other customer archetypes (most profitable customers, least profitable customers, channel partners, distributors, customers buying much more recently, customers buying much less recently, power users, leads lost, and so on), types of internal customers (purchasing, installers, engineering, users, key decision maker, repair and service technicians), geographical segments, customer segments, and more.

The following are the two potential examples highlighting ways to segment your customers for sample selection that I find both effective and simple:

| | Lead Users | Satisfied Customers | Dissatisfied Customers | Former Customers | Non-Customers |
|---|---|---|---|---|---|
| Segment 1 | | | | | |
| | | Lead Users | Satisfied Customers | Dissatisfied Customers | Former Customers |
| Segment 2 | N. America | | | | |
| Segment 3 | Europe | | | | |
| | Asia | | | | |

*Figure 5.1: Customer profile matrix*

The first one looks at customer types (**Lead Users**, **Satisfied Customers**, **Dissatisfied Customers**, **Former Customer**, **Non-Customers**) versus the different market segments you are targeting. By taking this approach, you can fill in the table with customers in each quadrant ensuring that key customers in each segment are being identified and earmarked for inclusion into your program. The second approach looks at customer types versus geographical location. Most of the time, you will find that needs and differences in other geographical areas will be just as pronounced as those in different market segments, making it all the more critical to include geographically dispersed customers if investigating an international product.

The reason I like using a variation of the matrices in the preceding diagram is that it forces you to include those customers who are not the typical customers that your company calls on all the time. If you only include the customers who are your traditional customers that the company knows very well (and by extension, they know and like you well), it will be much harder to create a new product that will help to expand your market to that large segment of customers that you are not selling to.

Of course, if you are expanding your VoC program to include customers you don't already have, how do you go about finding who they are? Some of these will be easy to find, and the sales team can potentially provide you with customers for whom they have not been successful in persuading. Of course, this information may not always be easy to get from the sales team for fear that your research could unearth additional issues the noncustomers have which go beyond product considerations.

The following are some thoughts as to where you could find potential and noncustomers to help fill in one of the preceding matrices:

> **Your company CRM**: Assuming your company has a CRM system that is actually used, this is a potential goldmine of lost opportunities and past customers, as well as an excellent place to identify your current customers. If your CRM system is robust, there may also be customer data in here about service and repair issues that customers have had as well as people who have gone through your call center. If not, I would also recommend seeing what customer information those organizations have as well.

> **Your website**: If your website is not linked to your CRM, this is another potential source of customers who, for one reason or another, thought enough about your company and product to investigate you, but did not ultimately buy.

> **LinkedIn groups and other online blogs**: This can be an excellent source of identifying potential customers that you do not currently have. Of course, if you spend the time absorbing what people are writing in their LinkedIn group or blog, you can also identify lead users based on what they write, whether they are using your products or not.

> **Tradeshows**: You will typically have a list of people who have visited your booth and expressed some level of interest, but you can also purchase lists from the tradeshow or event organizer if you do not already have it.

> **Hire a market research firm**: If you develop a persona around the type of person you wish to include in your research, these organizations can call around and solicit volunteers on your behalf in your industry.

> **Professional organizations**: Many industries have professional organizations or standards bodies that help drive the market. These individuals are often very knowledgeable about your industry and can offer great insight, if they're not a competitor. Be sure to discuss your needs with the organization management. They can provide the right guidance for contacting individuals and can often share ideas of who would be a good point of contact.

> **Magazines and other lists**: There are list brokers and magazines that offer access to their lists for a fee.

# How many customers must I interview?

This is a question everyone has, but there is no definitive number of interviews that I can offer to you. However, the following are some guidelines that may be helpful in determining the right number of customers for your project:

➤ The more strategic the product, the larger the number of customers you should target. If this product is key to the future success of the organization, you definitely want to make sure you have gotten it right and have a clear picture of the market. If you are interviewing customers regarding a minor modification or enhancement to an existing product, you would certainly not wish to invest the same level of time and money that you would if you were interviewing customers regarding the creation of a whole new product platform aimed at customers in a different market segment than that you are already working with.

➤ A consideration that many of us need to deal with has less to do with how many interviews *should* I do, but has more to do with how many interviews *can* I do? Interviews are a very labor- and resource-intensive pursuit, and while you may wish to visit 80 to 100 customers, realistically, it is unlikely your organization has the time, resources, or patience for such an endeavor. Keep in mind that the interview cost can be considerable when you add employee time, travel and lodging expenses, and then the additional backend costs for analysis and reporting. Firms constantly need to balance the question of the costs of additional interviews with the benefits of identifying a more robust set of identified customer needs, but it is helpful to consider that a VoC program of 30 interviews could cost an organization $30K to $100K when including time, travel expenses, and analysis. Make sure you understand what your budget is going into the process so you are planning effectively.

➤ As a rule of thumb, experts say you should do three or more interviews for each matrix block you have identified for your sample selection. If you look at *Figure 5.1*, we have five columns and three rows for each example. If you were doing three interviews for each block you would end up with 45 interviews! If we went even further with our matrices and said we wish to identify customers in three different segments for an international product, our matrix would look similar to *Figure 5.2*.

| | | Lead Users | Satisfied Customers | Dissatisfied Customers | Former Customers | Non-Customers |
|---|---|---|---|---|---|---|
| N. America | Segment 1 | | | | | |
| | Segment 2 | | | | | |
| | Segment 3 | | | | | |
| Europe | Segment 1 | | | | | |
| | Segment 2 | | | | | |
| | Segment 3 | | | | | |
| Asia | Segment 1 | | | | | |
| | Segment 2 | | | | | |
| | Segment 3 | | | | | |

*Figure 5.2: Large customer profile matrix*

As you can see here, the number of interviews would be much larger than an interview-based VoC would warrant (five different customer types x nine segment types x three interviews each = 135 total interviews), and one should either look at another research method or consider modifying the approach. Even though you may be interviewing different customer types and interviewing customers in other regions, there is inevitably a point of diminishing returns. Abbie Griffin and John Hauser did some research on this topic while at MIT. Using binomial distribution, they plotted the number of customers interviewed versus their identified needs. In their analysis, they showed that 30 customers would identify 90% of all the total needs. They also showed that 20 customers would identify over 80% to 85% of the needs, and a sample of 12 customers might uncover 70% to 75% of the needs.

Based on the research by Griffin and Hauser, and consideration of resources and time to market, you would probably be well served to target a number of interviews in the range between 20 and 30 customers for a completely new product initiative. Unless you are doing something as drastic as a fundamental overhaul of your entire business, which could warrant 40, 50, or even 60 visits, for most product- and service-centric VoC programs, 20 to 30 is a good starting point. You will probably find that, in many cases, when doing your own research the interviews start to become rather redundant somewhere between 15 and 20.

Of course, this does fly in the face of the experts' rule of thumb that if you are making a product for multiple segments and multiple markets, as illustrated in *Figure 5.2*, you may be best advised to consider a modified customer profile matrix that will hopefully give you a fair representation of the market, but not be so onerous and expensive that you would spend the next 2 years doing customer research. I have found that it is typically best to try and narrow your initial VoC program into those segments you deem the best fit based on the research you have done as part of your customer-selection process. Try to have three or four interviews in the cells you consider to be the most important customers for your research and fewer, if any, in the other cells. In *Figure 5.3*, you can see an example where we have determined that our most important market is small international manufacturers, but we have also added a few additional interviews with large manufacturers' lead users to compare and contrast against the small manufacturers in an effort to determine whether we need to have a potential second round with the large manufacturers as well:

| | | Lead Users | Satisfied Customers | Dissatisfied Customers | Former Customers | Non-Customers |
|---|---|---|---|---|---|---|
| N. America | Small OEMs | 3 | | 3 | | 3 |
| | Large OEMs | 2 | | | | |
| Europe | Small OEMs | 3 | | | 3 | 3 |
| | Large OEMs | 2 | | | | |
| Asia | Small OEMs | 3 | 3 | | | |
| | Large OEMs | 2 | | | | |

*Figure 5.3*

It is important not to try and shortcut this process and just interview the customers you think are the *best*. Laying out the tables we have shown in *Figures 5.1* through *5.3* will help you to clarify the entire potential customer base and further help you to find the most ideal representatives for your future market. The matrices have the additional benefit of providing a framework to explain your segmentation and customer interview selection process to your coworkers as well as your management, and also gives them the opportunity to add constructive feedback.

While every VoC program is different, and you must ultimately decide the correct number of customers to interview, I would offer the following guidance as a place to start (assuming budget is not a gating issue) when trying to develop your customer VoC program:

> ➤ For a new platform product in a market segment different from the one you already cater for, aim for 20 to 30 interviews

> ➤ For a new platform product in a market segment that you already cater for, aim for 12 to 25 interviews

> ➤ For a new product in an existing platform, aim for 10 to 15 interviews

> ➤ For a minor modification or enhancement, aim for 5 to 12 interviews

# Where should I interview my customers?

When discussing customer interviews, most people assume that you will be conducting the interviews at the customer's place of business. While this is typically where many interviews take place, there are a number of areas in which you can hold interviews:

> ➤ At your place of business
> ➤ At a neutral location
> ➤ At the customer's place of business

The following are some thoughts as to the positives and negatives of each.

## At your place of business

From a logistical and cost perspective, this is by far the best choice. If you can convince enough customers to visit your location, you can conduct many interviews with little cost. Even if you end up paying for the customer's travel, you still have the benefit of not loosing as much time out of the office as if you would have had to travel to each customer location. Having customers come to your site offers the additional advantage that the customer will not need to cut short the VoC if they need to run to another meeting, and it also means that many other members of your team can meet with the customers in addition to the customer interview team. Also, as the customer is already coming to your site, you can hold additional sessions with the customer to get feedback on other areas of your development roadmap, as well as the VoC-focused program; just be sure you don't try and blend another customer session directly into your VoC session. There should be clear delineation and ground rules (which we will cover in the next chapter) for the VoC session, which is considerably different than any other customer meeting.

## At a neutral location

Often, it is possible to coordinate customer interviews at an offsite location in conjunction with another event where the customer will already be in attendance. Tradeshows and conferences are prime examples. Holding customer interviews during these events have a number of advantages similar to holding the interviews at your place of business. First, there is a good chance that you will have other business at the conference or tradeshow and can accomplish additional sales and marketing tasks in the same trip, such as competitive analysis, attending conference sessions, or exhibiting.

As most of the time the customer will already be in attendance at these events, it is also unlikely that you will need to pay for things such as travel or lodging for the customers you are meeting. The other advantage, much like having the meeting at your site or location, is that the customer is *out of the office* and is less likely to shorten or cancel the meeting, and the possibility of the customer getting pulled out of the meeting when it is offsite is much lower.

Probably the largest advantage of meeting at a venue such as a tradeshow or conference is that you will likely have the opportunity to meet with a number of customers for the outlay of money and time, as opposed to only seeing one at a time if you are meeting at your location or the customer's site.

# At the customer's place of business

While there are a few negatives with visiting the customer's site as we discussed earlier, I have found that if you have the budget and resource availability, nothing can match the depth and richness of knowledge one can acquire by directly visiting a customer at his or her place of business.

In addition to the PR benefits of traveling to a customer's site, showing them how important they are to your research, there are two other rather significant advantages to an onsite interview that cannot be matched with an interview at your place of business or a neutral location:

> ➤ As you have already committed to the travel and living expenses required for most customer visits, you should also try and get a 360 degree view of anyone using your product or part of the value chain why not try and meet with three or four different types of users when visiting the customer location? Being able to get the viewpoint of the users, the purchasing department, the maintenance personnel, and the management of the organization you are visiting provides a much richer view of the customer than could be accomplished in only one interview, or even by interviewing all these customer types representing differing customers.

> ➤ If you are able to not just interview the customer at their place of business, but also actually see the customer using your product in their place of business, you will walk away with a much deeper understanding of the customer's needs. Quite often, a customer will not be able to recall an issue they have had in the past, but once put in front of your product, most of the time past experiences will bubble to the top of their mind. Additionally, during this phase of the interview you will also occasionally be able to learn just as much by watching the customer use your product as you do during the actual interview. We will cover more details of this part of the interview in *Chapter 6, The Interview Process – The Interview.*

# The interview team

When deciding on conducting the interviews, you can choose to source the interviews to a specialized third party that does market research, or you can choose to commit the manpower and resources from your own organization to conduct market research. Of course, there are obvious benefits of using a third party. They will be able to free up the amount of time you and your organization will have to commit to this initiative, and they also have expertise in formulating questions, interviewing customers, asking questions, and documenting customers' responses.

While this is certainly a viable option for a lot of companies with more financial resources than personnel, I generally do not recommend it (and no doubt you do not either, as you are reading this book). If you use a third party to do your customer research, you may be missing out on insights you may have gleaned if you held the interviews yourself. Typically, the market research teams are very knowledgeable about interviewing processes and can ask all the right questions and statistically interpret them, but they do not have the breadth and depth of product and application knowledge in the same way that you do and cannot hope to provide the same level of insights that you could. You will find that third-party researchers tend to do a pretty good job of answering *what* is important, but in almost all cases they do not answer the question *why*.

One might agree that there are problems with third-party researchers, but one might ask whether we can just have the sales force do the interviews. After all, they are already visiting the customers and already have a relationship. There are a number of problems with delegating customer research to the sales team:

> ➤ The incentive structure for most sales teams is driven by sales volume, and the task at hand will not produce any near-term sales revenue. This could end up resulting in sales focusing more on short-term changes to the products and less about long-term strategic changes. There is also a considerable danger that the VoC interview would turn into a sales call.

> ➤ Most sales people do not have the disposition to be successful in research, which is what the customer inquiry entails.

> ➤ There is a potential loss of consistency across the interviews with so many people involved.

> ➤ Sales may focus more on their best customers' views and less on getting a holistic representation of the market.

> ➤ The communication funnel from customer to research and development will get longer and, potentially, more convoluted through loss of critical information.

Some might say, "well....ok, if I can't get a third party to do it and I can't get my sales team to do it, I'll just have my marketing team do the customer interviews. After all, that is part of their job isn't it?" They should report back what the customers want and then engineering can design it and manufacturing can build it? Of course, the answer is "No"!

If your organization truly wants to become market focused, engineering cannot delegate all customer contact to the marketing organization and expect to receive all the market intelligence they require to build your next great product. *Figure 5.4* helps to highlight the issue:

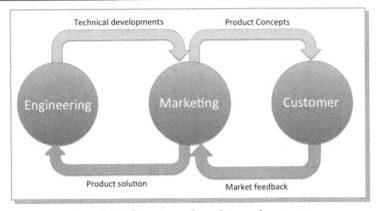

***Figure 5.4: Information exchange between departments***

In the preceding illustration, engineering (or another technical organization) creates a technical development or breakthrough and passes it to marketing, expecting them to package the new technology into a product concept to present to the customers. Customers provide feedback on how the product concept could be adjusted to provide more value and then marketing adjusts the concept into a new proposal before passing it back to engineering. While this process is very easy for engineering as they focus on doing research or producing *whatever marketing tells them*, it does not lead to the product breakthroughs that companies need. Marketing has to perform a two-way translation in this model that often results in a loss of information, a loss of time, and distortions. In many industries, in particular B2B and technology industries, engineering/R&D is too important to be isolated from the customers. Customers value direct contact with the technical staff, and many of the technical staff values visits to the customers, as long as it is structured.

I recommend that one or more teams of two individuals perform the customer interviews. One person should be from the marketing community and one from the engineering or technical community. If there are other objectives for the visit (input on logistics, documentation, usability, and so on), you may also want to include a third individual from one of those organizations. You will find during your interviews that marketing and engineering tend to pick up different things during the discussions with the customer and by having both the business side and technical side in attendance, you should be able to paint a more complete picture of the customer input after the session.

While I do highly encourage you to use marketing, technology, and, when the project warrants it, another department to take part in the customer VoC, I do not encourage you to include sales as part of your customer visit unless it is absolutely necessary. Customers may not believe this meeting is focused on research and may believe it is actually a thinly veiled sales call. Even if it is not, most of the time the salesperson will end up trying to turn it into a sales call as that is what they are best at. Another problem is that customers may not feel free to speak their mind when a salesperson is in attendance.

This is not to say that the salesperson should be left in the dark about the customer visit as this would go against how many organizations are structured. More often than not, sales owns the customer engagement and their ability to make a living is determined by how well the customer is managed. I would highly encourage you to liaise with sales to help find the best customers to meet the profile you have created, but I would also explain to them that it is necessary to meet with the customer without their attendance and reassure the salesperson that you will respect the customer relationship that has been established and that you will brief the salesperson after the interview is complete.

There are a number of noticeable advantages in using a team from both the engineering side and marketing side, in particular around technology products. Many organizations have a defined marketing department and engineering department. Often, these departments are at odds with each other with respect to what should be built. By working and living together during the interview process, often a beneficial side effect is that these two teams tend to work together better in the future as they have developed a more personal bond. Another factor, and this is a considerable one, is that by actually interviewing the customer together and hearing the same things that are said by the customer, I have found the actual development process that happens well after the interviews are complete tends to go much smoother. By interviewing the customer together, I have, working with my engineering counterpart, been able to develop the marketing specification and the engineering specification in tandem as we both heard and saw the same things. This can shave months off your development process as it greatly reduces the amount of back and forth spec wars, which happens in so many organizations.

If you are doing eight interviews or fewer, one team should be sufficient. If you are doing more than eight interviews, you may look to create multiple teams. Of course, there are positives and negatives to using more than one team. The positives are that you do not have to commit so much of your own time to complete the interviews and you should be able to do the interviews in parallel, thereby completing this program in less time. The downside is that you will need to train and coach more people to ensure the interviews are delivered in a consistent fashion with the right things emphasized during the discussions with the customers. With multiple teams, you also have the potential problem of differing interpretations and variation in data collection, which is why I prefer to use as few teams as possible to meet the objectives of the project and timeline.

# Customer's visiting process and buy-in

Once you have determined the statement of intent, objectives for the visits, a list of customers to visit, and confirmed the venues where you will hold the meetings, you now need to get the right level of organizational buy-in to make sure your program is properly funded and resourced. To do this, you will probably need the buy-in of your management team or your sponsor. As part of the buy-in process, it would be advisable for you to create the right level of expectations. I would consider putting together two additional things at a minimum to present to your management or sponsor:

> A budget
> A project plan showing key dates

The budget should include an estimate of resource commitment required (and could include their fully loaded cost if you have access to it), as well as an estimate of travel, meals, and lodging expenses. If you also require some sort of model or screen-mock ups for the interviews, or any other extraneous expenses, I would list them as well.

The project plan should provide visibility to the management team or sponsor of how long this process should actually take before something actionable will come out of it. I find it is critical to set this expectation lest the management might mistakenly believe that you will be done well before you have completed your interviews or your post-interview analysis. If you have access to a tool such as MS Project, you can create a **Gantt** chart. You can also find other free tools online to represent your high-level Gantt chart using programs such as Excel, as shown in *Figure 5.5*:

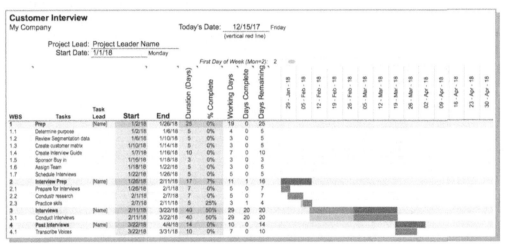

**Customer Interview**
My Company
Today's Date: 12/15/17 Friday (vertical red line)
Project Lead: Project Leader Name
Start Date: 1/1/18 Monday
First Day of Week (Mon=2): 2

| WBS | Tasks | Task Lead | Start | End | Duration (Days) | % Complete | Working Days | Days Complete | Days Remaining |
|-----|-------|-----------|-------|-----|-----------------|------------|--------------|---------------|----------------|
| 1 | Prep | [Name] | 1/2/18 | 1/26/18 | 25 | 0% | 19 | 0 | 25 |
| 1.1 | Determine purpose | | 1/2/18 | 1/6/18 | 5 | 0% | 4 | 0 | 5 |
| 1.2 | Review Segmentation data | | 1/6/18 | 1/10/18 | 5 | 0% | 3 | 0 | 5 |
| 1.3 | Create customer matrix | | 1/10/18 | 1/14/18 | 5 | 0% | 3 | 0 | 5 |
| 1.4 | Create Interview Guide | | 1/7/18 | 1/16/18 | 10 | 0% | 7 | 0 | 10 |
| 1.5 | Sponsor Buy in | | 1/16/18 | 1/18/18 | 3 | 0% | 3 | 0 | 3 |
| 1.6 | Assign Team | | 1/18/18 | 1/22/18 | 5 | 0% | 3 | 0 | 5 |
| 1.7 | Schedule Interviews | | 1/22/18 | 1/26/18 | 5 | 0% | 5 | 0 | 5 |
| 2 | Interview Prep | [Name] | 1/26/18 | 2/11/18 | 17 | 7% | 11 | 1 | 16 |
| 2.1 | Prepare for Interviews | | 1/26/18 | 2/1/18 | 7 | 0% | 5 | 0 | 7 |
| 2.2 | Conduct research | | 2/1/18 | 2/7/18 | 7 | 0% | 5 | 0 | 7 |
| 2.3 | Practice skils | | 2/7/18 | 2/11/18 | 5 | 25% | 3 | 1 | 4 |
| 3 | Interviews | [Name] | 2/11/18 | 3/22/18 | 40 | 50% | 29 | 20 | 20 |
| 3.1 | Conduct Interviews | | 2/11/18 | 3/22/18 | 40 | 50% | 29 | 20 | 20 |
| 4 | Post Interviews | [Name] | 3/22/18 | 4/4/18 | 14 | 0% | 10 | 0 | 14 |
| 4.1 | Transcribe Voices | | 3/22/18 | 3/31/18 | 10 | 0% | 7 | 0 | 10 |

**Figure 5.5: Customer VoC Gantt chart**

One might also consider putting all of the information you have acquired to this point into a more formalized project charter. In addition to the preceding two items, the charter should also document the overall scope of the project, the purpose of the set of visits, and the desired objectives from the visits. You should also document who will be part of the overall team and what their individual responsibilities are.

# The interview guide

A good interview should seem more like a natural conversation between two organizations and less like an interrogation. However, it is critical that you approach the discussion with a clear plan of the topics you are going to address and the feedback you wish to gather. A good interview guide provides the foundation for this process.

While it may seem counterintuitive, the absolute worst way to derive a customer's wants and needs during an interview is to simply ask them "*What are your wants and needs?*" or "*What are your requirements?*". When you do this, the customer will switch to solution mode and will start offering you suggestions for incremental changes to the current product based on things that are likely already available in the market.

If, for instance, you asked customers about their requirements for an automobile, they would talk about mileage, horse power, cup holders, integrated Bluetooth, Sirius, and other features, which would be great if you were just looking to create a "me-too" product in the market. If, however, you are looking to create new functions and features for the future wants and needs of customers, you will need to do the hard work of understanding customers more holistically and in a way that is structured and measurable. This is what the interview guide allows you to do better: understanding how your customer goes about accomplishing his assigned duties, what things prevent them from accomplishing those duties, and how your product or service can make them more successful.

The interview guide is meant to be more of an outline of the things you will discuss with the customer and less of a script. A successful interview guide will set the agenda for the visit and the stage for the interview showing a progression of topics starting with more general business topics and then gradually shifting to more specific topics. It takes a little time to build rapport with customers, so it is not advised that you delve directly into technical detail. Also, I have often found that we uncover new opportunities higher up in the discussion guide funnel before we have even begun to talk about products. *Figure 5.6* is an example of a discussion guide funnel I have found to be useful in the past:

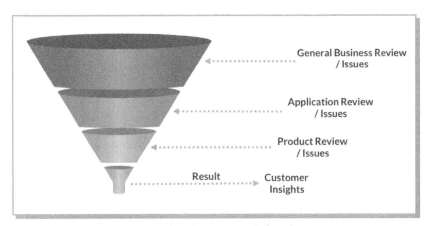

*Figure 5.6: Discussion guide funnel*

The interview guide should lay out the structure for your interview and should promote a smooth flow of topics. To create an interview guide, there are a couple of points worth keeping in mind as you go about creating your list of questions:

> ➤ Ask open-ended questions that have unlimited potential answers. In general, it is best to avoid closed-ended questions that have a predefined set of responses, such as yes or no, or A, B, or C. If you must ask closed-ended questions, only do so at the end of a section and only if they are necessary to get closure on a specific topic.

➤ Questions should be worded in such a way as to not give any clue to the interviewee about what the "right" answer is.

➤ "What", "How", and "Could" questions are good ways to open a question. "What problems have you experienced in the past?" "How does this product help you achieve your goals?" "Could you tell me more about a time when this product did not work the way you were expecting?"

➤ "Why" questions can be used, but one must be careful. "Why" questions can help you better understand motivation on the part of the user, but they can also be perceived negatively and can sound like criticism. "Why do you use the product in that way?"

➤ "Can", "Are", and "Do" question should be avoided. They tend to elicit a positive or negative response only. You are always better off asking more open-ended questions that start with something like "Describe".

When developing your interview guide, it is best to start by using a flip chart and capture all the questions you wish to ask a customer. Once you have done that, it is then possible to try and group similar questions to see if you can ask one summary question that will address the main issue you are trying to discuss. Instead of asking:

➤ What are the negative cost issues you've had with the current computer system?

➤ What maintenance issues have you had with the current computer system?

➤ What ordering issues have you had with the computer system?

➤ What software issues have you had with the current system?

➤ What hardware issues have you had with the current system?

➤ What workarounds have you had to devise for the current system?

You could simply ask:

➤ Tell us about the problems you have had with the computer system

If, for some reason, the customer does not answer some of the burning questions in your mind, you can always ask a follow-up to help provide more clarity.

Once you have created a list of summary questions, you can then try and group the questions to create a logical flow for your interview. As I said before, try and start with the environment or business and then continue to drive deeper toward product-specific questions. Ideally, one topic leads to the next through the entire conversation. It is good to lay out the flow for your interview, but be prepared to follow the interviewee and deviate from your path if it looks like the conversation is going that way. You can always circle around later to pick up anything you may have missed.

I have found that something like the following works well in understanding the larger business issues and eventually driving to the product-specific issues:

1. Introduction
   - ➢ Purpose of visit and introduction of team

2. General
   - ➢ Overall business review, challenges, opportunities
   - ➢ Types of equipment used today
   - ➢ Changes to the business in the future
   - ➢ Factors driving consideration of new purchase

3. Application
   - ➢ Current applications and processes
   - ➢ Opportunities and issues with current applications
   - ➢ Future applications and processes

4. Product
   - ➢ Problems in using and installing current product offerings
   - ➢ Problems in purchasing, ordering, and receiving current product offerings
   - ➢ Problems in supporting, training, documentation, and so on, relating to current product offerings
   - ➢ Needs not being addressed by current product offerings
   - ➢ Enhancements required for current product offerings
   - ➢ Prioritize relative importance of each need

5. Wrap-up
   - ➢ Summarize findings
   - ➢ Probe for additional insights or input
   - ➢ Review if there is anything else customer wishes to add or bring up

While this shows the general flow of a discussion guide with a list of topics to discuss, I have found it is often helpful to construct specific questions for each section. This ensures that there is a level of consistency from interview to interview, that all key points are addressed during the interview and, as we will talk about in the next chapter, that clues are also provided as to what may have been missed by your fellow interviewers.

When you are constructing the discussion guide, care must also be given to not end up with pages and pages of questions. In general, you should target the interviews to be close to 60 minutes and typically no more than 2 hours in length. With this amount of time, two to four pages is typically the right length for an interview guide.

When you are completed with your interview guide's first pass, I highly recommend distributing your interview guide to the other team members to get feedback on the structure, flow, and level of detail.

# Scheduling interviews

We have already discussed how to find the right customers for your VoC program, but once you have developed your list, it is necessary to contact them to set up your VoC session. One alternative is to use an outside resource to help you schedule your interviews. There is value in using an outside resource to schedule your visits as appointment setting is a specialized skill and there is a considerable time commitment involved in setting up 20 to 30 interviews. However, I have found that setting up the interviews myself helps me to better control the expectations of the customers and begins developing the relationship with the customer that can help reduce any potential awkwardness during the first meeting. Making the calls myself also allows me to screen the potential interviewees to make sure they are a good fit for the program. Sometimes the company is the right company to interview, but the person I am contacting is not. By doing the interview scheduling myself I have the ability to ascertain whether this is the right individual, and if not, try and get a referral to someone else in the organization. Even if he is the right individual, he can often also refer me to other disciplines or people within his organization from which I would like to receive input. Quite often, they will even make the introduction for you to the other individuals, thereby greatly increasing your credibility to the people you do not know.

Regardless of whether you choose to do it yourself or have a third party do it, there are a few key things you should keep in mind when setting up the calls:

> **Set the customer's expectation for the meeting**: Customers may not be used to these types of research meetings and they need to understand that this is not a sales call, and your only objective is to listen and learn so you can better understand their needs.

> **Share with them the agenda for the meeting**: Make sure they understand why you are doing this research and why this would be a good investment of their time. Sometimes you may need to offer some additional "carrot" to get their participation, such as sharing with them your future product roadmap or a strategic briefing to solidify their participation.

> **Set a time expectation**: Tell them how long you expect the meeting to last.

> **Try and schedule a tour or demo**: While the main purpose of the trip is the face-to-face interview, seeing how the customer is using your product or similar products in their facility or application can often be more illuminating than the actual interview.

# Summary

In this chapter, we have done a deep dive into preparing for the face-to-face customer interview. We have outlined the things you must do before you begin to have your first meeting to help ensure your VoC program will get off to a good start. In this section, we covered the following topics:

> **Plan**: Developing an understanding of what will be involved in a customer interview program

> **Visit purpose**: Creating the statement of intent for your customer VoC program and why it is important

> **Selecting customers to visit**: Leveraging the customer segmentation you have already done and how to select who you are going to interview, how many customers you should interview, and where you will conduct the interviews

> **Interview team**: Selecting who should and should not be part of the interview team and why

> **Customer visit process and buy-in**: What information you should gather together to help convince your management as to the value versus the cost of a VoC program

> **Interview guide**: How to develop the interview guide, the main areas on which to focus, and the ideal structure of the questions

> **Scheduling interviews**: How to schedule the interviews with the customer and the critical things you must do when arranging the meetings

Once you are armed with the preceding information, it is time to think about how the actual meeting will proceed, what the roles and responsibilities of the participants are, and the dos and don'ts for the customer interviews. This information and more will be covered in the next chapter.

# >6

# The Interview Process – The Interview

*"You'll learn more by meeting a real, live customer and spending an hour with him than you can learn from fifty research studies or analysts' reports."*

*– Adrian Slywotsky, The Art of Profitability*

In *Chapter 5, The Interview Process – Preparation*, we discussed developing a plan to do a VoC, how to leverage the resources within your organization, and the methods to engage with the customers outside your organization you wish to interview. Inside your organization, we made sure you had clear goals and plans as to why you are doing a VoC program, and how to gather the data to present to your management to justify the costs and resources. We also talked about how to create an interview team and how to select who should, and should not, be on the team, as well as how to develop an interview guide and structure the customer discussion. External to your organization, we discussed leveraging the customer segmentation you had done previously to select qualified customers to visit. Lastly, we reviewed scheduling the interviews with your customers and how to get them to buy in to the interview session.

In this chapter, we will take the next logical step and talk about the details of the actual interview. We will go beyond the topics covered in *Chapter 5, The Interview Process – Preparation*, as we dive into the various roles and responsibilities of the interview team. We will talk about how to assign the "best" people to these roles and discuss the responsibilities of each role within the interview. We will also spend a good amount of time on best practices as we talk about the various dos and don'ts when conducting customer interviews.

# The VoCMOT

This is the moment you have been building up to. This is the VoC Moment of Truth. You have gotten approval from your management to pursue a customer VoC and have received funding. You have segmented your market and selected the key customers you wish to interview. You have painstakingly developed a robust interview guide, have scheduled appointments with your customers, and have hopefully received permission before you arrive to record the interview and have even signed an NDA when customers required it. Now is the moment of truth, as the actual face-to-face customer interviews you will do are the heart and soul of the customer VoC and the lifeblood of the new product development process.

# Review logistics

Before we can begin to undertake our VoC program, we should review everything you need to prepare, and execute, your actual face-to-face interviews.

Before making your first customer visit, the following should already be in place:

> Developed, in full, a customer visit calendar

> Gave advance warning to customers if you need data they possess in their systems

> Made sure you have a good introductory statement

> Reviewed your interview guide and made sure you fully understand the questions, and if you have multiple teams, everyone else understood the questions as well

> Practiced your questions and honed your interview skills

> Team members assigned by functional roles in teams to get the most out of the interviews

> Decided on team roles and best practices

# The key to a successful VoC – robust data

The key to a successful VoC program only appears after all the interviews are over. It is only then that you can analyze all the responses to all the questions you have asked your customers and begin to see patterns emerging, or "aha" moments where you understand some of the nuggets your customers need, but they never thought to ask for, and you never thought to produce. Of course, to have the ability to see these patterns and experience these epiphanies, you need to have a detailed record of all your customer visits.

While there are a number of impressions and key moments in the interview you will remember with clarity, you cannot rely on your memory alone when conducting any VoC interview. Having a detailed record of the interview via written notes is imperative to capture what the customer has articulated. This is especially important as you look to analyze 10 or more interviews and attempt to compare and contrast how the various respondents have answered a specific question.

In addition to having a record of every interview, the additional benefit of note taking is that you can dissect your notes for the later analysis by cross-tabulating the data and cutting and pasting from multiple interviewee answers to specific questions.

While it is possible to "free form" the note taking, it is better to use the interview guide as a template for the note taking. This ensures two key results for the interview. One, there will be no questions missed inadvertently, and two, it is very easy to match the customers' responses to the questions in real time. Often, during the course of an interview, a customer might "answer" a question as part of another answer. When this happens, it is very easy to assign the response to a specific question in real time if you have a structured guide that you are already intimately familiar with. It is much more difficult to do this after the fact when you are conducting multiple interviews in a short amount of time.

Most people will print out the interview guide with space between questions where they can write answers as the customers answer them. While this certainly does work, a trick when note taking is to align all the questions on the side of a sheet instead of having the questions on a sheet of paper with a lot of white space between them. There is still a lot of room on the right side of the page for responses, and if necessary, you can continue the notes on the back of the sheet. This will allow you to include more questions on each sheet and it also seems to be easier to find specific questions when the interview "bounces around" as your eye does not have to travel as far.

Another way to capture notes for an interview that is likely to move from topic to topic, and not in a linear fashion the way you designed the interview guide (as most do), is to draw several squares on your notes and assign a different topic to each one. As the customer moves from topic to topic, you will be able to quickly keep up and put the notes in the right section. While this is effective to capture key points and assign their relative categories on the fly, I prefer to have the individual questions represented and place the responses with the questions asked. See *Figure 6.1*:

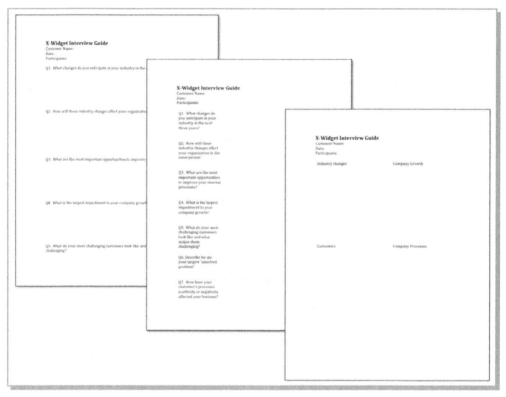

*Figure 6.1: Three potential ways to arrange interview notes*

If these suggestions don't make sense, try them out and you will probably find one of them will match your note taking style.

If you are using an app or a program to take notes in the meeting, try preloading the interview guide and using it as a template for the collection of responses. Make sure to pre-number the questions and be intimately familiar with where each question is in the interview guide for those times when the interview does not follow the linear fashion you had originally laid out. This will allow you to very easily jump to the specific question to record the responses. It is also helpful to color code the questions separately from the answers so the questions will always stand out. This is very useful when you are searching for the specific question you are hoping to assign the response to:

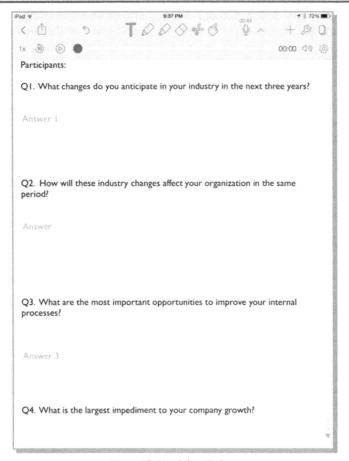

*Figure 6.2: Notability iPad app*

# Audio recording and transcriptions

When in the process of interviewing a customer, you will be very busy trying to ask questions of the customer to draw out their unarticulated needs, capturing all the customer's salient points, as well as observing subtle clues and gestures the customer makes when responding to a query. All in all, there is an awful lot going on and the challenge of your job is to collect as much of it as possible, which can become increasingly difficult with note taking alone.

Unfortunately, it is often impossible to capture everything and this is why, whenever possible, you should ask a customer's permission to audiotape or videotape the interview. Explain to the customer that you want to record the interview because their input is extremely valuable to you. In most cases, you will find that the customer is perfectly willing to allow you to do this and they often forget that the recorder is even on during the interview. If they prefer that you do not, of course, you should proceed by taking notes only, but you will be amazed at the additional information that is to be found in the recordings of your customer visits if they do allow it.

Invest in a decent-quality digital recorder if you are planning on recording interviews. These devices have built-in condenser microphones and many of these offer directional capabilities, allowing you to have one microphone pointed at the interviewer and one at the interviewee. Tascam and Zoom both have a range of recorders that should give you good results at a reasonable price.

With the proliferation of smartphones and smart devices, it is no longer necessary to set up a recorder sitting in the middle of the room when wishing to record a meeting. However, depending on where you are in the room and what other ambient noise is in the room, you may lose quite a bit if using your smartphone to do the recording.

However, if you are inclined to take notes on an iPad or computer during the interviews, there are also a number of apps/programs that allow you to record the audio of the meetings at the same time. These programs offer the ability to sync your note taking with the audio that is being recorded and will also provide a backup if something happens to your higher-quality recording. This is a large benefit when reviewing your notes and finding that you missed a key piece of information. No longer do you need to listen to a whole interview or jump from place to place in the audio recording. By clicking on the pertinent section of the notes you have taken, you can play back the audio that was recorded at the very same instant you wrote the note.

By using such a program, you have the additional benefit of double-checking where you have assigned a response. Sometimes in the heat of the interview, it is possible to put a response to a different question. In case there is any question about where the answer should go, a real-time recording of the context and the customer's real-time response can greatly aid in after-the-fact data cleansing.

# Video recording

Video recording is another excellent way to capture the interview in such a way that it can be analyzed for more information. Video recording has an additional benefit over voice recordings in that you can better see and review your customer's facial expressions and mannerisms when certain questions were asked and as they delivered their answer. While it is possible to share audio and video with others outside of the interview team after the fact, video seems to be more engaging and offers a richer viewing experience. Of course, the same rules apply to video recording as for audio recording in that you must get the customer's permission before actually recording the session.

While tape recording or videotapes do have their place for pinpoint analysis, they are not ideal for cross-tabulating or summarizing the results of a meeting. For this, you still need a robust collection of written notes that are fully indexable.

If you are able to record many of your sessions, you may end up with hours upon hours of recordings, which could be very time consuming to review. Most often, video and audio recordings are better used as a vehicle for pinpoint analysis where you need to go back and review a particular customer's answer for clarity. Again, an app, such as the aforementioned Notability program, is a large asset as you can go back to the specific answer and hear exactly what the customer said when answering that question just by clicking on the customer's answer.

# Interview roles and responsibilities

It is imperative that you walk into any customer interview with not only a clear idea of why you are conducting these interviews, but also a crystal clear understanding of everyone's responsibility in the customer VoC and what role they are going to play.

There are two key roles when conducting a customer interview. First is the role of the moderator. This individual "executes" the interviews. The second role is that of a "listener/note taker" whose responsibility is primarily to take good notes from the session. If you have the benefit of additional people in the interview (but please, not too many), they can act as "observers."

# Moderator role and responsibility

The moderator acts as the quarterback in the interview process. It is their responsibility to execute the interview by introducing the topics of discussion, asking most or all the questions, and guiding the interview from one topic to the next with smooth transitions. The absolute last thing a customer wants during an interview is to have three or four members of the visiting organization each pursuing their own agenda, bombarding them with rapid-fire questions that have no semblance of order or consistency. You will find that customers will be more at ease and will be able to provide better insight when they understand that one individual is in charge, most of the questioning comes from that one individual, and the interview is structured and has clear transitions. It is best practice for the moderator to set the stage from the very beginning of the interview by explaining that they will be leading the interview so the customer has a clear expectation who is in charge. So the customer further understands the mechanics of the interview, the moderator should also explain the functions of each of the other team members. This also helps to solidify the fact that the moderator is the leader of the interview.

If you are the moderator, the key thing to keep in mind is to get the customer talking and express their needs using their own language. Your role as the moderator is not to be their best friend, it is not to have a conversation with them, nor is it to start a dialog. The role of the moderator is to "facilitate" an interview.

The moderator will use the discussion guide as a road map for the interview, but must also be keenly aware of the necessity of not getting trapped by the interview guide and losing track of the time and/or not be willing to stray from the interview discussion guide. The moderator must decide how much time to spend on each topic, whether there are further useful nuggets of information to be had by probing a little deeper, or whether to cut a topic short if it is not applicable to the interviewee or not yielding the necessary information. The moderator must also be tuned in to the customer as much as possible. Often, it is better to let the customer "lead" the interview and discuss the things they want to discuss when they want to discuss them, instead of when they appear on your interview guide. As long as you get all the questions answered, it usually does not matter in which order the questions are asked.

As the quarterback of the interview, it is also the moderator's duty to bring in other members of the team at key points if their contribution is required or warranted. But it is necessary for all the members of the interview team to recognize the responsibility of the moderator and allow them to play the leadership role, even if their role in the organization is less than other members of the team.

The moderator typically comes from the marketing or product management part of the organization. These members often have less of a technical nature than the engineering side of the organization and also tend to have more of a business view. While technical acumen can be helpful for being a moderator, the more critical skills of a moderator are good communication and the ability to build a rapport with customers. Often, the marketing and product managers have more experience and training in this regard than other more technical parts of the organization, which is why the product management or marketing groups lead the interviews. As a side note, while it is acceptable to have multiple moderators on a team and to share the responsibility, there is more consistency from interview to interview in keeping the same moderator.

# Listener/note taker responsibility

The role of the listener/note taker is about being the archivist of the meeting more than anything else. Their role is to capture all the salient points and customer responses to the questions being asked by the moderator. They must also be able to not only write verbatim what the customer says during their response, but must also be able to capture the customer's most critical priorities and the emotional nuances that the customer expresses in the tone of their voice or cadence of their response.

The listener/note taker's role is not to help moderate the questions, but often the note taker may need to ask for clarification or elaboration to make sure that the question is fully answered and documented so as to perform the later analysis.

The note taker must also be sure to take notes in such a way that it is easy to digest the most salient points of the interview immediately after the interview is complete, as well as have the ability to pull specific questions' responses from multiple interviews when all the interviews are complete. Again, try following one of the methods discussed previously by leaving lots of white space either between the questions or to the right of the questions so it will be easy to assemble *all* the responses to any given question after the interviews are complete.

The note taker must also keep track of which of the key questions have been asked and answered, and which ones have not. If the customer ends up "leading" part of the interview, then the questions will likely be discussed out of order and the moderator may not be fully aware of which ones have been addressed. Often, it will be your job toward the end of the interview to inform the moderator which key questions are still open and awaiting a response from the customer.

You may ask, "Why do I need to take notes if I am recording the interviews?" The rationale is driven by post-interview analysis. It is much easier to try and compare how a customer responded to a particular question when it is all in written form and categorized based on the question being asked. If all you had was a recorded record of the interviews, it would be a very labor-intensive process to review as many as 30 recordings to see how each customer answered Question 15. If you have a written record of each interview and have all the answers categorized by question, it is a very easy and efficient process to analyze 30 different respondents and perform some rudimentary analysis across the sample population. It is a simple clerical task to create detailed reports by simply cutting, copying, and pasting each interview answer to the appropriate question.

Even if you pay for a transcription service (which will end up being very expensive), you will have a much larger amount of text to wade through and still will not have the answers categorized with their respective questions. The best way to document the interview is to use your written or typed notes as the basis for your post-survey analysis and use the recording to go back and review the rich content when you need to understand in more detail the nuances of how the question was being answered.

# Observer

If your interview team has more than two members, you should assign the remaining members the task of being observers. If you only have two team members in the interview, then the role of the observer would also be filled by the note taker.

Of course, everyone on the team needs to act as an observer in some capacity. From when you arrive in the lobby, how you are greeted, whether the work environment is formal or casual, to whether the offices are luxurious or not; these all give you little clues about the company culture. Additional tell tale markers are how the management team interacts within their organization, how they interact with others, and whether there is a strong and formal hierarchy within the organization. All these clues provide insight into your customers and customers' organizational value systems.

The role of the observer is to process the interview in its entirety. They do not need to take notes (unless also assigned that duty in the case of only two members being on the interview team), nor do they need to moderate the discussion or keep the interview on track. They can fully take in and process what the customer is saying during the interview and build a mental model of what the customer is saying and why. The observer should also be looking for the non-verbal clues that indicate what the customer is actually thinking, not just the words they are using. Voice changes, mannerisms, and gestures all provide clues about the customer's unarticulated needs or concerns.

# Interview introduction

Before beginning an interview with a customer, it is necessary to set the stage and refresh the customer's memory relative to the purpose of the customer interview.

The moderator should lead the discussion and introduce themselves along with their position and, specifically, how their position relates to the customer VoC. Next, the moderator should introduce the rest of the team and provide details of their backgrounds, applicability to the customer VoC, and their roles in the interview. Having the moderator perform this extra step helps to further solidify their role in the VoC as being the person responsible for interacting with the customer, but if the situation warrants it, you can also have each team member introduce themselves.

After all the team members have been introduced, provide a brief overview of the customer VoC project and the purpose behind the customer interviews with enough information so that the customer understands the value they can bring to the project, but also an understanding of what the customer interview is not (a sales call, technical troubleshooting, pricing discussion, and so on). Of course, if you are dealing with an irate customer for one reason or another, it may be difficult for them to turn off their attitude of "I'm gonna tell them a thing or two when they show up." In this case, it is best to allow a 10–15 minute discussion where they can express their displeasure with your product, support, pricing, and so on, and get it off their chest before beginning the actual interview. But please, try to address the customer's issues well enough so they will be able to focus on your interview questions, but do not spend your entire visit dealing with the customer's issue, thereby defeating the original purpose of the visit.

As a part of the introduction, emphasize that only a few customers have been selected, and if warranted, tell them why they were selected. Explain that notes are going to be taken, how they will be used, and that they will be confidential between the customer and your organization or project team, but that they could be part of a follow-up that you might distribute to all the customer participants so they may see how others in their peer group also responded to some of the open issues. Lastly, if you will be recording or videotaping the interview, double-check to make sure this is okay with the customer.

# Moderator tips

One of the key attributes of a good moderator is the ability to engage in "passive listening." This skill communicates to the customer that you are paying attention to the speaker and are engaged. Some tips for passive listening are:

> **Make good eye contact**: Much like leaning in, good eye contact tells the customer you are interested in their views.

> **Have a good posture**: Do not slouch in your chair. If anything, try to sit slightly forward in your chair. It shows you are interested in everything the customer is saying.

➤ **The interview seating arrangement**: Whenever possible, try to sit around the corner from the customer. This is less formal than sitting directly across from the customer, but more effective than sitting next to the customer. When you sit next to a customer, while you are technically closer and less formal, you also are unlikely to fully see the customer's expressions.

➤ **Keep your emotions and opinions in check**: It is good to encourage the interviewee by nodding your head in agreement and saying "uh-huh." It is not good to react to something you hear that you do not agree with and physically react by shaking your head, frowning, rolling your eyes, and so on.

➤ **Do not feel the need to fill the silence**: Some people are more deliberate in their answers to your questions and may take a little longer to fully articulate their response. Do not jump in to try and complete the sentence for the customer if they should pause while answering. When you think the interviewee is done talking, wait a moment before asking the next question.

While passive listening is an absolute requirement for a good interviewer and must be deployed in every customer VoC, some interviewers also believe *active listening* has a place in a VoC session and can actually help you to get more out of an interview. When actively listening, the moderator will often explore what the customer has said by paraphrasing what the moderator thought they heard. The benefit of active listening is that customers often feel like they have actually been heard and understood and are therefore more likely to continue to share their thoughts. Active listening can also help an interviewer clarify a customer's meaning and can be used with "probing" to help uncover a customer's underlying needs. Active listening can also provide additional benefits to the interview by pausing the questioning process and thereby allowing the note taker to catch up. Lastly, active listening can be used effectively by an interviewer to summarize the key takeaways the customer has shared and to provide an effective transition to the next interview topic. Do, however, be aware that active listening used ineffectively can interrupt the customer's train of thought, mislead the customer into believing the items that are paraphrased are more important than those that aren't, and inject the interviewer's own bias into the discussion by paraphrasing terms that aren't necessarily consistent with the customer's view.

While we have covered some of these items previously, it is worth capturing some of the other tips and best practices for a moderator to have the best possible customer session:

➤ Your role in the process is as an interview facilitator. As such, your task is to provide the line of questioning and the environment, enabling the customer to pull deeply-embedded insights to the surface for you to analyze and document.

➤ You should spend no more than 25% of the time talking, ideally closer to 10%. The vast majority of the time you are talking is to ask questions and clarify responses. The remaining 75–90% is allocated to receiving the customer's insights.

➤ Be prepared for non-linear thinking on the part of the customer. You should allow the customer to lead the discussion within reason, but you must also be able to bring the interview back on track to ensure you are getting the information you require.

> ➤ Always use the customer's context, not yours. Use the customer's point of reference when asking questions and phrase the questions in such a way that you allow the customer to share their world.

# Ladder of abstraction

A moderator will often find the information gleaned in response to a question is not adequate to take meaningful action. Specific examples or relevant facts and experiences are not what people usually give when answering a question. More often they tend to speak in generalities that are the result of their own emotions, opinions, and conclusions, resulting in senseless statements with no context or reference. Part of the role of the moderator is to continue to drive them toward the level of detail that will allow the organization to address the root of the customer's initial response.

If you are in an interview you might hear the customer say something like "your current product is too expensive" when asked his impression of your current product. Upon reflection, you may find that your product is actually LESS expensive than your competition and you choose to disregard what the customer said as you perceive him as being uninformed, or just trying to get a better deal. But what the customer might have meant was that your transportation costs were higher than the competition, that your product was more difficult to use than the competition—which required more training expenditure on the part of the customer—or that the difficulty and resulting cost to install your product is significantly more than the competition, which drives up the total cost of the product. The initial response does little to help you understand the current perceptions of your product. Only by diving deeper and asking what the customer means are you able to understand the problem the customer has and potential ways to fix it.

During the course of your interviews, you will hear customers using emotionally-charged words or expressing opinions by using words such as great, poor, easy, hard, and expensive. Your task is to move the interviewees beyond their initial statements to a more specific, actionable response by exploring the connection between features, benefits, and values. Continue to ask things like: "Why is that great?", "If you had that feature, what would it do for you?", "What are the consequences of not having this function?", "How does that affect you?", and more.

# The five whys

The five whys is an effective tool in helping you to move your customer down the ladder of abstraction. The five whys is a simple approach for exploring root causes and instilling a "find the root cause, not the symptom" mentality. Invented by Japanese industrialist Sakichi Toyoda, the idea is to keep asking "why?" until the root cause is arrived at. The number five is a general guideline for the number of whys required to reach the root cause level, but asking "why?" five times versus three, four, or six times is not a rigid requirement.

Of course, we don't want to just keep asking the customer "why, why, why" for fear we will sound like a three-year-old child. Instead, we can find other ways to continue to drive down from the stock answer by peeling away layers of information until we get to the valuable insights about the customer's problem or unarticulated need by asking things such as "Can you tell me more?" or "Why is that?" You can also use the customer's last answer to probe a little deeper: "You said that the product was difficult to learn, and this is because the customer interface is poor. Can you describe ways in which the menu interface is poor?"

Ultimately, the intent of the five whys is to get to a level where you get specific, actionable input that you can use in developing product features and requirements. By doing this, you will establish and be able to focus on the root problem your customers are trying to solve.

An example, as shown in *Figure 6.3,* from DMAIC tools website, shows how the five whys can help uncover a customer problem where the wrong item was shipped to a customer:

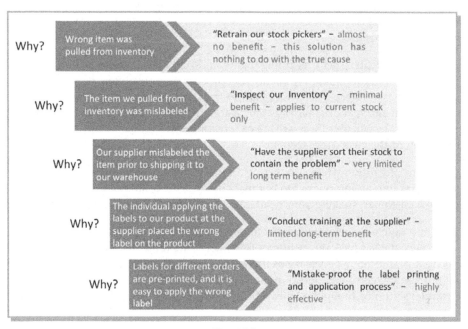

*Figure 6.3*

# Note taker tips

People who are starting out on their first VoC programs often are not sure how much to write down and how to keep track of attributing comments to different speakers. While there are benefits to understanding the customer's responses and the context of their words, this is not your primary responsibility. Your main responsibility is to provide a verbatim transcript of the interview session, capturing the customer's responses in a way that sounds like the customer speaking; in other words, capturing the customer's voice.

To do this, you need to try and write down the interviewee's responses without attempting to interpret or translate their responses in any way. Try to capture as much of what has been said as possible. Any change you make to the words the customers says takes time and thought. Attempting to process and summarize what the customer has said tends to put you into the interview and this is not what you want. When you try and summarize what the customer has said, you end up drawing upon your own knowledge and experiences and that could color or change what the customer truly meant. This is particularly true if a customer says something you know to be false, and you may leave it out of the interview entirely. To avoid imparting your judgments or experience into the interview, it is safer to just write down as much of what the customer says in as much of its entirety as you can capture.

Something else that may seem a little unnatural at first, but offers additional benefits during the later phase of deconstruction of the interviews, is to always keep the original pronouns as they are used. If the person says, "I had an issue installing your controller," that is exactly what you should write. You should not say, "They had an issue installing our controller" or "had issue when installing controller." By keeping the original pronouns in the interview notes, you will always know it is the customer who is speaking and what their words are.

It will often be difficult to get everything that is said verbatim; however, getting key customer quotes is an integral part of the VoC process. It is absolutely necessary to identify those key passages where the customer makes a salient point. Make sure you do write it verbatim and mark the passage the customer said using quotation marks so there is no question as to whether these are the exact words shared by the customer or your interpretation of the customer's feedback.

One last word of caution when conducting an interview is to never let your feelings or emotions enter into an interview. Do not react to what the customer says by frowning, correcting a customer, shaking your head, and so on. Simply write or type what you hear.

Even the best note takers will invariably miss a point or two during an interview, and while it is acceptable to ask the customer to repeat something that has been said, it is best to only do it if absolutely necessary as this can interrupt the flow of the interview. Often it is better to ask any clarifying questions at the end of the interview, as this will not impact the customer's train of thought or flow of the conversation.

# Don'ts for the interview

We have talked about a lot of the things one must *do* to have a good VoC session, but it is equally important to highlight some of the key *don'ts* when conducting a customer VoC:

> **Talking more than the customer**: We have been blessed with two ears, but only one mouth. Keep this ratio in mind when performing a customer VoC. You are there to ask the customer's perspective and learn, but you are not there to teach. A good rule of thumb is to try and get the customer to talk at least twice as much as you do, and getting the customer to talk 90% of the time is even better.

➤ **Forgetting basic meeting manners**: Be on time, courteous, attentive when the customer speaks, send thank you notes, and so on.

➤ **Treating the VoC guide as a rigid agenda**: The VoC guide is just that, a guide. Feel free to let the discussion take its natural course based on the customer's lead. As long as you get the information you came for, it is not typically important in which order you receive it.

➤ **Having more than one person asking questions**: This could create confusion about the various roles and the customer might feel like they are being ganged up on.

➤ **Interrupting the customer**: This really should be obvious, but always, always, let the customer finish their train of thought and fully express their answer. Do not feel the need to fill a perceived vacuum by saying something when it is not necessary.

➤ **Asking useless questions**: Years of experience has shown that questions such as, "How much would you pay for this product feature?" or "What features do you wish to see in this product?" are generally throwaway questions and customers rarely answer them in a way that is actionable by the interviewer.

➤ **Asking leading questions**: These types of questions are often biased to satisfy your own assumptions or beliefs and offer little vale to the engagement. Questions such as "Don't you agree that this product is better than any competitive product at the same price point?" don't really help to uncover customer needs and lead to assumptions that you are manipulating the discussion to validate the answer you already have in your head.

➤ **Asking loaded questions**: Loaded questions tend to introduce a subtle influence that could result in a biased response. Don't ask, "Do you favor stiffer industry regulations to reduce $CO_2$ emissions that will save lives?" Instead ask, "Should industries be more regulated when it comes to $CO_2$ emissions?"

➤ **Using ambiguous words**: Words can have different meanings for different people. Don't ask, "What time do you usually eat dinner?" Instead ask, "What time do you normally dine in the evening?"

➤ **Using acronyms or industry jargon that the customer is not intimately familiar with**: Nothing helps to derail a question or line of thinking more than when the customer does not understand the question. In the best case, it forces the customer to ask, "What did you mean by that?" In the worst case, the customer won't ask what you meant for fear of appearing uninformed and will answer what it is they "thought" you meant by your buzzword or industry jargon, and it will not be what they were actually thinking.

➤ **Use examples that consist of response alternatives**: Don't ask, "What data acquisition systems, such as portable hand held barcode readers, did you purchase last month?" Instead, ask, "What data acquisition systems did you purchase last month?" or if needing more specificity, you could ask, "What portable data acquisition systems did you purchase last month?"

> ➤ **Expect the customer to remember specific numbers or times**: Sometimes we like to know exact numbers to aid in our after-interview analysis, but it is often difficult to recall, or we expect an answer that is more specific than can be expressed.

> ➤ **Use outsiders to do VoC**: Although some would differ here, specifically professional service firms who include VoC as an offering, the information you can gain from a customer is much too valuable to be done by a third party.

> ➤ **Fall victim to the Satchmo principle**: Musician Louis "Satchmo" Armstrong was once asked how he was able to play the trumpet so masterfully. He responded, "I don't know, I just do it." This is the basis of the principle. Once you learn something, it is very difficult to remember what it was really like not knowing it. The same is true for your products and technology. You spend all your day thinking about your product and you are very familiar with it, and to you it seems easy to use and understand. Your customers, on the other hand, may find it overwhelming because they only use it occasionally or rarely. Be careful you do not assume your customer is stupid or not as skilled as you for not knowing as much about your product or market as you do. You must eliminate all preconceived notions driven by your experience and the experience of those that you work with, and learn to look at the customer's input through their eyes. If the customer tells you that something is difficult to use or confusing, it is!

# Observational VoC

Many times when interviewing a customer, it is difficult to really understand what it is like to be in the customer's shoes. Sometimes we don't have the right amount of experience in the customer's world to relate to some of the things they are saying. Other times, they are not able to fully explain what we need to know.

You will find, when interviewing a customer about their experiences, that sometimes they are just too close to their own issues to see the big picture. Other times, they have learned how to get around the various roadblocks and obstacles we have created for them by making poorly-defined products, and they have learned to accept their situation and the status quo. And still other times, you will find that customers just "don't know what they don't know." Of course, this is why we do the VoC in the first place. If the customers could just tell us what we need to build so we could sell them tons of equipment to make them more successful, they would; unfortunately, they cannot.

Unfortunately, even conducting a rich VoC session with a customer is not enough to truly understand what they see and what they are going through. This is why ethnography or observational VoC is such a valuable component to doing a VoC for so many industries. Only by watching a customer interact with their environment, with your products, and with your competitor's products do you begin to understand their world, their problems, and their roadblocks to success. Observational VoC helps us, as VoC practitioners, begin to make sense of the "messy world" of the customer. Often customers will tell us one thing during a VoC session, but their true needs become much more apparent when you can watch the customer trying to interact with products in an effort to accomplish a goal.

Take a case study that could have been done for TV remote controls:

| During the customer VoC the customer said the following: | Proposed offering based on customer VoC: |
| --- | --- |
| ■ I need a remote that is a universal remote to control all my AV devices<br><br>■ I need a sleek black design |  |
| **When observing the target customers:**<br><br>■ Watched TV in the dark<br><br>■ Constantly checked the TV guide and switched channels<br><br>■ Family had favorite channels they watched often<br><br>■ Would misplace remote in the dark<br><br>■ Younger members of family used smartphone for everything else<br><br>■ Had a number of other smart devices that were not AV that they needed to control | |
| **The observational VoC solution:**<br><br>■ Two different ways to control the AV equipment was preferred<br><br>■ Parents preferred to use a dedicated remote and children preferred to use a smartphone app<br><br>■ Not black in color, so easy to see buttons in the dark<br><br>■ Not black in color, so less likely to misplace remote in the dark<br><br>■ Able to control thermostats, lights, dimmers, and door locks from apps<br><br>■ Easy to save favorite channels |  |

*Figure 6.4*

If you are able to conduct an observational VoC during your interview, try and keep the following things in mind as you observe the customer:

> Make sure you try to observe the customer in as close to their natural environment as possible. Try to observe the customer's behavior without interfering with their activities.

> If allowed, take a video of the way the customer uses/interacts with your products. If you are not allowed to record the video yourself due to security concerns, ask if you were to leave a camera whether the customer would be willing to record and edit the file before sending it to you.

> Try and identify exactly what problem the customer is trying to solve.

> Are they able to solve the problem completely with the offering they are using (whether it is yours or someone else's)?

> What does the customer have to do to make the current offering work for them?

> How could your offering make their ability to solve their problem faster, cheaper, and more effective?

> Is the customer using your products or offerings in ways you did not imagine?

> How will improving your offering affect the customer's bottom line or productivity?

# Practicing the interview

Like any new business skill, you will likely not be a master of VoC the very first time you try it, and like any other new business skill, practice will help you perfect the craft. The customer visits you are undertaking mean spending hours of time to find the right customers, identify the right contacts, and set up the meetings. Now you are spending money, both in time and expense, to go out and meet with your customer face to face. The absolute last thing you want to do is waste all this considerable time and expense because you do not want to practice your interview.

It is good to create teams in your organization and practice on some of your co-workers before setting out on your first interview. You will learn a lot, both in regards to your own capabilities and potential areas for improvement, as well as opportunities to brush up in the actual interview guide.

When you decide that you are finally ready, after practicing a number of times with your co-workers, you will also want to make sure you start the interview process with a few customers who are not the ones at the top of your prioritized list. If you are still going to stumble (after all the considerable practice you have done), it is better to do so with less important customers so your most critical customers see the close-to-perfect you.

# Perfecting the interview

It is not unusual to find that the guide you have taken days to develop and hours to practice is not quite right. You should hold a quick debrief after every interview (or at least after the first five interviews) to determine what works in your guide and what doesn't. These sessions should be held with all of the team that took part in the interviews. Are the questions you wrote understandable to the customers, or are customers sometimes confused by what you are asking? Does the flow of the questions and the transitions make sense, or do you need to change them? Do the questions yield the type of information you are looking to get from the customer, or do you end up with superficial responses that are not actionable by the project team at the conclusion of the interviews?

If you are handling multiple teams, make sure that you coordinate with the other teams and discuss whether they had the same issues with their interviews. Regardless of whether they did, if you change one discussion guide, make sure all the discussion guides are changed to better ensure future consistency.

# Concept testing

Many times during the course of customer interviews, some ideas or concepts begin to emerge based on what the customers have told you thus far.

Many times, it is possible to take the information you have learned so far and begin to make drawings, sketches, screen mock-ups, or models made from wood, stereo lithography, or 3D printing models. This helps to crystalize what you have heard so far and also provides a basis for further market research. At this point, it is often helpful to add a section to the visit agenda at the completion of the interview to test some of these new concepts with customers to see how well they might fit their needs.

The purpose of concept testing, then, is to help predict the success of a new idea or concept before it enters the design stage, where real money and resources are allocated by getting customer reactions to the proposed offering. In my experience, I have found that customers will have a much easier time pointing to a concept that you already have and then explaining what they like, what they dislike, and why. Concept testing has a number of advantages; here are some:

> Get real-time feedback on concepts
> See if a concept is intuitive
> Minimize engineering spend and waste
> Uncover potential problems with your offering
> Leverage customer feedback to modify your strategy and plans
> Trade-offs between functional design choices
> Understand market attractiveness
> Understand potential adjunct uses and markets

➤ Receive supplier advice

➤ Explore manufacturing issues before the design phase

➤ Iterate ideas and features quickly

While concept testing can be another valuable tool in refining your VoC input, there are a few caveats that you should employ when adding concept testing to your repertoire:

➤ Don't take too long to develop the prototype.

➤ Don't make the concepts overly complicated. Keep it as simple as possible to convey your concept.

➤ Don't get fixated on a really nice prototype model. Sometimes all that is required is a sketch. Actually, you should start with a sketch and move to a prototype model only if you are getting consistent feedback after showing the sketch.

➤ Don't make it too real. If the customer perceives it looks *too good*, they will assume it is already in development and that it will be something they can order soon.

# Following up

Part of the process you are engaging in with a customer when doing an interview is designed to be beneficial for both parties. Certainly, we are keenly aware of the benefits you will receive based on the ability of your past and future customers to help guide you in making successful products and services that they will pay you money for. Of course, the customers also get the benefit of helping to direct a new product offering that will be more closely aligned with their needs by providing input during the development process.

To ensure that you have understood the customer correctly, and documented the key takeaways to be truly reflective of what the customer said, it is often advised to provide a follow-up email/letter to the customer highlighting some of the key findings and observations discussed during the interview. This has the double benefit of double-checking what the customer has said as well as providing you with an opportunity to thank them for their time. This further tells the customer that you were listening to what they had to say and value their input. This helps keep the customer engaged in your process, which could lead to follow-up dialog on one of the key points, providing additional insight.

Further, the small gesture of a follow-up helps solidify the relationship between you and the customer and will make it more likely that they will continue to be a subject for future market studies or analysis.

# Summary

This chapter leverages the analysis and research we have covered in previous chapters relative to which customers to target, what questions to ask, how to coordinate a customer visit program, and how to assign team members for your VoC program. We learned the various roles and responsibilities of each of the team members and how you must choose a moderator to act as the quarterback of your VoC visits. We also learned how the supporting members of the interview team are equally important in taking valuable notes and how to observe the customers during the interview to yield the most robust data, which can be analyzed after the visits are compete. We also talked about best practices for the interview session as well as a number of *don'ts* that can undermine the success of your initiative. Lastly, we discussed the benefits of observational VoC, as well as how to use concept testing during the interview process.

Now that your interviews are complete, only half the work is done. Now you must apply the observations you have made as part of the VoC session to future product decisions. To do this, you will need a repeatable set of methods and tools to analyze the data you have collected, which we will cover in *Chapter 7, Understanding the Customer's Voice.*

# >7

# Understanding the Customer's Voice

*"If we're building the wrong product really efficiently, it's like we're driving our car off a cliff and bragging about our awesome gas mileage."*

*–Eric Ries*

In *Chapter 6, The Interview Process – The Interview*, we focused on the actual interview details and structure. We talked about the various roles and responsibilities of each of the interview team members, how to select team members for the interview team, and how to get the best out of each team member. We focused on the all-important interview itself, how best to interact with the customer, and how to execute the interview to get as much meaningful data as possible from the limited time you will have with the customer. While that chapter focused on the most important phase of data collection, this chapter will delve into a number of tools and processes you can use as part of your VoC toolkit to drive new product decisions using the data you have gathered.

In today's business environment, companies cannot just assume they know what customers want—they must know for sure, which is why we undertook the actions described in the preceding chapters. Now, we are beginning to have a better understanding of what customers want, but the challenge is to then provide products and services to meet and exceed customers' desires. Business leaders have struggled for years to meet this very challenge.

You have now completed the interview process and are ready to move to the next step. You have an abundance of notes and possibly audio tapes, photos, and videos. The challenge is to make sense of all the input you and your team have received from the customers during your extensive rounds of interviews.

It is very possible you will happen upon an "aha" moment and your customer interviews will yield an almost obvious new product development that will help catapult your business to the next level. More often than not, though, you will have assimilated a great deal of customer data, observations, issues, and responses that you must now try and turn into meaningful product requirements so the organization can leverage the investment they have made into the VoC program, and take the data you have collected thus far and turn it into actionable products and services.

To do this, we will need to have a process that will help us organize and codify our observations into new products and services. Without a process, you run the risk of having only a small sub-segment of the customer's input actually making its way to the product decision step, and often it is only the most convincing or vocal of the team members who get their interviews into this step when there is no process. You need to make sure all input is considered and evaluated to ensure you are making effective product design decisions.

What we need is a process to take the customer's images, statements, and voices and transfer them into an engineering specification that can be used to create our product. If we simply share what the customer said with the development team, we will likely not get what we, or our customers, envision. You have probably seen a version of the graphic in *Figure 7.1* before:

*Figure 7.1*

This happens when there is not a clear documented process of taking the customers' voices and images and transferring them through a process that can convert them into a meaningful, functional specification that the engineering team can build. The high-level view of the process we will use in taking the needs of the customers and turning it into a functional specification are shown here (*Figure 7.2*):

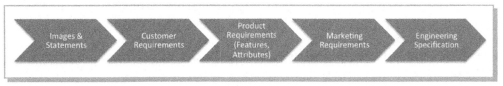

*Figure 7.2*

We will also leverage many of the tools used in six sigma, QA circles, and as part of the project management office that can also be used as part of the innovation process. While much of the work in QA revolves around doing root cause analysis of a problem, often one can see how these same philosophies of understanding a customer's problem and how to solve it are directly related.

# Consolidating the customer's voice

After all the interviews are complete, and as soon as possible, it is time to bring together the various data input the teams have received and try to summarize key customer findings and identify key customer trends.

If you have followed the process laid out in this book, you should already have a good set of notes from each interview (at a minimum). The first step in our consolidation process is for everyone to consolidate all their own information from the interviews they have each attended. This is done individually and before the groups meet to discuss their findings. Everyone who has participated in the group interviews must do this without any discussion among the team members. If you had three teams with three members on each team, you would have nine sets of notes that were developed individually, separate from each other, that capture the messages each team member heard from the customers from their own individual perspective.

The first step in the consolidation process is to review your own set of notes (or the notes made by your team) and begin by highlighting key customer insights and observations that were the most relevant to you from the interviews you attended. Review your notes, transcripts, videos, and so on multiple times, and use a colored highlighter to select the key passages in your notes that best represent your customer discussions in support of your customer visit objectives. Transcribe key takeaways from videos, photos, and anything else onto a separate sheet of paper and highlight all these as well. Make sure each page of your notes is numbered (as we will need this in a later step). At the end of this step, you should have a fair number of passages highlighted.

Review your highlighted notes and remove those that are clearly duplicates or not relevant.

The next step is to transfer your highlighted key passages onto yellow sticky notes. Start by reviewing all the passages you have highlighted in the previous step and assign a point value to each passage from 1 to 5, 1 being the most important and 5 being the least important. Transfer all the passages that scored 1, 2, or 3 onto a yellow sticky note while eliminating redundant or duplicate items. Review your notes and see if there are any of the fours and fives that you think are key enough that should also be shared during the meeting with the rest of the team, and transfer them as well. When you are done, it is very likely you will have in excess of 50 yellow sticky notes and you could easily have more than 100.

Before you transfer your notes to a yellow sticky note, you must also ensure that there is a protocol for writing each of the notes on the sticky notes and that everyone follows the same process. Following is a suggested process for creating sticky notes for your VoC feedback, but you may choose to do something different. Again, what is important is that you have a consistent, repeatable process that is used by all members of your team:

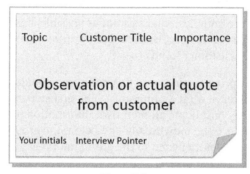

*Figure 7.3*

When using the yellow sticky note process, as shown in *Figure 7.3*, it is best to use a 3x5 Post-it note. Make sure all participants write horizontally, legible only on the front in block letters, and have the sticky side on top. Follow a set protocol such as the one shown in *Figure 7.3* and explained here:

> ➤ **Topic**: This is the topic of conversation used in your interview guide that precipitated the customer quote or observation.

> ➤ **Customer title**: We are looking for the customer's functional area to better understand the context of the quote or observation. We do not need the customer's name, but you and your team should agree on the "customer codes" to be used here to identify specific types of customers.

> ➤ **Importance**: This is an agreed-upon key signifying the level of importance or priority of the quote or observation from the customer's perspective. You and your team must decide what to put here, but a value of *H=High, M=Medium,* and *L=Low* tends to work well. If you do not use a *H, M, L* indication and choose something else, the key point is to make sure it is something simple and easily understood by all members of your team. Often you will be able to use the one, two, three code you used in step 1 to indicate the level of importance in this step, but not always.

- ➤ **Quote or paraphrase from the customer**: This is what the customer told you. What we are trying to get here is the customer's voice—something that expresses a customer's need or desired outcome. It is best to use actual customer quotes, and when doing so, use quotation marks. If you don't have direct quotes, still record what the customer said on the sticky note but do not put the observation in quotes. Whenever possible, place the observation in a positive requirements form and ask for each statement to include a verb and a noun. Try to limit the quote or observation to two lines and certainly no more than four lines.

- ➤ **You're initial**: This could also be your first name and last initial. We are simply looking for a way to trace the quote or observation back to you.

- ➤ **Interview pointer**: An agreed upon code tracing this quote back to a specific place in your notes. Often this code will include a page number and specific interview number allowing the team to trace the quote or observation to a specific location in your notes.

*Figure 7.4* is an example of a sticky note that has been completely filled out as part of this exercise. As shown in this figure, try to keep the lower right-hand corner of the sticky note blank:

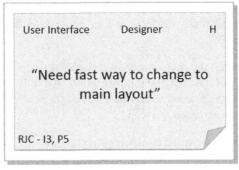

**Figure 7.4**

The quotes or paraphrases you transferred from your customer notes to your yellow sticky notes are considered *customer statements*. If you had the additional benefit of being able to observe how your customer uses your product or the environment where they might use your product, you probably also walked away with some distinct images in your head about the shortcomings your product has that could also be addressed by a new product or solution. This could have come about by processing the customer interview in totality, as opposed to a specific statement your customer made. Record any images you felt were pertinent and important as a result of your customer interview. Agree on a process for differentiating whether what you are recording is a customer statement or an image. As an example, you could use a different color pen for images versus statements, or perhaps a small green dot on each note that is an image.

Once you have transferred your key statements and images from your customer interview onto the yellow sticky notes, you are ready to start to prepare for the next step, where you will bring the team together to consolidate all the customer statements and images.

# Prioritizing the customer's voice

You have completed the multitude of interviews, market research, focus groups, and surveys, and now you find yourself drowning in quotes and observations, but without some structure, all you will have is a mountain of information.

What is required is a way to gather these large amounts of data (ideas, criticisms, opinions, and issues) and organize them into an actionable plan. This is where an affinity diagram can offer the practicing marketer a base-level way to organize these large groups of data into groupings based on their natural relationships. This tool is very popular for brainstorming, but can also provide value by providing the first step in making sense of the volumes of information you may have collected.

In the late 1970s, the US government commissioned an exercise to study effective group decision-making. In this exercise, they asked 30 military experts to study enemy intelligence data and to try to determine the enemy troop's movements.

Each expert analyzed the data and created a report. The commission then scored each report on the accuracy of how well each one actually predicted the troop's movements. They found that the average military expert only scored 7 out of 100 elements correctly. Each expert then reviewed all the other experts' reports and rewrote their initial assessment. The average accuracy for these revised reports went up by 72 points to a total of 79 out of a possible 100.

What was different between the first time they completed a report and the second report? The experts did not have any new information. All they had was the combined perspectives of all the other experts. When they added those additional perspectives to their own, their accuracy increased ten fold.

When designing new products, most companies' resources are limited. It becomes necessary to find some way to prioritize all the things you and your customers want you to do. The answer probably resides inside the customer VoC you have done, but how to get all these perspectives into a prioritized list is a challenge for most organizations.

To do this, we turn to a popular technique that has been around for thousands of years, which is the grouping of data based on natural relationships. This is referred to as an affinity diagram, which is also often referred to as "the KJ-method" after its inventor Jiro Kawakita.

Like the proceeding example, the affinity process is used to bring organization to the data you have collected and provides two key outcomes that are critical for VoC and the innovation process:

> ➤ **Sifting through large volumes of data**: Often the interviews create a large list of unsorted data as a result of documenting multiple segments and customer needs.

> ➤ **Encourage new patterns of thinking**: An affinity process is an excellent way to get people to react at a "gut" level instead of intellectually dissecting the customer input. This is especially true when using the tool for brainstorming as it allows the participants to input ideas without criticism, which often yields creative ideas that are outside the traditional business or marketing areas.

Affinitizing your data is a process performed by a group or team to channel the various perspectives and opinions of customers they have interviewed in an attempt to meld these insights into logical groupings. In this case, it is done by the interview teams who have just transferred their set of customer observations and quotes onto yellow sticky notes. Ideally, there should be no more than five or six participants per affinity team with a maximum of 10, so you may need to break into smaller groups initially and come back together at a later step.

At this point, you have organized all your notes, audio clips, video clips, photos, and diagrams from all the interviews you have done. You have highlighted your notes from all the interviews and prioritized the key messages from the customers. You have also transferred each of these key quotes or observations to a yellow sticky note using an agreed upon protocol and you likely have somewhere between 50–100 yellow sticky notes. You are now ready to move to the next step, where you can start driving out the key customer product attributes using an affinity diagram. This next step is a critical part of the process and can easily take a half to a full day, but can be done in much less time depending on the nature of the exercise. This is a critical step and should not be short-changed:

➤ Determine the focus question. Each session will have a focus question, and you can use the same data to answer different questions. Some potentials questions could include:

  ➢ What requirements do our customers have for our next-generation widget?

  ➢ What are the biggest obstacles to our product selling?

  ➢ What new service offerings do we need to provide?

  You can only do one at a time, so it is best to pick the most important one first.

➤ Call a meeting to review everyone's customer interview observations and consolidate your sticky notes. Ensure that all the people who went on the customer visits attend the meeting and have filled out the yellow sticky notes. This is critical and there can be no exceptions. Limit the participants to only those people who have actually participated in the customer interview and a facilitator if needed. If your management insists upon attending the meeting but have not actually done the customer interviews, they must participate as observers only. They have not done the interviews so any input they have would more than likely be based on their own bias.

➤ Make sure that you have ample space for the teams to work together on the affinity process. It is recommended that you bring a number of flip charts and a roll of paper, if available, to construct your affinity diagram. If you have a roll of paper, cut two pieces of 5 to 6 feet and tape them to one or two walls to construct your "board."

➤ Assign one person who may have done previous exercises with affinity diagrams to the facilitator role.

> ➤ One at a time, have each person read their observation, quote, or image from their sticky note and have them place it on the board. Others cannot debate or question the contents of the sticky note, but can ask for clarification if it is needed.

> ➤ Once all the sticky notes have been placed on the board, have everyone go up to the board to review all the observations and quotes.

> ➤ Have everyone look for any sticky notes that are duplicates, and in silence have each team member place the duplicates on top of each other so the original observation or quote still shows. The duplicates do not have to say the exact same thing, but should have the exact same meaning. Once all the duplicates have been found, allow everyone to talk to make sure everyone is in agreement that the duplicates are indeed duplicates, and if not, separate them again. Have the team pick the best statement that represents this observation or need and place it on the top (see *Figure 7.5*):

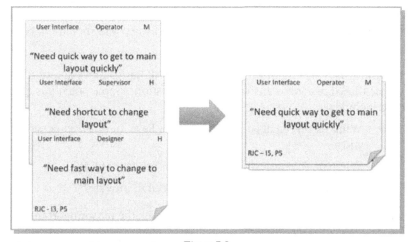

*Figure 7.5*

When you have finished, you could easily have 200 or more sticky notes on the board. The goal now is to determine the most critical 20–50 statements that best answer the original focus question. To do this we will have to narrow down the large number. When this is complete, we expect to have closer to 20–30. The next steps will help us narrow down the extensive number of notes to something much more manageable.

> ➤ Taking turns, have everyone move, one at a time, the sticky notes they consider the most important to another section of the board or to another board on another wall. Have the participants group the sticky notes roughly into the topic categories from the discussion topics we used in the discussion guide (and are at the top left of the sticky note if you followed the protocol we described earlier) as they move them to the new board. During this process the participants will notice yellow sticky notes that are trivial or irrelevant and these should not be moved to the new board.

➤ Examine and remove all yellow sticky notes that only have technical information, such as specifications, or are a description of a new feature. The remaining sticky notes should only have customer voices that express a customer need or desired outcome. Do not discard the yellow sticky notes that had specifications or features, but put them aside for future use.

If you still have in excess of 30 sticky notes at this time, you will need a way to systematically reduce the number using a group prioritization technique:

➤ Have each member of the team place a red dot on the items they feel are more important. If a red dot is already on the card you would have picked, choose another card that does not yet have a red dot that is also important in your mind. Continue doing this until all the important cards are marked. Remove the unimportant ones to be used later for reference.

➤ If you still have in excess of 30 cards, divide 30 by the number of members of your team and round it up. This is the number of picks each person will have. If your team has 7 people, *30/7=4.3*. In this case each person gets 4 picks from the board, which would result in 28 voices. Again, keep in mind your goal is to walk away with 20-30 picks for the entire team.

➤ One at a time, have each person go to the board and pick what they consider to be the most important voice on the board. Have them repeat this process until voices are picked or excluded because no one feels they are important enough.

➤ Have each team member place their saved yellow sticky notes on a new board one at a time and read the statement aloud and explain why they picked this yellow sticky as one of the key voices.

# From voices into customer requirements

You have now limited your focus on the 20-30 most pressing customer voices. You now need a way to group these disparate thoughts and images into a cohesive set of requirements that can be deployed in your new development. Have everyone review the yellow sticky notes that were picked. You should now have a robust set of customer voices from your interviews and you should begin to develop a sense of your customers' main concerns and requirements.

We now need a method to convert your customers' voices, key concerns, and images into requirements. For this we will use a "translation worksheet." This tool allows us to reframe each customer voice into specific performance requirements for the product or service you are investigating. This part of the process is critically important. Customers often describe their needs in vague language or in terms that they are already familiar with, or even worse, they tell you the solution they need. This step helps us to identify the requirements necessary to develop the solution the customers actually require.

To begin, we will take the final set of yellow sticky notes and transfer the customer statements or voices onto the translation worksheet as shown in *Figure 7.6*. You will create a worksheet for all the voices. If you are translating all voices into customer requirements, you may also wish to split up into teams to do the translation work as it can take a fair amount of time:

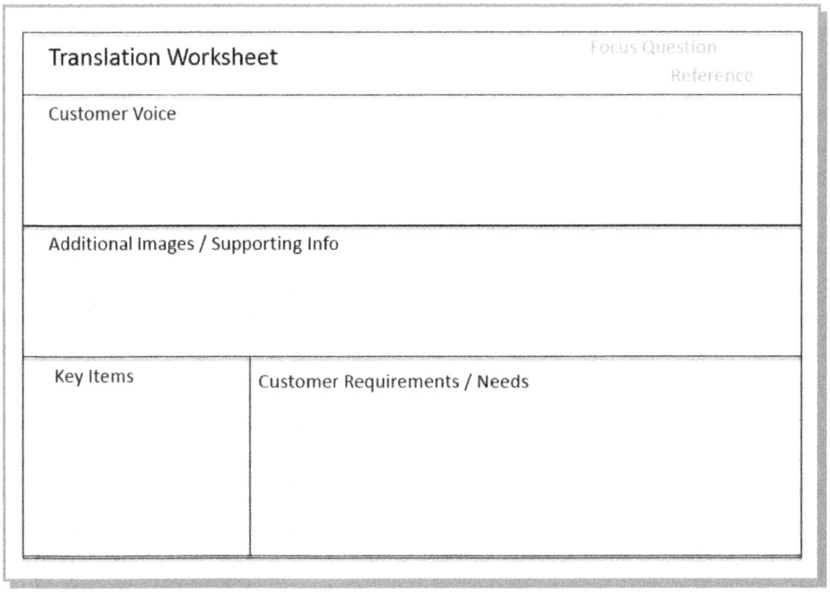

| Translation Worksheet | Focus Question Reference |
|---|---|
| **Customer Voice** | |
| **Additional Images / Supporting Info** | |
| **Key Items** | **Customer Requirements / Needs** |

*Figure 7.6*

The following is a description of each section of the translation worksheet:

> **Focus question**: You need some way to link this worksheet to the focus question you are trying to address. Stating the focus question as part of the sheet or some other way to group these worksheets is good practice.

> **Reference**: Having some way of going back to your notes or yellow sticky notes is also good practice and should be adopted as part of your process. It is simple to transfer the reference from your yellow sticky directly to the worksheet that addresses this need.

> **Customer voice**: This is a verbatim sentence, statement, phrase, or group of sentences taken from the yellow sticky note.

> **Images**: Add any additional images that you saw or heard during the customer interview or site visit that supports the customer's voice. Sometimes, this image can be constructed by the team as they visualize themselves in the customer's world and doing what the customer does.

➤ **Key items**: These can be any issues or considerations that come to mind when you think about this specific customer voice. Key items often serve as the link between the customer voice and the actual requirement statement. There are no hard and fast rules about what is or is not a key item. Use this area on the worksheet to free-associate recording key words, sentences, or other images that come to mind. This area can also include outside items such as research reports and historical data and analysis in support of the customer's voice.

➤ **Customer requirements/needs**: This is a concise one-sentence statement that clearly describes the function or product attribute you will need to address the customer voice. It is likely that you will need more than one requirement statement to address the customer voice.

Before filling out the customer requirements/needs section, it is good to step back and review the types of needs and what makes up a good requirement. A good customer requirement/needs statement should have the following criteria:

> **1. Identify a functional need** - The requirement must identify a functional need, not a product solution. A functional need tells us what the solution should do while the product solution tells us how it should be accomplished.
>
> **2. Make your customer requirement/need as specific and clear as possible** – imprecise or vague terms allow for differing interpretations. Use simple sentence structure
>
> **3. Phrase your customer requirement / need in a positive language.** Do not use language that includes "does not" or "will not"
>
> **4. Use multivalued language when describing your need.** A multivalued requirement allows an individual to measure something along a scale. It is not a binary or a yes/no attribute and often adds more a higher level of specificity even thought you may think the opposite.

*Figure 7.7*

Writing a good requirement statement often takes multiple iterations. It is often helpful to write down your first impression of a requirement statement and then attempt to refine it to meet the requirement statement criteria in *Figure 7.7*. It is also good practice to ensure you do not use "and" in your requirement statements. The use of "and" usually indicates more than one customer requirement.

The following example illustrates a customer requirement for a ruggedized laptop:

| Translation Worksheet | What needs do you have in a laptop? |
|---|---|
| | RJC – 14, P3 |

**Customer Voice**

"I need a robust laptop that won't leave me hanging. I have to finalize my customer report at the end of the day, every day!"

**Additional Images / Supporting Info**

He is on the road at the job site every day. His laptop get banged around at the construction site and has gotten knocked off the table and he lost at least one hard drive

| Key Items | Customer Requirements / Needs |
|---|---|
| • Durable exterior<br>• Durable interior<br>• Rugged construction<br>• Must stand up to high abuse | • Computer shall withstand abusive handling while in a construction vehicle<br>• Computer shall withstand being dropped from a 3'-6" table onto concrete and still operate |

*Figure 7.8*

As you can see from the translation worksheet, the quote from the customer was not enough to determine the customer requirement/need, but by understanding the other things the customer said, as well as seeing the customer's site, we were able to create a much more robust image than with the customer voice alone.

As you are undertaking this exercise, do not be surprised if you interpret customer requirements differently than others on your team. We have different perspectives and have interviewed different customers, so this should not be a surprise. Explore these differences and, if necessary, create two requirements. Again, it is more than likely you will get multiple requirements from a customer voice and these opportunities should be fully vetted as part of this exercise.

It is also worth noting that you will often uncover potential solutions as you are performing this analysis. Do not try and force these solutions into requirements; simply put them aside for review later in the process.

When you are finished with your translated worksheet, move on to the next one. If you get stuck on a particular worksheet, put it aside and come back to it later.

# Sorting and prioritizing the customer's requirements

At this point, you have transformed the customer voices into a high-level set of requirements with supporting quotes, statements, and images. We now need to discuss how we can go about solving the various customer requirements we have received and prioritized and turn them into product requirements. This is where an understanding of both the customer and the associated product and company technology can pay off in developing a first-of-its-kind solution.

If you started with 30 or so voices and translated them into customer requirements/needs, you likely have 40-50 requirement statements. Before we continue further, we need a way to narrow our focus so we can allocate our resources to the requirement statements that will do the most to delight our customers and maximize our investment. To narrow our focus, we will assess our requirement priorities using a process very similar to the process we used to convert customer voices into customer needs:

1. Transcribe all the customer requirement statements onto yellow sticky notes like we did earlier in the chapter.

2. On a whiteboard or butcher block paper, write your focus statements, such as, "What are the key customer needs for XXX?"

3. Post all the yellow sticky notes on the board.

4. Have individual members move all the requirements, which they feel are important, from one board to another, and remove the ones that were not moved.

5. Have each team member place a red dot on the bottom right-hand corner of notes they think are worth keeping. Only one dot per note.

6. Take down all the notes without a dot.

7. Add a second dot and continue the exercise until there are fewer than 30 notes remaining.

8. Divide 30 by the number of people on the team and round to the next whole number. This is the number of picks each member gets.

9. Each person picks the note that is left on the board that they feel is the most important, reads it aloud, and explains to the group why it is important.

This continues until we have our specified number of statements.

Now that we have our 20-30 key customer requirements, we need to group and prioritize them:

➤ *In silence*, instruct everyone to review all the statements on the board and read them several times.

➤ Have each member try to create a mental image of the meanings as opposed to just reading the words.

> ➤ Have everyone move the sticky notes around on the board so as to create logical groupings of needs. Start by looking for two ideas that seem related in some way. Look for ideas that are related to those you already grouped and add them as well. Look for other ideas that are also related to each other and create new groups with them. As an example, one group of Post-its might all have to do with the "performance characteristics" of a printer (like speed), while another may focus on the "user interface," another may talk about "communications," and yet another deals with "additional functions" such as scanning or faxing. The goal is to do this process quickly and without a lot of agonizing. Go with gut reactions to find the interrelationships. It is possible that these needs will cross over into other topic discussions, which is okay, but it should not happen that often if you have a good discussion guide structure.

> ➤ If a team member does not like where an idea is grouped, they can move it. You can always move it back. If a consensus cannot be reached, make a duplicate sticky note and place one copy in each group.

> ➤ Typically, you should have no more than two to three yellow sticky notes in a group. Keep moving requirements around until you have 8-12 groups.

> ➤ Stop when there is little or no movement of sticky notes.

> ➤ Ideally, all the ideas can be sorted into related groups. If there are some loners that do not fit into any of the groups, do not try and force them into groups where they do not belong. Let them stand alone in their own group (see *Figure 7.9*):

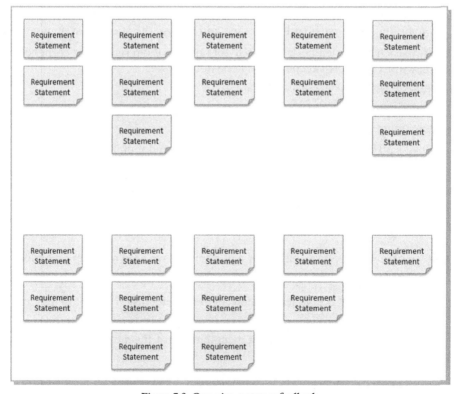

*Figure 7.9: Grouping customer feedback*

Allow everyone to talk. Have the team discuss why certain things are grouped together by answering the question, "Why are these particular sticky notes together?" Allow these groups to get combined if there are duplicate themes or broken apart if it appears there is the possibility that more than one theme is represented by the group. Anyone can nominate two groups that should be combined, and we will vote on whether or not to combine them. If anyone dissents, we discuss among the team why, or why groups should not be combined. After this, we will take another vote to see whether we should combine the groups, but again, the vote must be unanimous to combine them.

Make sure there were no key requirements that were missed. If so, add them, but do not use this as an opportunity to add back in your "pet" requirements.

Have the team discuss the groups and come up with a level 1 title for each that best defines the common theme in each group. Review key words or phases in each group to see what they have in common. These titles should be written in the same language as the original requirement statements, but should be at a slightly higher level of abstraction. If at all possible, use an existing quote as a level 1 title if it adequately addresses the entire need. If there is no customer requirement that addresses the entire group need, create one using the collective requirements from the yellow sticky notes.

Care must be taken so as not to try and describe everything in the group with the group title. The group title should only capture what the requirements have in common as shown in *Figure 7.10*. For this reason, it is likely there should be the word "and" in the level 1 title:

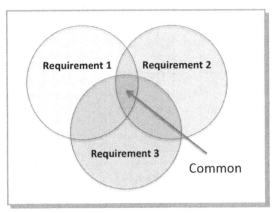

*Figure 7.10*

> Write the level 1 title for each group on a yellow sticky note in large, red block letters and place it above the group. If there is a yellow sticky with a customer requirement on it that is being used as a group level 1 title, draw a red block around the customer need and move it to the top of the group.

> If you have any groups that only have one sticky note, draw a red box around the customer need and use this as the group header. If you have any loners that did not fit into another group before, check if they now fit into a group once the title has been decided.

When you are done, you will have something that looks like *Figure 7.11*:

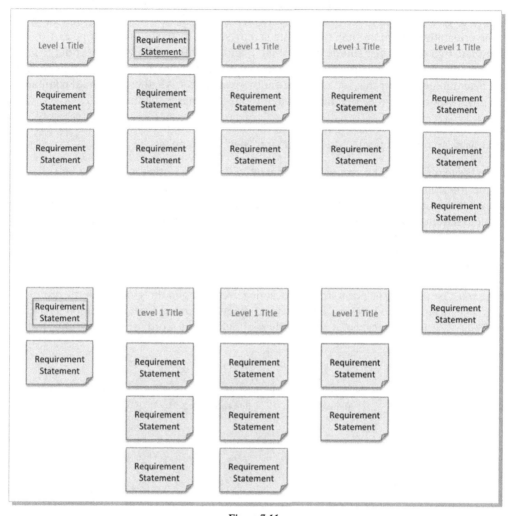

**Figure 7.11**

Once the requirements are grouped like in *Figure 7.11*, we will look for ways to group the level 1 titles into common larger themes:

> ➤ Stack the groupings so the top level 1 title or individual requirement statements show.

> ➤ Look for groups of two or three titles that share common traits, like we did with the individual requirements.

➤ Repeat the cluster analysis, like we did previously, by allowing the team to silently move the stacks around into common themes at a slightly higher level of abstraction. Make sure to avoid cause and effect relationships.

➤ Allow the team to move them back and forth until there is no more movement.

➤ Have the team decide on a second level title that captures the common theme for each group. These higher-level titles will help you capture overall issues and will help in communicating these items to senior management and other managers.

➤ Have the team write a second level title on a yellow sticky in blue block letters, using the same philosophy as before, by focusing on the words or phrases that reflect what the level 1 titles have in common, and place it above the group.

When you are finished, you will have something that looks like *Figure 7.12.*

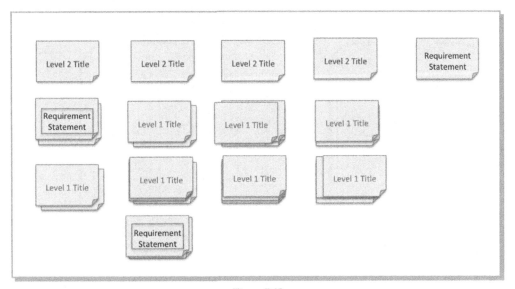

*Figure 7.12*

Once we are finished with this step, we need to lay out our completed affinity diagram so we can see the complete picture of what our customer interviews have told us:

➤ Have the team take the level 2 stacks with the level 1 and requirement yellow sticky notes to a separate board or piece of paper. This will be the final affinity sheet.

➤ Deconstruct the yellow sticky notes so you can see each individual sticky note, but it still retains its cluster.

➤ Draw a black line around each level 1 grouping.

➤ Draw a blue line around each of the level 2 groupings.

When complete, you should have something similar to *Figure 7.13*:

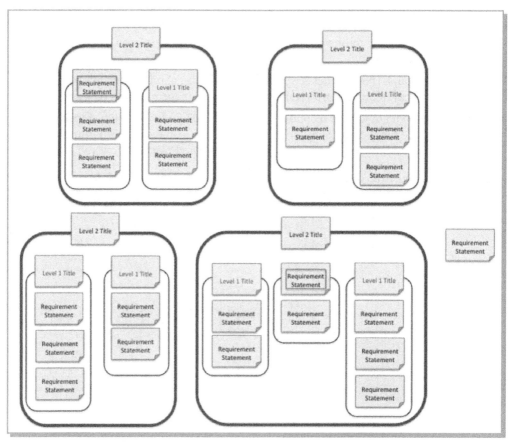

*Figure 7.13*

> When complete, have each participant take a piece of paper and write down the names of three level 1 headers that best address the focus question or are the highest priorities in addressing the focus question. If participants have trouble narrowing it down to three names only, have them start with five and scratch two off (yes... it really works).

> Now, have everyone rank their three choices from most important to least important on their paper where they have written the header names. This tends to be easier than trying to do both steps at once.

> Have each participant go up to the board, and on the level 1 note put three stars on their first choice, two stars on their second choice, and one star on their third choice. When complete, each participant will have marked a total of six stars on the level 1 notes.

Add up all the stars on each level 1 header and determine the first, second, and third most important or appropriate. Color in the background of the first choice with a red hash, the second choice with a blue hash, and the third choice with a green hash. Once this is complete, discuss the findings with the group and try to agree on a common conclusion. If you do, write it on the upper right-hand corner of the chat. Have everyone sign and date the final affinity diagram in the lower right-hand corner. Your final affinity chart should look similar to *Figure 7.14*:

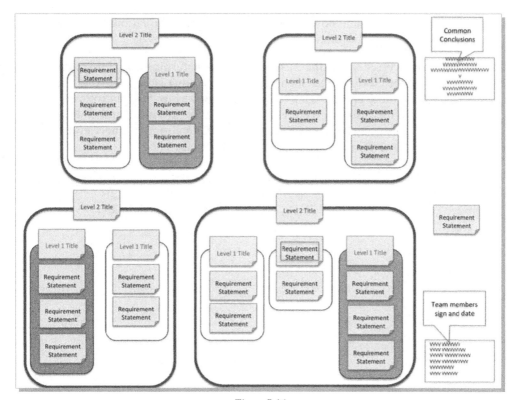

*Figure 7.14*

# Summary

Previous to this chapter, we discussed how best to get customer insights, feedback, statements, quotes, and images, which, collectively, we refer to as the customer voices. In this chapter, we reviewed how to transform the voices of multiple interviews into something that is actionable by your organization. We reviewed the best way to capture and share key insights with your interview team using the sticky note concept. We talked about having a post-interview meeting where all parties can come together and share the insights they have received, and how to merge the voices from the various interviews into one superset of data using the affinity process.

This chapter also discussed taking the customer voices and turning them into customer requirements using the customer statements, images, and other keywords. After this, we reviewed using the affinity process again to help us group key feedback into clusters that provided structure to the customer requirements. Lastly, we prioritized and ranked the customer requirements using both the insights we had gotten from the interviews, as well as from a feedback mechanism to get a wider view of the customer.

In the next chapter, we will take the next step in the process by turning our customer requirements into actionable marketing documents, technical requirements, and ultimately solutions for our customers.

# 8

# Validating the Customer's Voice

*"The great thing about fact-based decisions is that they can overrule the hierarchy"*

*–Jeff Bezos*

In *Chapter 7, Understanding the Customer's Voice*, we discussed how to make sense of all the information we gathered during our interview process. We reviewed how to highlight our interview notes, and take those highlighted passages and transfer them to yellow sticky notes. We do this, of course, so we can group and prioritize the customer's needs we have been told about. After this, we transferred the most important 30-50 customers' voices and, through our translation worksheet, turned the customer voices into rudimentary requirements. We then performed another affinity process on these customer requirements and further reduced the number to 20-30 of the customers' most important needs. We grouped and prioritized the most important requirements.

When that is complete, you will have prioritized what *you think* the customer has told you are the most important customer requirements. You will have done this, of course, by interviewing a representative sample of your customers and while this is a very good beginning, it is also worth considering doing a more detailed analysis to see whether your assumptions are correct.

The process we described in *Chapter 7, Understanding the Customer's Voice* helped us to understand customer requirements. What this process did not do was help us understand which of these product attributes or requirements were the most important to the customer, which product attributes were an absolute "must-have" in the eyes of the customer, and which of these would have a higher influence on customer satisfaction than the others.

At this point, it is often necessary to assemble the information you have gotten this far and then go back to some of the same customers, or different customers, to help you prioritize what needs to be done and why.

# Linkert scale

Since you have extracted the customer requirements from your interviews and images, it will be very easy to now take the customer requirements you have generated and make a questionnaire to help ascertain the real level of importance of each requirement. Your customer interviews probably consisted of 20-30 face-to-face meetings. To make the importance survey reliable, we recommend you survey 100-150 customers for each market segment you are targeting.

While most surveys get a 3-5% response rate, you really need to ensure you are getting a good cross-section of your customer base and are aiming for a 50-60% response rate. This will require some work with your marketing team to make sure customers are properly notified about the survey, that there is a proper incentive for their participation, and that there is a follow-up after the survey for those who did not respond.

The importance questionnaire format is shown in *Figure 8.1*. In this questionnaire, we list each of the possible requirements and have each customer rank each of them on a scale of 1-9, from *not at all important* to *extremely important*.

| How important would it be if... | Not at all important | | Somewhat important | | Important | | Very important | | Extremely important |
|---|---|---|---|---|---|---|---|---|---|
| Requirement 1 | 1 | 2 | 3 | 4 | 5 | 6 | 7 | 8 | 9 |
| Requirement 2 | 1 | 2 | 3 | 4 | 5 | 6 | 7 | 8 | 9 |
| Requirement 3 | 1 | 2 | 3 | 4 | 5 | 6 | 7 | 8 | 9 |
| Requirement 4 | 1 | 2 | 3 | 4 | 5 | 6 | 7 | 8 | 9 |
| Requirement 5 | 1 | 2 | 3 | 4 | 5 | 6 | 7 | 8 | 9 |
| Requirement 6 | 1 | 2 | 3 | 4 | 5 | 6 | 7 | 8 | 9 |
| Requirement 7 | 1 | 2 | 3 | 4 | 5 | 6 | 7 | 8 | 9 |
| Requirement 8 | 1 | 2 | 3 | 4 | 5 | 6 | 7 | 8 | 9 |

*Figure 8.1: Linkert scale*

When the questionnaires are returned, add up the ratings for each requirement and divide the total by the number of respondents, in order to determine each requirement's average rating. This will give you a prioritized list, as determined by your customers, of each of the customer requirements you have identified.

# Kano model

The preceding example illustrates a common survey instrument, which is used to ascertain the relative importance of one requirement versus another using a scale of five to nine points from the lowest degree to the highest. This tool is also often used in conjunction with a rank order scale, which asks customers to rank each requirement from 1-$N$ so the company can identify the highest-ranking requirements.

The problem with this methodology is two fold. In many circumstances, the customers will say virtually every requirement is *important* or *very important* to them. There is no downside to ranking virtually everything as important or very important.

The other problem with this tool is there is no way to know which and how many requirements absolutely have to be in the product. Nor is there any way to know which requirements will be competitive differentiators and will delight the customer, resulting in them buying your product rather than the competition's.

These questions can be difficult to answer, but thankfully there is a tool to help us understand what functions or features *need* to be in a product, as well as which functions or features will delight our customers. This tool is called the Kano model.

Dr. Noriaki Kano, a Japanese professor and international consultant, first developed the Kano model. In the late 1970s and early 1980s, he laid the foundation for an approach to quality creation. Dr. Kano questioned the traditional ideal of customer satisfaction that *more is better*—that the better you perform on each product or service attribute or criteria, the more satisfied your customers will be. Instead, Dr. Kano held that performance in all product and service attributes is not necessarily equal in the eyes of customers. Better performance in certain categories of attributes produces higher levels of satisfaction than other categories. He wanted to explain and demonstrate how different classifications/ categories of customer requirements and features have the ability to satisfy customers in different ways. By better understanding how customer requirements impact customer satisfaction, we can do a better job of taking the feedback we've received from our customers, and find the best features that will increase their satisfaction, thereby resulting in their choosing our product over the competition.

Before we discuss how to incorporate the Kano model into your customer VoC process, it is necessary to understand the components of the Kano model and how it helps us define needs and delighters.

The model begins with looking at customer satisfaction or perception. The Kano model draws customer satisfaction on the vertical axis and goes from total satisfaction or delight, to total dissatisfaction or frustration. The following image is a representation of the scale on this axis:

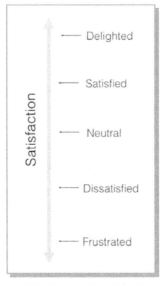

*Figure 8.2: Kano model satisfaction axis*

You may see this and think you must always be at the top of that scale in the **Delighted** area of the graph. While this is a noble goal, you will find it is a whole lot harder than you may think to occupy that space in a customer's mind, especially in a consistent way.

The horizontal axis represents the functionality the product delivers, or what the user gets when evaluating customer perception. You can also look at the horizontal scale as a function of how much effort a company put in to develop the product, the level of investment in the development of the product, or how well the functionality has been implemented in the product:

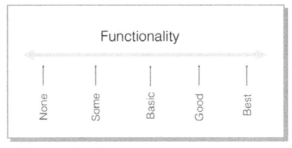

*Figure 8.3: Kano model functionality axis*

Together, the level of customer satisfaction versus the level of functionality gives us a good understanding of how our customers feel about out product's features. Let's see these features in detail:

> ➤ **Performance**: When we talk about product features, many people believe most or all of the features are based on a linear curve, as shown in the yellow line in *Figure 8.4*. The more we get of any one feature, the happier we are with the product— things like the mileage we get with our automobiles, the life of our cell phone battery, or the speed of our internet connection. The more we get, the higher our satisfaction and the better we feel about the product or company (assuming it doesn't cost us more to get it). Conversely, the less these requirements are satisfied, the more dissatisfaction the customer feels. Examples of this include such things as price, noise, space in an airline seat, and many more:

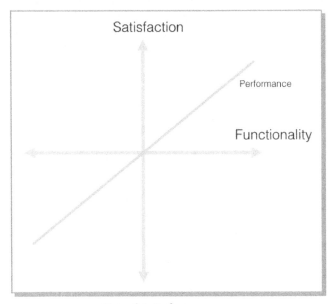

*Figure 8.4: Performance curve*

As you can see, this a linear function and there is a direct correlation between how much additional functionality is added (say, mileage), and the level of our satisfaction. These too are often the product features that customers think about when describing an ideal product. They are likely to say they want a car with better mileage, a phone with a better battery, or internet speed that is faster. These are considered *spoken* needs.

It is worth noting, however, that higher levels of functionality also typically equate to the level of resources or investment that must be made to deliver it:

> ➤ **Must-Be**: These are the features that the customer expects to get and are often taken for granted or assumed to be in the product. These are the obvious expectations your customers have for the product, and if it does not have them, it will be considered to be incomplete, or just wrong or bad. These features are called Must-Bes or Basic Expectations. These are going to be the same features that all your major competitors also have in their products. Having these features in your products will not make the customers more satisfied; they just won't be dissatisfied. Our cars should have brakes and windshield wipers; our hotel rooms should have windows and running water, and be clean. When booking a hotel, you do not request a clean room. You just expect that it will be clean. If this basic need isn't met, you are disappointed. As these are expected features, a customer rarely articulates them and they are considered "unspoken" needs.

You can see this curve in *Figure 8.5*. Notice how it is very easy to add a little investment to increase customer satisfaction, but it is also worth noting that satisfaction never crosses into the positive side of the graph, regardless of how much more is invested. Once a basic level of satisfaction is met, it is impossible to increase customer satisfaction by an additional amount, regardless of the resources or time investment:

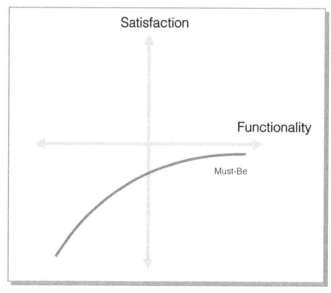

*Figure 8.5: Must-Be curve*

➤ **Indifferent**: In terms of these features, most customers simply do not care whether they are present in our product or not. Customer satisfaction remains neutral in either case. It really doesn't matter how much effort we put into these features—customers don't care. Another way to think about these features is these are the features that we really should avoid working on or committing resources to. For the vast majority of customers, we will never get payback for the money or effort expended. Good examples of **Indifferent** features would be the advanced features on our phone that most people never use—even if they could find them:

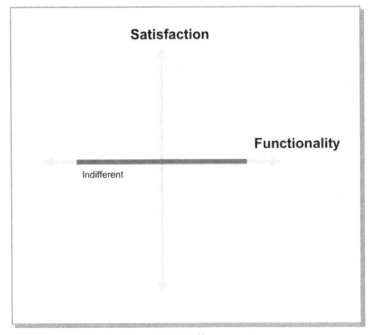

*Figure 8.6: Indifferent curve*

➤ **Attractive**: These are arguably some of the most important features you can put into a product. These are the unexpected features that, when a customer experiences them, create a positive reaction. This curve might be called delighters or exciters instead of attractive. This is the curve where many product innovations lie and where you can find your Competitive Differentiators or **Unique Selling Propositions (USPs)**. They tend to delight a customer when they are present, but as the customer is not "expecting" them to be present, when they are not there the customer is not disappointed with the product. Examples of delighters include things such as the first iPhone or the Nest smoke detector. When it first came out, the iPhone had a totally new interface and offered music, a phone, and a mini computer all in one package. The Next smoke detector has the ability to be silenced by simply waving your hand at it. Consumers did not expect these things, so the needs were never "spoken," but once they were introduced to the market, customers loved the new functionality.

This effect can be shown on the curve in *Figure 8.7*. You can see how incremental investments into functionality can have a large effect on customer satisfaction. Of course, you can also see that additional investments beyond a certain point may not even fall on the curve and you could be making investments that will yield no additional return.

Exciters don't have to be a whole new platform or product that changes the landscape the way the iPhone did. I remember taking a drive with my fiancée, who had just purchased a Range Rover. It was March, and the clocks had just changed to Daylight Savings Time. My fiancée asked me to change the two clocks in her car—both the analog clock and the digital time readout—while she was taking me to the airport. Since the car was new and neither of us knew how to change the clocks, or were willing to read the manual, I thought I'd tackle the digital dashboard display as I was pretty confident I could navigate the menu structure to make that change. The analog clock I was less confident about, as there appeared to be no dials or switches to advance the time.

As suspected, I was able to navigate the menus and make the changes to the dashboard time readout without looking through the manual. Much to my amazement, when I changed the time reading on the digital display, the analog clock hands magically moved forward on the face of the clock to mirror the time that was on the digital display. This is a good example, as it shows something does not need to radically change the way we use or interact with a product; it just has to be something that, when exposed to it, customers would say, "Wow... that is really nice!" Of course, if the exciter is for a whole new platform or product category, and ends up being a big innovation, this can also yield explosive results for a company, like the iPhone did for Apple:

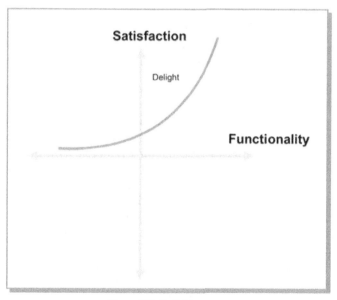

*Figure 8.7: Delighter curve*

➤ **Reverse**: There is another category that is not part of the traditional Kano model, but it is one you should be aware of. It is the **Reverse** category, and it is something you want to ensure is not a part of your offering. These are the features that cause dissatisfaction with customers when they are present, and satisfaction or indifference when they are not.

Examples of this are the little additional programs that are often packaged with a new PC, or the Microsoft paperclip helper, Clippy. Most people did not like the little assistant and found it especially annoying as there was not an easy way to turn him off:

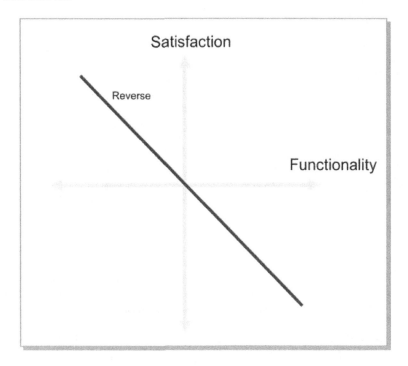

*Figure 8.8: Reverse curve*

*Figure 8.9* shows the complete Kano model. No doubt, if you were able to question customers on where your current product features lie, you would be able to see that many probably fall into the **Performance** and **Must-Be** categories. Hopefully, you don't have many that fall into the **Indifferent** category, and you have none that would fall into the **Reverse** category:

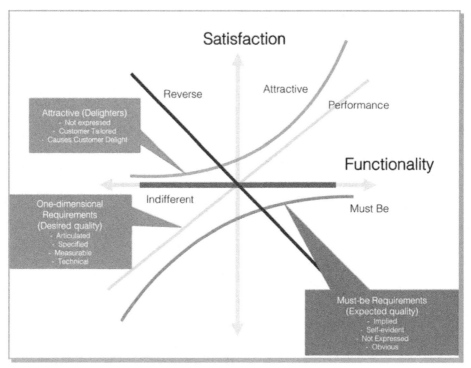

*Figure 8.9: Complete Kano model*

> **Delight decays over time**: When contemplating the Kano model, it is important to understand that what delights customers today will be asked for tomorrow and expected the next day. Delight only lasts a short time, and continuous innovation must be introduced to keep your innovative status in the open market. There are countless examples of new innovations that, when introduced, were completely novel or revolutionary. Again, think back to the first time you saw an iPhone with its swipe interface and the introduction of the App Store, where you could download programs that turned your phone into something altogether different from a phone. Shortly after the iPhone was introduced, people started asking for similar features in competitive phones, and now a smartphone without the same capabilities as the original iPhone doesn't stand a chance in the market. Of course, the iPhone is but one example. Think about power steering and anti-lock brakes in your car, wireless internet in your hotel room, a remote control for your TV, and many more. These were all innovative features when first introduced, but now if you buy a car without power steering, book a hotel without internet, or purchase a TV without a remote, you would consider the product to be inferior.

You can see in *Figure 8.10* how delight decays over time. The key point to remember is that any analysis you do at any given point in time is simply a snapshot of today's reality. The market does not stand still, and customer expectations are ever-changing. The more time that passes after the snapshot you create today, the less valid it will be:

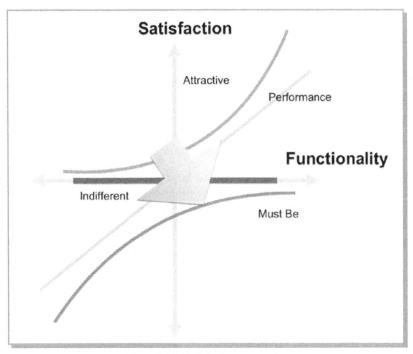

*Figure 8.10: Delight decays over time*

Now that we understand the components of the Kano model, the question is, how do we use it as part of our VoC process, and how can we plot our current and future products on the Kano model to understand our current position in the market, as well as those things that will delight our future customers?

In order to uncover our customers' perceptions of the features we have in our product, or are contemplating for a future release, we use a Kano questionnaire, also known as a Kano survey. The way a Kano questionnaire works is we construct a pair of questions for each feature or function we wish to evaluate. The first asks our customers how they would feel if they had this feature (a functional question) and the second asks them how they would feel if they did not have the feature (a dysfunctional question). For each of these questions, the customer has to choose from five possible responses to each question:

➤ I like it that way
➤ I expect it that way
➤ I am neutral
➤ I can live with it that way
➤ I dislike it that way

Let's use an example to illustrate the point. The following might be the types of responses we have gotten from potential customers for a set of downhill snow skis:

*Figure 8.11: Requirements for downhill skis*

Taking the first customer request, **Good grip on hard-pack snow**, we could turn this request/feature into two questions we could ask other customers. The first functional question would be something like this: "If the edges of your skis grip the snow well on hard-packed ski runs, how do you feel?" The second dysfunctional question would be: "If the edges of your skis don't always grip the snow well on hard-packed ski runs, how do you feel?" The customer would then choose one of the five responses for each question:

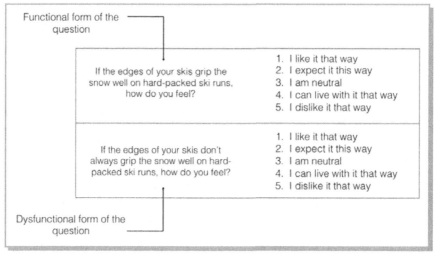

*Figure 8.12: Functional/dysfunctional questions*

How the functional and dysfunctional questions are answered tells us a lot about customer attitudes and preferences. If the customer answers the functional question with an "I expect it that way" response and the dysfunctional question with an "I dislike it that way" response, it is something that *must be* in the product. If the customer answers a functional question with an "I like it that way" response and the dysfunctional question with an "I expect it that way" or a "neutral" or an "I can live with it that way" response, is it something the customer is not expecting and would be a delightful feature in the product. If someone says they dislike the functional question and likes the dysfunctional question, they are clearly not interested in what we are offering and probably wish for the opposite. This is a new category, and it is called **Reverse**. If you get a large number of people responding with **Reverse** responses, you may wish to switch your functional and dysfunctional questions around.

It is also worth noting that you may sometimes get conflicting responses to some of your questions. As an example, if your customer responds "like" to both the functional and dysfunctional question, these answers are clearly suspect and you would have a "questionable" answer. Some of these are to be expected, but if you are getting too many, you probably need to re-evaluate your question text.

The following is what a traditional Kano matrix would look like:

| Customer Requirements | Dysfunctional | | | | |
|---|---|---|---|---|---|
| **Functional** | I like it | I expect it | Neutral | I can live with it | I dislike it |
| I like it | Q | A | A | A | P |
| I expect it | R | I | I | I | M |
| Neutral | R | I | I | I | M |
| I can live with it | R | I | I | I | M |
| I dislike it | R | R | R | I | Q |

*Figure 8.13: Kano matrix*

The Kano matrix provides an evaluation table that combines the functional and dysfunctional answers in rows and columns to get to a specific Kano category. Every answer pair leads to one of these categories. The keys for each of the cells in *Figure 8.13* are as follows:

> ➤ **A**: Attractive or delight

> ➤ **M**: Must-Be

> ➤ **I**: Indifferent

> ➤ **P**: Performance (one-dimensional)

> ➤ **R**: Reversal

> ➤ **Q**: Questionable result

While this is the traditional model, I find the model put forth by Fred Pouliot makes a little more sense and adds two additional questionable answers at locations (2,2) and (4,4), which looks like the following:

| Customer Requirements | Dysfunctional | | | | |
|---|---|---|---|---|---|
| **Functional** | I like it | I expect it | Neutral | I can live with it | I dislike it |
| I like it | Q | A | A | A | P |
| I expect it | R | Q | I | I | M |
| Neutral | R | I | I | I | M |
| I can live with it | R | I | I | Q | M |
| I dislike it | R | R | R | I | Q |

*Figure 8.14: Pouliot's Kano model*

I believe it is important to have a baseline understanding of how each category is derived from each pair of customer responses:

➤ Must-Be features are features that a customer will dislike if they are not present.

➤ Attractive or delight features are identified when a customer likes having a feature they did not expect.

➤ Performance features are the ones that a customer likes having and dislikes not having. Typically, a customer feels *more is better.*

➤ Indifferent features are ones where the customer would respond that they can take it or leave it. You will have a hard time getting customers to pay for features that are in this category.

➤ Questionable features are ones where a customer contradicts the functional and dysfunctional form of the question (for example, liking both). This is often indicative that the question was phrased incorrectly, or the customer misunderstood the question, or they simply made a mistake when answering.

➤ Reverse features are ones that a customer likes not having or dislikes having. As an example, when booking a holiday travel package, some customers want a completely planned itinerary, while other customers would prefer few to no pre-planned events.

In addition to answering the Kano questionnaire, I find it is also helpful for the customer to rank the individual feature/requirement to determine the relative importance of this feature versus the others as part of the questionnaire. This will aid in establishing customer priorities, as well as understanding the level of satisfaction each feature brings to the customer.

# Using the Kano model as part of your VoC process – Kano questionnaire

Now that you understand the Kano model and the Kano questionnaire, no doubt you are asking: how does this tool relate to the VoC work we have done thus far, and how would one incorporate the Kano model into a VoC program?

As you may have already guessed, we can easily leverage the output of our requirements from the process we discussed in *Chapter 7, Understanding the Customer's Voice* and use it as a basis for our Kano survey. Before we do that, however, we must decide how we will administer our survey. As would be expected, the preferable method for administering a Kano survey is by conducting additional customer interviews—either by going back to the customers we interviewed previously, engaging with different customers, or a combination of the two. If that is not an option due to budget constraints, you can also send out a mail or email survey to your customer base. As you can imagine from our previous discussions on surveys, there are advantages and disadvantages to going down this route. The advantages are you can question a large number of people at a relatively small expense. The disadvantages are the response rate will likely be very small, no additional "discovery" will occur during the process, and there is no opportunity to explain any questions the customer may have.

To create the Kano survey, we will take the customer requirements we identified at the end of *Chapter 7, Understanding the Customer's Voice* and construct functional and dysfunctional questions for each of the features identified, just as we did for the downhill ski requirements earlier in this chapter. In *Figure 8.15*, we see what a typical questionnaire might look like.

As important and revealing as the Kano model is, it only shows the extent of customer satisfaction or dissatisfaction when features or requirements are met or not met, but does not show the importance in terms of the value the user or customer attaches to the product requirements or features. Satisfaction and importance are not the same. While satisfaction deals with the performance of the requirements, importance has to do with the expected perceived value of the requirements.

For this reason, in this example, in addition to asking functional and dysfunctional questions, we also ask the customer to rank the individual requirement or feature to determine the relative importance of each feature. Notice that we ask all three questions before moving to the next topic:

## Customer Questionnaire

### Questionnaire

Name: _____

Company Name: _____

Job Title/Function: _____

Date questionnaire completed: _____

Interviewer's name (if applicable): _____

| No. | Question | Answers (select with a X one choice only) |
|-----|----------|---------------------------------------------|
| 1A | If the edges of your skis grip the snow well on hard-packed ski runs, how do you feel? | x 1. I like it<br>2. I expect it<br>3. I'm neutral<br>4. I can tolerate it<br>5. I dislike it |

| No. | Question | Answers (select with a X one choice only) |
|-----|----------|---------------------------------------------|
| 1B | If the edges of your skis don't always grip the snow well on hard-packed ski runs, how do you feel? | 1. I like it<br>2. I expect it<br>3. I'm neutral<br>x 4. I can tolerate it<br>5. I dislike it |

| No. | Importance | |
|-----|------------|---|
| 1 | How important is it that the edges of your skis grip the snow well on hard-packed ski runs? | 7     Importance Rank from 1-9 |

| No. | Question | Answers (select with a X one choice only) |
|-----|----------|---------------------------------------------|
| 2A | If your skis turn quick on the snow, how do you feel? | x 1. I like it<br>2. I expect it<br>3. I'm neutral<br>4. I can tolerate it<br>5. I dislike it |

| No. | Question | Answers (select with a X one choice only) |
|-----|----------|---------------------------------------------|
| 2B | If your skis don't always turn quick on the snow, how do you feel? | 1. I like it<br>2. I expect it<br>3. I'm neutral<br>4. I can tolerate it<br>x 5. I dislike it |

| No. | Importance | |
|-----|------------|---|
| 2 | How important is it for your skis to turn quick on the snow? | 6     Importance Rank from 1-9 |

*Figure 8.15*

# Using the Kano model as part of your VoC process – Kano analysis

Once you have completed all your Kano surveys, you can summarize all the responses in an evaluation table, as shown in *Figure 8.16* (note that this is only a partial image; the number of questions and customers should be considerably more than what is shown here):

## Customer feedback

| | | User 1 | User 2 | User 3 | User 4 |
|---|---|---|---|---|---|
| Functional | 1A. If the edges of your skis grip the snow well on hard-packed ski runs, how do you feel? | 1 | 2 | 1 | 1 |
| Dysfunctional | 1B. If the edges of your skis don't always grip the snow well on hard-packed ski runs, how do you feel? | 5 | 3 | 3 | 5 |
| | Q1 Grade | P | I | A | P |
| | Importance (scale 1-9) | 9 | 7 | 9 | 8 |
| Functional | 2A. If your skis turn quick on the snow, how do you feel? | 1 | 2 | 3 | 4 |
| Dysfunctional | 2B. If your skis don't always turn quick on the snow, how do you feel? | 5 | 5 | 3 | 3 |
| | Q2 Grade | P | M | I | I |
| | Importance (scale 1-9) | 5 | 5 | 6 | 7 |
| Functional | 3A. If the skis can be used on all areas of the mountain including groomed and ungroomed trails, how do you feel? | 3 | 2 | 2 | 2 |
| Dysfunctional | 3B. If the skis cannot be used on both groomed and ungroomed trails, how do you feel? | 5 | 4 | 5 | 4 |
| | Q3 Grade | M | I | M | I |
| | Importance (scale 1-9) | 4 | 6 | 6 | 6 |
| Functional | 4A. If the skis come with free tuning and edge sharpening for life, how do you feel? | 1 | 1 | 1 | 1 |
| Dysfunctional | 4B. If the skis don't come with free tuning and edge sharpening for life, how do you feel? | 4 | 3 | 4 | 4 |
| | Q4 Grade | A | A | A | A |
| | Importance (scale 1-9) | 5 | 6 | 4 | 6 |

*Figure 8.16: Evaluation table*

Once we have collected all this feedback, we need to summarize it further. The easiest method is to evaluate and interpret the answers according to the frequency of responses, as shown in *Figure 8.17*. As you can see in this image, we total up the number of *A, M, I, P, R*, and *Q* to fill in this table. The final grade for each question is whichever response gets the greatest number of votes from all the customers who have participated in our survey. In this case, we see that having good edge grip is a Performance attribute, skiing on all areas of the mountain is a Must-Be attribute, and skis with free edge sharpening and tuning would be a product differentiator in the market with an Attractive or Delight attribute.

You will often find that you may have groupings of responses that point to two different results if you have not done adequate segmentation before administering the questionnaire. As an example, edge grip and the ability to ski on groomed and ungroomed trails might be Must-Be attributes for an expert skier, but novices might see edge grip as a Performance attribute and may be Indifferent to using the skis to ski on anything but a groomed trail:

| Features | Grade | Importance | A | M | I | P | R | Q |
|---|---|---|---|---|---|---|---|---|
| The edges of your skis grip the snow well on hard-packed ski runs | P | 8.25 | 1 | 0 | 1 | 2 | 0 | 0 |
| Skis turn quick on the snow | I | 5.75 | 0 | 1 | 2 | 1 | 0 | 0 |
| Skis can be used on all areas of the mountain including groomed and ungroomed trails | M | 5.5 | 0 | 2 | 2 | 0 | 0 | 0 |
| skis come with free tuning and edge sharpening for life | A | 5.25 | 4 | 0 | 0 | 0 | 0 | 0 |
| Feature #5 | -- | 0 | 0 | 0 | 0 | 0 | 0 | 0 |
| Feature #6 | -- | 0 | 0 | 0 | 0 | 0 | 0 | 0 |
| Feature #7 | -- | 0 | 0 | 0 | 0 | 0 | 0 | 0 |
| Feature #8 | -- | 0 | 0 | 0 | 0 | 0 | 0 | 0 |
| Feature #9 | -- | 0 | 0 | 0 | 0 | 0 | 0 | 0 |
| Feature #10 | -- | 0 | 0 | 0 | 0 | 0 | 0 | 0 |
| | Grade | Importance | A | M | I | P | R | Q |

A = Attractive or Delight
M = Must be
I = Indifferent
P = Performance
R = Reversal
Q = Questionable result

*Figure 8.17: Frequency of responses*

If the individual product requirements cannot be assigned to a specific category due to a large number of votes in more than one category, it is helpful to consider the following rule:

$$M > P > A > I$$

Simply put, the Must-Be requirements are the most important and will yield product dissatisfaction if not met, so in the case of a tie between Must-Be and something else, Must-Be wins. The next most important variables are the Performance characteristics, followed by the Attractive characteristics, and lastly the Indifferent characteristics. When deciding between various Attractive attributes in your product decisions, the decisive factor is how important they are to the customer. This can be determined by evaluating the self-stated Importance attribute in the customers' responses.

Based on this discussion, one might ask if there is any way to measure customer satisfaction using the tools in the Kano model. Fortunately, Charles Burger and his associates determined a way to leverage the Kano model to help us understand the level of customer satisfaction when a specific attribute is present and the level of customer dissatisfaction when a specific attribute is missing.

They determined that the best way to calculate the level of customer satisfaction is to add the Attractive and Performance columns, and divide by the total number of Attractive, Performance, Must-Be, and Indifferent responses. For the calculation of the average impact on Dissatisfaction you would add the Must-Be and one-dimensional columns, and divide them by the same divisor as in the previous example:

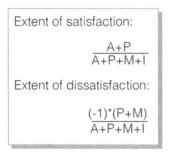

Extent of satisfaction:

$$\frac{A+P}{A+P+M+I}$$

Extent of dissatisfaction:

$$\frac{(-1)*(P+M)}{A+P+M+I}$$

*Figure 8.18*

The dissatisfaction equation is multiplied by (-1) in order to emphasize the negative influence on customer satisfaction if this attribute is not fulfilled. The extent of satisfaction ranges from 0 to 1; the closer the value is to 1, the more the attribute influences customer satisfaction. A customer satisfaction score close to 0 signifies there is little influence on customer satisfaction resulting from this attribute. For the customer dissatisfaction score, if the number approaches -1, the influence of this attribute on customer dissatisfaction is very strong if the attribute or feature is not fulfilled. A value close to 0 signifies that this feature or attribute will not cause a great deal of customer dissatisfaction if it is not met. The completed satisfaction/dissatisfaction table is shown in *Figure 8.19.*

| Features | A | M | I | P | R | Q | Satisfaction | Dissatisfaction |
|---|---|---|---|---|---|---|---|---|
| The edges of your skis grip the snow well on hard-packed ski runs | 1 | 0 | 1 | 2 | 0 | 0 | 0.75 | -0.50 |
| Skis turn quick on the snow | 0 | 1 | 2 | 1 | 0 | 0 | 0.25 | -0.50 |
| Skis can be used on all areas of the mountain including groomed and ungroomed trails | 0 | 2 | 2 | 0 | 0 | 0 | 0.00 | -0.50 |
| skis come with free tuning and edge sharpening for life | 4 | 0 | 0 | 0 | 0 | 0 | 1.00 | 0.00 |
| Feature #5 | 0 | 0 | 0 | 0 | 0 | 0 | 0.00 | 0.00 |
| Feature #6 | 0 | 0 | 0 | 0 | 0 | 0 | 0.00 | 0.00 |
| Feature #7 | 0 | 0 | 0 | 0 | 0 | 0 | 0.00 | 0.00 |
| Feature #8 | 0 | 0 | 0 | 0 | 0 | 0 | 0.00 | 0.00 |
| Feature #9 | 0 | 0 | 0 | 0 | 0 | 0 | 0.00 | 0.00 |
| Feature #10 | 0 | 0 | 0 | 0 | 0 | 0 | 0.00 | 0.00 |
| | A | M | I | P | R | Q | Satisfaction | Dissatisfaction |

A = Attractive or Delight
M = Must be
I = Indifferent
P = Performance
R = Reversal
Q = Questionable result

*Figure 8.19: Satisfaction/dissatisfaction table*

Using the aforementioned techniques, you should have a good idea of your customers' priorities. You now have an understanding of your customers' priorities, their must-haves, the things that could drive satisfaction by being improved, and the differentiators that could delight your customer. The next step, although optional, can also provide a little more illumination in terms of how importance can drive increased satisfaction. I find it is worthwhile to multiply the satisfaction and dissatisfaction scores by the importance score. This should give you a more weighted view of the customer satisfaction score (as shown in *Figure 8.20*):

| Features | Grade | Importance | Satisfaction | Dissatisfaction | Satisfaction | Dissatisfaction |
|---|---|---|---|---|---|---|
| The edges of your skis grip the snow well on hard-packed ski runs | P | 8.25 | 0.75 | -0.50 | 6.19 | -4.13 |
| Skis turn quick on the snow | I | 5.75 | 0.25 | -0.50 | 0.67 | -2.88 |
| Skis can be used on all areas of the mountain including groomed and ungroomed trails | M | 5.5 | 0.00 | -0.50 | 1.00 | -2.75 |
| skis come with free tuning and edge sharpening for life | A | 5.25 | 1.00 | 0.00 | 0.00 | 0.00 |
| Feature #5 | -- | 0 | 0.00 | 0.00 | 0.00 | 0.00 |
| Feature #6 | -- | 0 | 0.00 | 0.00 | 0.00 | 0.00 |
| Feature #7 | -- | 0 | 0.00 | 0.00 | 0.00 | 0.00 |
| Feature #8 | -- | 0 | 0.00 | 0.00 | 0.00 | 0.00 |
| Feature #9 | -- | 0 | 0.00 | 0.00 | 0.00 | 0.00 |
| Feature #10 | -- | 0 | 0.00 | 0.00 | 0.00 | 0.00 |
| | Grade | Importance | Satisfaction | Dissatisfaction | Satisfaction | Dissatisfaction |

*Figure 8.20: Weighted satisfaction/dissatisfaction table*

# Summary

In the previous chapter, we learned how to take the volume of data we generated in our customer interviews and turn it into a list of requirements that our customers told us they valued. In this section, we dove deeper into this data by engaging with the same customers, or other customers, and we had them help us to prioritize these features and requirements. In addition to prioritizing these features and requirements, we also learned how to apply the Kano model as part of our customer review process to better understand the different ways customers value the attributes in our products, and learned how to differentiate between the Must-Bes, the Performance features, the things the customers are indifferent about, and the things that will delight them. We also talked about how to identify the things that caused customer satisfaction or dissatisfaction with our products, and how to measure the level of each.

In the next chapter, we will bring all of our analysis together to help us understand how we can incorporate customer feedback into our product development process, use customer feedback to convince senior management of the need for these product features, and lastly use this information to price, position, and sell our product in the marketplace using our customers' own words.

# 9

# Completing the Circle – Using the Customer's Voice in Your Organization

*"The pathway to profitability? It lies in fully understanding the customer."*

*– Adrian Slywotsky, The Art of Profitability*

In *Chapter 8, Validating the Customer's Voice*, we really dove into the discussion of customer satisfaction and how to measure it. In this chapter, we will discuss the various ways in which the **Voice of the Customer** (**VoC**) can affect and drive product and business decisions within your organization. We will be reviewing methods and tools that will help your team take the information gathered from your interviews and apply them to business and product issues. We will help you determine the right set of customer requirements for your product, and demonstrate how to turn them into requirements and features, how to prioritize those requirements and features, and how to determine how well your organization can deliver on those requirements and features. We will also discuss how to price your products and create a value proposition that delivers on the features requested. This information will help you build the business case for your VoC-driven products, and aid in convincing your senior management to fund your development initiatives and provide the basis for developing sales tools for the marketing and sales organizations to close business.

# From voices to product requirements – types

After all the customer research you have done, you will probably have a pretty good idea of what will resonate with your customers, and what will not. However, it is not enough that you know these things in your own head. More importantly, for your organization to use the knowledge you have gathered from your VoC sessions, you will need to find a way to express this wealth of customer understanding so that the organization can consequently make changes to the product roadmap, engineer specifications, and marketing material. To do this, the first thing we must do is to determine customer requirements in a way that is digestible by the rest of the organization.

Customer requirements express what the customer will be able to accomplish, what the product will be able to do, or how the product will be able to satisfy the customer's need to achieve something. Product requirements are not specifications or descriptions of how a product meets customer needs, but are merely statements of what the customer will be able to accomplish, be able to do, be able to obtain, or be able to resolve as a result of your product or service.

Developing product requirements is typically the responsibility of product management or marketing in an organization. These product requirements take the form of an MRD (see *Chapter 2, VoC in the Product Development Process*), and are given to engineering, whose responsibility is to take the requirements received and create a document describing how the design specification will satisfy this customer's needs.

As mentioned previously, the reason most products fail is because the customer requirements are not wholly or accurately expressed. Either this is because the organization did not undertake sufficient customer research, or the team did conduct effective customer research, but the translation from the customer's voice to the product requirements was flawed.

When we think about developing product requirements, many other elements must be considered, and stakeholders must be involved. These stakeholders are internal stakeholders in the business, as well as customer stakeholders who are also participating in purchasing, installation, commissioning, maintenance, usage, disposal, and justification. There are a number of different types of requirements we should consider when developing a product, but there are two that come to mind immediately: functional and non-functional requirements.

*A functional requirement describes what a product or offering should do, while a non-functional requirement places constraints on how the system or product will do, or how it will relate to a quality the product will have... In essence, how the product will work for the customer.*

A company's e-commerce site must send an email whenever a particular action is initiated by a customer – for example, when a visitor to the site signs up to join the email list, they change their shipping address, they place an order or initiate a return, and so on. A non-functional requirement for this example would be that the customer must be notified within an hour of the time the condition changed state.

Another example of a functional requirement would be: "A car's overhead light will turn on when the door opens." The associated non-functional requirement would be "how long the light will stay on after the door closes" and "how bright the overhead light will be.".

Examples of functional requirements include:

> Business rules
> State changes
> Authorization
> Certification or regulatory requirements
> Legal requirements
> Reporting requirements

Some common non-functional requirements include:

➤ Operation

➤ Usability

➤ Performance – response time, accuracy, throughput, repeatability

➤ Look and feel/interface

➤ Serviceability

➤ Capacity

➤ Interoperability

➤ Maintainability

➤ Manageability

➤ Recoverability

➤ Reliability

➤ Scalability

➤ Security

In addition to the two previously mentioned requirement types, product managers should look at two additional requirement types: business requirements and constraints.

Business requirements relate directly to the business outcome the customer desires. Many times, this is expressed directly or indirectly in the form of economic value to the customer. For example, the customer may wish to increase their efficiency, reduce overhead, or enhance their productivity to contribute to reducing their overall costs.

Some possible examples of business requirements include:

➤ The customer shall increase efficiency by a minimum of 4%

➤ The customer shall be able to use 10% less internal resources

➤ The product will be able to reduce the total cost of ownership for the customer by 15%

Constraints are limitations or strict guidance the product team has in place when developing the product. These create boundary conditions that the product must adhere to. Examples include:

➤ The total cost of manufacturing shall not exceed $25.25 per unit

➤ The product must conform to the Apple Homekit specification

➤ The product shall interface and exchange data with an SQL database

# From voices to product requirements – characteristics

Whether you are writing functional requirements, non-functional requirements, business requirements, or constraints, your requirements must meet certain characteristics to be beneficial to an organization. The characteristics of good requirements are:

> ➤ Attainable
> ➤ Valuable
> ➤ Concise
> ➤ Design free
> ➤ Complete
> ➤ Clear, consistent, and unambiguous
> ➤ Verifiable
> ➤ Traceable
> ➤ Measurable
> ➤ Atomic
> ➤ Prioritized

## Attainable

I have always been a believer in pushing the development team to the very edge of their capabilities, resulting in products they did not even believe they could create. However, there is a fine line between pushing the team to the limits of their abilities and asking for the impossible, or for something the organization is not able to support with the right resources. The result will be a frustrated development team and friction between the development team and the marketing/business team.

## Valuable

While this is obvious, it is also worth emphasizing that any requirements that are documented and given to the development team must do the following:

> ➤ Solve a customer's need or address a customer's problem
> ➤ Meet the criteria as derived from the customer interviews
> ➤ Address real market problems, not simply the need of one customer

# Concise

Requirements that are concise are easy to read and understand by all interested parties, including management and development teams. They also help minimize ambiguity in terms of what needs to be accomplished, and they identify the problem (or problems) that must be addressed. To be concise, it is also best to limit your requirements to be no more than 30-50 words.

# Design free

If you are, or ever were, an engineer or are technically minded, you will find this to be particularly challenging. When faced with a problem, it is very easy for us to jump to an immediate solution or potential solutions without fully understanding the requirements. Even though you think you know what needs to be built to meet the perceived customer's issue, one needs to focus on why the customer needs it, and let the development team design the solution. In the next section, we will talk about how you must describe the "what's," and the development team will be tasked with how they will determine the "how's."

# Complete

Your requirement statement must fully articulate what the customer or user will be able to do, accomplish, or experience with the product or service you will create as part of this development. If at all possible, it is also good practice to include forms of measurement whenever possible.

# Clear, consistent, and unambiguous

You need to write requirements using grammatically correct language that is logical and easily understood, with the intent that all members of the team will have a clear and consistent understanding of what is being asked for in the requirement statement. Strive to remove all vagueness and ambiguity from the requirements you write, so that there is only one interpretation from anyone on the development team who might review them.

Another characteristic that is worth checking is to ensure the requirements you write are also consistent with your business strategy. If your requirements run counter to the business strategy, your odds of getting approval for your project are diminished.

# Verifiable

As we mentioned in the introduction to this section, the main reason we write requirements is to communicate to the development team and the rest of the organization what the customer requires, and what needs to be done to satisfy the market. If we cannot verify that what ultimately is delivered to the market meets the original needs expressed by the customer, we will have no way of knowing whether we have been successful or not.

# Traceable

Each requirement statement needs to be able to tie back to a customer input that you have collected during your research.

# Measurable

The requirements must be written so the final product can be tested, analyzed, inspected, or demonstrated so as to ensure that it meets the needs of the original customer input. As an example, "The cable modem will be able to download at a minimum of 100 Mbps." Only in this way is it possible to verify whether the product or system met the requirements or not.

# Atomic

Each requirement needs to be a single specific market need. If the requirement statement you write contains two or more requirements, it must be rewritten to convey only one thought, or the requirement statement must be separated into multiple requirements. If your requirements say, "The computer must support a USB and an HDMI output," these needs must be separated and written as two unique requirements. If not, you run the risk of satisfying only a part of the requirement when the project is complete, and you may end up only solving a portion of the market needs.

# Prioritized

While many customers will consider *all* their requirements to be the top priority, that is far from possible. For a list of requirements to be actionable by the organization, there must be a priority assigned to each requirement, so that the development team can understand the relative importance of each individual requirement statement to the others.

The preceding two sections were necessary to provide you with an understanding of the types of requirements, as well as what characteristics make for a good requirement. If you have responsibilities for the product management function and are writing the MRD, this section should be a good reference for you.

We are now ready to take the output from our affinity exercise and turn it into something actionable by the organization. Actual requirements that engineers can use to develop your new product.

# Getting the requirements into engineering – QFD

Now that we have developed a consistent way of putting our requirements down on paper for the rest of the organization to understand, we must now work to develop a way to express our requirements to engineering. This must be done so they can understand what it is we are asking for, what must be done by the organization to fulfill those requirements, and who will do it and when, so they can go about creating our new product.

To do this, we will turn to a tool called QFD. QFD originated in Japan in the late 1960s, during a time when Japan was trying to break away from its notoriety of product development through copying and imitation, to a product development process based on originality. At that time, the Japanese automobile industry was in a state of evolution, as they were growing rapidly and needed to create multiple model changes to keep up with demand. As a result, Japanese companies began to understand the importance of design quality to ensure the rapid developments would not fail when they were delivered to the end customers. Unfortunately, there was no process to impart design quality into the front end of a product, only a way to check quality at the end of the line during manufacturing, after the new products were already produced.

This new concept is called hin shitsu (Quality), ki nou (Function), and ten kai (Deployment) – that's **Quality, Function, and Deployment,** which we have acronymized to **QFD**. While the translation means little to us on the surface, the three words taken together mean meeting customer requirements, determining what must be done to meet the requirements, and who will do what action at what time to meet the requirements.

The concept of QFD originated in the late 1960s, but it was not until 1972 in the Mitsubishi Kobe Shipyard in Japan, where they were building supertankers, that it was fully deployed. The new process by Mitsubishi ensured that every step of the construction process would be linked to fulfilling a specific customer requirement. As each need was identified, the design team developed potential solutions to solve the customer's identified need. The needs were called the "Whats" and the means of addressing the need were called the "Hows."

The team began by thinking there was a clear one-to-one relationship between each What and each How. Unfortunately, it quickly became apparent that many times the Hows impacted more than one What, and often in very conflicting ways, as shown in *Figure 9.1*:

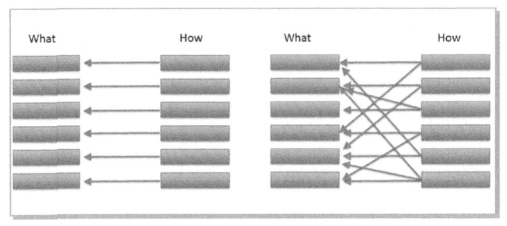

*Figure 9.1: Whats versus Hows – originally conceived versus reality*

To overcome this, the team at Mitsubishi put customer demands on the vertical axis of a matrix (the Whats) and the methods by which these demands would be met (the Hows) on the horizontal axis of the same matrix, to see the relationships of the methods in relation to the various customer demands:

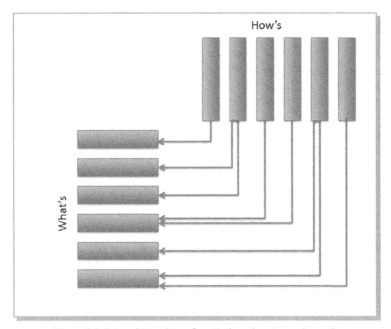

*Figure 9.2: Interrelationships of methods and customer demands*

This was recognized as a breakthrough in the way to visualize customer needs versus product development. The process was widely adopted by many Japanese and global companies, including Toyota, Nippondenso, Nissan, Komatsu, Honda, Ford, GM, Chrysler, HP, Xerox, Dow, and many more. Since that time, QFD has progressed well beyond a two-axis matrix simply showing Whats and Hows, and now has the ability to present a number of design considerations in a graphical form. Additionally, it was discovered that QFD could also be an effective tool in developing component requirements, operational requirements, and working procedures resulting in aiding communication between design and manufacturing departments, identifying potential failure modes, developing new technologies, and reducing product cost.

QFD is often presented using a QFD matrix otherwise known as the *House of Quality*. The term "House of Quality" originated as the structure of the diagram resembles that of a house. The House of Quality uses a planning matrix whereby we can define what a customer "wants" versus what the organization is willing and able to deliver. A basic House of Quality matrix has the following form:

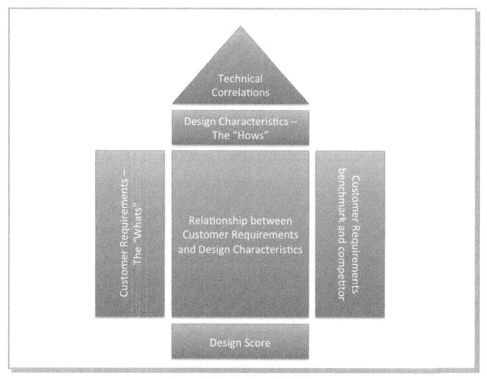

*Figure 9.3: The House of Quality*

The main sections of the House of Quality are as follows:

> **Customer requirements**: The "Whats" – this is the first section of the House of Quality (HoQ) to be completed, and is a structured list of the customer's requirements generated through the VoC.

> **Customer requirements benchmark and competitors**: Quantifies the customer's requirements and the performance of competitive products.

> **Design characteristics**: The "Hows" – this section is also referred to as the "Voice of the Company" and is generated by the design team who identify all the measurable characteristics of the product that they perceive are related to meeting the customer's requirements.

> **Relationships between customer requirements and design characteristics**: This section allows the design team to quantify the interrelationships between the customer requirements and the design characteristics. This is the most critical part of the HoQ and is the most time-consuming.

> **Technical correlations**: Used to identify where the technical design considerations support or impede one another.

> **Design score**: This is the last section to be completed, and it summarizes the results from the HoQ and may also include technical priorities, competitiveness, and potential targets.

To better understand how one can use QFD and the HoQ in a real-world situation, it may be best to use an example for illustrative purposes. The example we will use was originally developed by the University of Warwick, but I have taken the liberty of updating the content with changes in technology, market demand, and my own viewpoint.

In our example, we will take the role of an airline seat manufacturer, and discuss the steps we would undertake in our VoC and QFD process to design a seat to be marketed to the airlines. To begin the QFD, we will leverage all the work we have done previously in our VoC research. As a summary, we must:

> Determine the targeted market segments

> Determine who is our customer and the customer value chain (our customer's customer)

> Create a list of customer requirements through various VoC processes in the customer's own words

> Consolidate and rewrite customer requirements based on the first section of this chapter

In our example, we have already determined our market segment and potential customers as the airline companies servicing the economy flier market. Our customer's customers are their economy passengers. The potential list of requirements for our customer and our customer's customer, which we have generated from our VoC, might look like the following:

# Airline feedback for airline seat

- Customer must "feel" safe in the seat
- Fire-retardant material
- Built-in life preserver
- Quality seatbelt
- Meets all FAA regulations
- Color consistent with brand
- Low purchase price
- Easy to retrofit
- Durable material
- Lightweight
- Easy to replace
- Easy to move
- Low profile, allowing more passengers per plane
- Easy to clean
- Stain-resistant fabric
- Will not soak up spillages

# Passenger feedback for airline seat

- Moveable armrest
- Wide armrest
- Plentiful legroom
- Lumbar support for all body shapes
- Knees do not hit seat in front
- Seats do not hit passenger behind
- Seat back can be adjusted
- Seat back adjustment will not slip
- Seatbelt feels secure
- Seat feels stable and does not bend easily
- Pleasant color
- Clean
- Not stained

- ➤ Enough room to use laptop fully opened
- ➤ Tray is easy to pull out/push back in
- ➤ Magazines easy to remove/replace
- ➤ Place for water bottle
- ➤ Tray indent or hole for coffee
- ➤ Built-in entertainment for long haul flights
- ➤ Stream to own device (iPad, phone) for shorter flights
- ➤ Good selection of current movies, TV, and music
- ➤ Power for laptop
- ➤ USB power for phone/iPad

While it is great to have such a rich set of input from our customers, we also need some way to prioritize and assign how important each of these characteristics are to the customer, or else all will be treated as equal. Without some way to understand the relative importance of one item to another, we will end up allocating our resources like peanut butter, and ultimately, the customer will not get what he or she needs.

To do this, we will undertake an affinity process. During this process, we will place each requirement on a card and use the affinity process to group these requirements into like groups, and then create secondary requirements. This could include groupings for "Passenger comfort in the upright position", "Passenger comfort in the recline position", "Purchase price", "Entertainment", "Ergonomics", and so on.

Performing another affinity process on the secondary groupings would yield our primary groupings of "Passenger comfort", "Safety", "Human factors", "Technology", and "Cost".

In our example, this might look like the following:

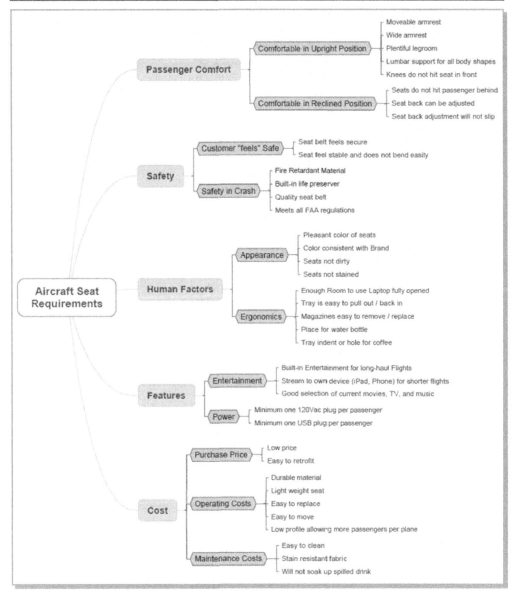

*Figure 9.4: Aircraft seat primary, secondary, and tertiary requirements*

The primary processes are shown in the blue boxes. The secondary features are illustrated in the purple boxes, and the tertiary features, which reflect our customer feedback, are illustrated on the right side of each of the secondary features.

To get the relative importance, we will deploy a technique similar to the process we described in *Chapter 4, Gathering the Customer Needs for Your Product* by using a customer survey to help us weight each customer requirement. To do so, we will construct a sheet similar to *Figure 9.5*, where we will represent all the customer feedback showing the secondary and tertiary requirements. From this point, we will ask a group of customers to distribute 100 points over all the secondary items only. This forces the customers to think about the relative importance of each secondary requirement relative to each other. Once this is complete, we then ask the customers to allocate each of the secondary points to the associated tertiary requirements, which will give us the necessary granularity and priority we require. In the example that follows, I have only done the first two primary requirements, so you can understand the format. Normally, I would have included all five primary requirements. When you complete this work yourself, you should do all the primary requirements on one sheet, unless there is a specific reason not to do so:

| Primary | Secondary | Points | Tertiary Requirements | Points | Sum |
|---------|-----------|--------|-----------------------|--------|-----|
| Passenger Comfort | Comfortable in Upright Position | 22.0 | Moveable armrest | 3 | |
| | | | Wide armrest | 2 | |
| | | | Plentiful legroom | 9 | |
| | | | Lumbar support for all body shapes | 3 | |
| | | | Knees do not hit seat in front | 5 | 22.0 |
| | Comfortable in Reclined Position | 15.0 | Seats do not hit passenger behind | 5 | |
| | | | Seat back can be adjusted | 7 | |
| | | | Seat back adjustment will not slip | 3 | 15.0 |
| Safety | Customer feels Safe | 4.5 | Seat belt feels secure | 2 | |
| | | | Seat feels stable and does not bend easily | 2.5 | 4.5 |
| | Safety in Crash | 14.0 | Fire Retardant Material | 4 | |
| | | | Built-in life preserver | 3 | |
| | | | Quality seat belt | 2 | |
| | | | Meets all FAA regulations | 5 | 14.0 |
| . | . | | " | | |
| | | | " | | |
| | | | " | | |
| | Total | 100 | Total | 100 | 100.0 |

*Figure 9.5: Customer requirements scoring*

Once we complete this exercise, we can begin to build our QFD model. As you will see, the exercise we just performed will provide input to the engineers about what needs to be built, and also provides a baseline from which to measure when we do the competitive analysis section of the QFD matrix.

Taking the above information and transferring it to a QFD matrix would result in a customer requirements section as follows:

| | | | "Customer Requirements" or "Whats" Tertiary Requirements | Weight/ Importance |
|---|---|---|---|---|
| Passenger Comfort | Comfortable in Upright Position | | Moveable armrest | 3 |
| | | | Wide armrest | 2 |
| | | | Plentiful legroom | 9 |
| | | | Lumbar support for all body shapes | 3 |
| | | | Knees do not hit seat in front | 5 |
| | Comfortable in Reclined Position | | Seats do not hit passenger behind | 5 |
| | | | Seat back can be adjusted | 7 |
| | | | Seat back adjustment will not slip | 3 |
| Safety | Customer feels Safe | | Seat belt feels secure | 2 |
| | | | Seat feels stable and does not bend easily | 2.5 |
| | Safety in Crash | | Fire Retardant Material | 4 |
| | | | Built-in life preserver | 3 |
| | | | Quality seat belt | 2 |
| | | | Meets all FAA regulations | 5 |

*Figure 9.6: Customer requirements with importance*

Now that we have a list of all the customer requirements, it is worthwhile for us to do a comparison regarding how well our current (or future) offering meets the needs of the customer, as well as how well each of our competitors meet those needs. For this example, I have ranked our current offering versus the competition on a scale from 1 to 5 for each customer requirement, as shown on *Figure 9.7*. To aid your understanding, you can also map the benchmarks for each competitor graphically, as shown. As before, if at all possible, it is far preferred to have users perform the competitive benchmarking, by allowing them to rank your current offering versus the competitor's offerings, themselves.

This can be done during the survey you used to get the importance scoring. Having the customers do this scoring also helps to ensure you are accurately reflecting the perception of the market:

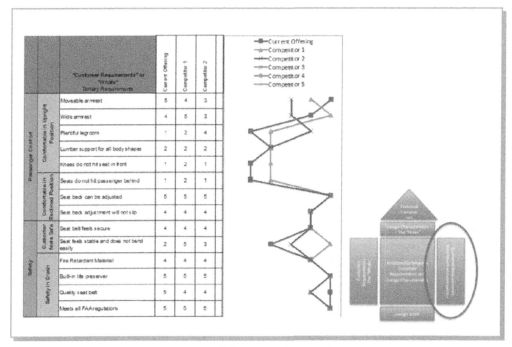

*Figure 9.7: Competitive benchmark*

Now we have both the customer requirement and the competitive benchmark. By placing both halves together, we can see the relationship between customer requirements and importance on the left, versus the competitive offerings on the right in our QFD matrix, as shown in *Figure 9.8* (we have cut out the middle section of the QFD, as nothing exists there at this time):

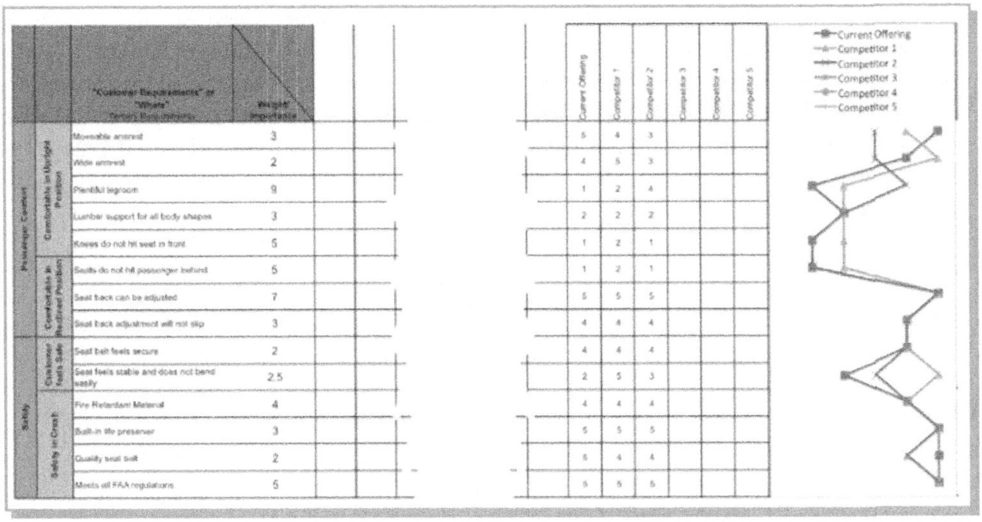

*Figure 9.8: QFD requirements versus competition*

Now that we have the customer requirements and the competitive benchmarks, we must determine the design characteristics that must be deployed in the product to ensure customer satisfaction. This is otherwise known as the "Hows", as this section tells us how the design team will address the needs outlined in the customer requirements section.

To develop the design characteristics, I recommend the VoC team and the engineering team sit together for a brainstorming session. To brainstorm the design characteristics, start with one secondary requirement and its associated tertiary requirements to brainstorm how the engineering group could fulfill the need for design characteristics. Try to generate as many ideas as possible that affect at least one of the tertiary requirements. But one rule must be strictly adhered to, and that is each design characteristic must be measurable in some form. If it is not measurable, it cannot be optimized and cannot be used to ensure customer satisfaction.

As an example, using our aircraft seat shows how we would start to brainstorm various parameters such as the height, width, hardness, space, and so on of the armrest, seat back, and seat cushion, to meet the defined customer need. *Figure 9.9* shows a representative sample of what the output might look like after doing the first two secondary requirements, comfort in upright position, and comfort in the recline position. If you were actually doing this exercise in real life, you would need to do the remaining secondary and associated tertiary requirements:

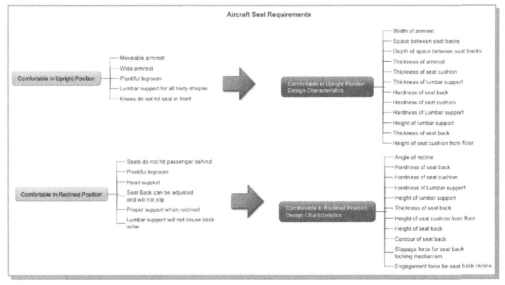

**Figure 9.9: Design characteristics brainstorming**

Once the brainstorming sessions are complete, you would have a similar list of design characteristics for each of the secondary requirements we defined earlier. From this point, we would gather all the design characteristics the team has generated and categorize them into like groupings, with a heading for each. In our example, we'd have groupings for such things as armrest, seat back, seat cushion, fabric, mounting hardware, seatbelts, services, and many more, when we are done.

The following figure shows a hypothetical result for the first two secondary requirements:

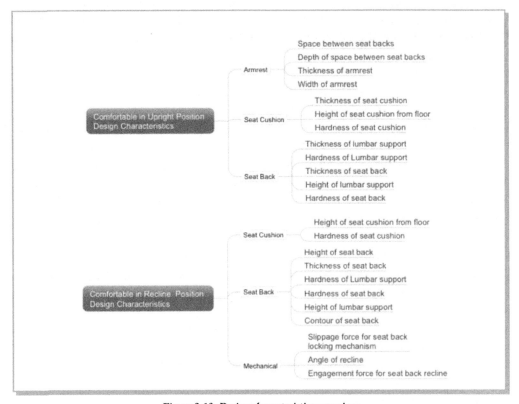

*Figure 9.10: Design characteristics groupings*

We would then take the various design characteristics from each of the secondary customer requirements, and group them together where the groupings are the same.

In our example, you can see that there are design requirements on the seat back and seat cushion for both secondary requirements shown in *Figure 9.10*, so we would group them together as shown in *Figure 9.11*, with all the design requirements for armrest together, all the requirements for seat cushion together, and so on:

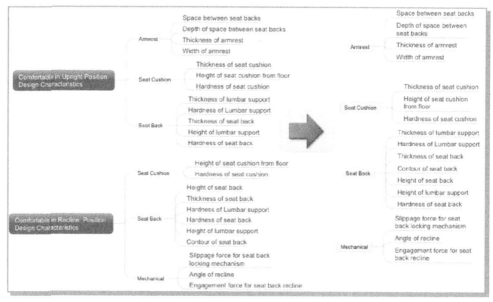

*Figure 9.11: Merging the design requirements*

From here, we would take the sum of all the requirements for armrest, seat cushion, seat back, mechanical, and so on, and move them to the top of our QFD matrix (the "Hows") as shown in *Figure 9.12*, with the secondary design requirements placed above the tertiary requirements:

| | | | Armrest | | | | Seat Cusion | | | | Seat Back | | | | |
|---|---|---|---|---|---|---|---|---|---|---|---|---|---|---|---|
| | "Customer Requirements" or "Whats" Tertiary Requirements | Weight/ Importance | Width of armrest | Space between seat backs | Depth of space between seat backs | Thickness of armrest | Thickness of seat cushion | Hardness of Seat Cusion | Height of seat cushion from Floor | Thickness of Lumbar support | Hardness of Lumbar support | Height of lumbar support | Thickness of seat back | Contour of Seat Back |
| Moveable armrest | | 3 | | | | | | | | | | | | |
| Wide armrest | | 2 | | | | | | | | | | | | |
| Plentiful legroom | | 9 | | | | | | | | | | | | |
| Lumbar support for all body shapes | | 3 | | | | | | | | | | | | |
| Knees do not hit seat in front | | 5 | | | | | | | | | | | | |
| Seats do not hit passenger behind | | 5 | | | | | | | | | | | | |
| Seat back can be adjusted | | 7 | | | | | | | | | | | | |
| Seat back adjustment will not slip | | 3 | | | | | | | | | | | | |

*Figure 9.12: Adding the Hows to the top of our matrix*

When this is complete for all the design requirements, we now have the structure to allow us to understand the relationship and the importance between all the customer requirements and the company's design requirements. This next section, the relationship matrix, is the meat of the QFD, and it is important that the team take the necessary time to discuss, understand, and build as much consensus as possible between the VoC interview team and the rest of the design team.

In this step, we will evaluate every intersection from the customer requirements and the design requirements, and determine how much of a relationship exists between the Whats and the Hows:

*Figure 9.13: The relationship matrix*

We then must provide a weighting to every intersection, to represent whether there is a strong relationship, a mediocre relationship, a weak relationship, or no relationship. If there is a strong relationship, we will give the intersection cell a value of 9. If there is a mediocre relationship, we will give it a 3. If there is a weak relationship, we will give it a 1, and if there is no relationship, we will leave it blank. As shown in *Figure 9.13*, there is a strong relationship between the customer requirement of "Plentiful legroom" and the design requirement of "Height of the cushion from floor". As such, we would place a *9* in this cell.

We can see what the upper-left side of our matrix might look like when it is completed in *Figure 9.14*. As you can see, it is not unusual that no more than 20–30% of the relationship matrix would have any values in the intersecting cells, and there should rarely be any instance where more than 50% of the relationship matrix has values:

| "Customer Requirements" or "Whats" Tertiary Requirements | Weight Importance | Width of armrest | Space between seat backs | Depth of space between seat backs | Thickness of armrest | Thickness of seat cushion | Hardness of Seat Cusion | Height of seat cushion from Floor | Thickness of Lumbar support | Hardness of Lumbar support | Height of lumbar support | Thickness of seat back | Contour of Seat Back | Height of seat back | Height of lumbar support | Hardness of seat back |
|---|---|---|---|---|---|---|---|---|---|---|---|---|---|---|---|---|
| Moveable armrest | 3 | 3 | 3 | 3 | 3 | | | | | | | | | | | |
| Wide armrest | 2 | 9 | 3 | 1 | 1 | | | | | | | | 3 | | | |
| Plentiful legroom | 0 | | | | | 1 | | 9 | | | | 3 | 3 | | | |
| Lumbar support for all body shapes | 3 | | | | | | 3 | | 9 | 9 | 9 | 3 | 3 | 9 | | |
| Knees do not hit seat in front | 5 | | | | | | | 1 | | | | | 9 | 3 | | 1 |
| Seats do not hit passenger behind | 5 | | | | | | | 1 | | | 1 | | 9 | 3 | | 1 |
| Seat back can be adjusted | 7 | | | | | | | | | | | | 1 | | | |
| Seat back adjustment will not slip | 3 | | | | | | | | | | | | | | | |

*Figure 9.14: Completed relationship matrix*

The next piece of the HoQ matrix is the technical correlations. This piece of the HoQ matrix serves to highlight relationships between the various design requirements. Symbols are used to show strong positive correlation, positive correlation, negative correlation, and strong negative correlation, as illustrated on the legend in *Figure 9.15*. This is the triangular piece on the top of the HoQ matrix, and helps to derive the "House of Quality" moniker. As before, the matrix is completed by moving along the intersections of the various design requirements and recording whether it has a positive or negative correlation with each of the other design requirements as shown.

As you perform the analysis, keep in mind whether the two design requirements have a positive or a negative correlation with each other. If we look at the far right of *Figure 9.15*, we can see **Thickness of seat back** and **Contour of seat back**. At first, you may think this is a strong positive correlation, but upon reflection you would see that the goal is to have as thin a seat back as possible, and the addition of adding contours for the seat back contradicts the goal of a thin seat back, so we have scored this a strong negative correlation:

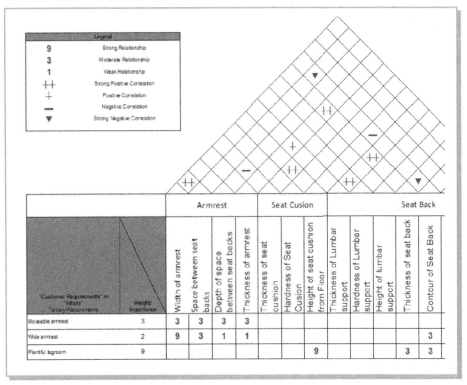

*Figure 9.15: Technical correlations*

While I do find this section of the HoQ interesting, I think that it does not add as much value as the other sections, and consider it an optional section when you are first getting started with your HoQ matrix.

The next section is the design score, and is one of the key outcomes of using the HoQ matrix. What we are really trying to do with the HoQ matrix is to understand the various inputs we have received from our customers, and then, with the assistance of our design team, attempt to ascertain the priority and impact of doing the various design efforts and how it will ultimately impact customer satisfaction. If done correctly, the design score should help you in creating that understanding.

To get our design score, we will need to multiply the customer importance rating times by the relationship matrix score for each of the design requirements. The formula would look like the following:

*Design score = Sum (Customer importance x relationship matrix score)*

Looking at the design requirement for width of armrest, we see in *Figure 9.16* that moveable armrest had a customer importance ranking of 3, and wide armrest had an importance of 2. Multiplying those scores with the relationship matrix scores shows that our formula would look like the following for the width of armrest design requirement:

*Design score = (3x3 + 2x9) = 27*

If we continue this process for all the other cells in our example, we would see the following if all we were evaluating was the passenger comfort requirement. In an actual case, you would need to add the other customer requirements and design requirements as well, but they have been omitted here for clarity and understanding:

| | | Armrest | | | | Seat Cushion | | | | | | Seat Back | | | | |
|---|---|---|---|---|---|---|---|---|---|---|---|---|---|---|---|---|
| "Customer Requirements" or "Whats"... | Weight/Importance | Width of armrest | Space between seat backs | Depth of space between seat backs | Thickness of armrest | Thickness of seat cushion | Hardness of Seat Cushion | Height of seat cushion from Floor | Thickness of Lumbar support | Hardness of Lumbar support | Height of lumbar | Thickness of seat back | Contour of Seat Back | Height of seat back | Height of lumbar support | Hardness of seat back |
| Movable armrest | 3 | 3 | 3 | 3 | 3 | | | | | | | | | | | |
| Wide armrest | 2 | 9 | 3 | 1 | 1 | | | | | | | 3 | | | | |
| Plentiful legroom | 9 | | | | | 1 | | 9 | | | | 3 | 3 | | | |
| Lumbar support for all body shapes | 3 | | | | | | 3 | | 9 | 9 | 9 | | 3 | 3 | 9 | |
| Knees do not hit seat in front | 5 | | | | | | | 1 | | | | 9 | 3 | | | 1 |
| Seats do not hit passenger behind | 5 | | | | | | | 1 | | 1 | | 9 | 3 | | | 1 |
| Seat back can be adjusted | 7 | | | | | | | | | | | | 1 | | | |
| Seat back adjustment will not slip | 3 | | | | | | | | | | | | | | | |
| **Design Absolute score** | | 27 | 15 | 11 | 11 | 9 | 9 | 81 | 37 | 27 | 32 | 117 | 79 | 9 | 27 | 10 |
| **Relative score** | | 5.4% | 3.0% | 2.2% | 2.2% | 1.8% | 1.8% | 16.2% | 7.4% | 5.4% | 6.4% | 23.4% | 15.8% | 1.8% | 5.4% | 2.0% |

*Figure 9.16: Design score*

In this scaled-back example, we can see that **Thickness of seat back** scored a 117 and represents 23.4% relative to everything else, making this the number one design requirement we must address to provide the most satisfaction to our customers. **Height of the seat cushion from floor** scored an 81, and even though we see that a number of other design requirements would actually address more customer requirements, **Plentiful legroom** was such an important customer requirement that solving this need is our second most important design consideration.

In addition to translating customer requirements into design requirements, I hope you will see how powerful a tool this is for your organization. Most companies have no problem gathering requirements from customers, and most if not all companies have more requirements than their engineering and design teams have time for. This tool has the advantage of aiding teams both in translating customer requirements into design requirements, and also an understanding of a method to prioritize those design requirements to provide as much customer satisfaction as possible, as quickly as possible, with the limited resources of the organization.

In addition to the outcome of creating a customer-driven product based on the VoC analysis you have created, QFD also offers the following benefits to the organization:

➤ **Competitive analysis**: Analyzing other products in the marketplace against the customer identified needs and develops an understanding of which areas we hold the lead and must maintain our advantage, areas we lag and must improve, and areas where we can gain a competitive advantage

➤ **Reduced development time**: The likelihood of design requirements changing late in the development process are greatly minimized, and the amount of time on insignificant features is minimized

➤ **Reduced development costs**: Minimizing changes late in the development process reduces development time as well as warranty and product support costs

➤ **Meeting market window**: By minimizing development time and changes made late in the game, we also have a much higher likelihood of getting the product to market in time to meet the market window

➤ **Documentation**: A knowledge base is built during the QFD process, and a record of decisions and justification is recorded

While it is beyond the scope of this text, it should also be noted that additional QFD attributes such as competitive technical benchmarking, establishing engineering targets, engineering characteristics importance, and degree of technical difficulty are all components that can be added to aid in your analysis. The QFD tool can also help you develop product strategies by identifying where your product excels. Also, there are three additional Houses of Quality that can be deployed within your organization that help identify specific action items a company can take, and which processes and control variables must be identified and deployed.

# Pricing

Once you have completed the QFD and you have agreed which design characteristics your product will have and when, you must begin the analysis of determining how to price your new offering. Setting the correct price for your offering is critical to a product developed through VoC. Set the price too high, and the sales team will have difficulty closing sales, your revenue targets will not be met, or the customers will not purchase your offering at all. Set the price too low, and you will leave margin behind, or even worse, operate at a loss. Price ends up being the number one factor that dictates whether your offering will succeed or fail in the marketplace. While this is not a book on pricing, it is my desire that you will begin to understand how customer VoC can drive pricing decisions, and as a result, you will incorporate *value* questions into your VoC research.

When setting price, you need to look for the best, or what could be considered the optimal price, to maximize your profitability. That does not mean that you are looking for the highest price possible to sell your offering. Neither does it mean that you should be evaluating your costs to build your product and then, using cost-based pricing, merely adding an arbitrary percentage above the cost to derive the price. Also, it does not mean analyzing what your competitor charges and matching their price, although that can be a valuable data point.

Unfortunately, this is often how marketers go about pricing their products. The following two illustrations show the most common pricing methods:

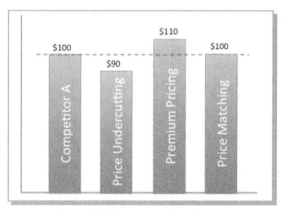

*Figure 9.17: Competition-based pricing*

In the first example, the price is derived from what the competitor(s) is (are) charging. One tactic would be to slightly undercut your competitor, particularly if they had a better market presence than you. In the other case, you might actually charge a slight premium if you have higher brand equity than your competitor. Or you might just match the competitor's price in an effort to be another alternative, without having to defend why you are charging more than the competition, or charging less and potentially leaving money on the table:

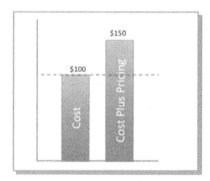

*Figure 9.18: Cost-based pricing*

In the second example, the price is set based on the cost to manufacture or deliver the product in what is known as cost-based pricing. In these cases, marketers analyze the cost of the product, and then add a fixed amount to meet the margin goals of the business or corporation.

While some might argue that the first approach may be considered market-based pricing as your pricing is determined by what the competitors are charging, neither of these examples can be regarded as value-based pricing.

Simply put, the most optimal pricing strategy is one based on value, and not purely competition or costs. Only by understanding the value your product brings to the customer can you truly price effectively. This is why a good customer VoC is so essential for the pricing process.

If you have done your VoC correctly, you probably have a pretty good idea of the pains that the customers have when using your competitor's or your products. You probably also understand the benefits that the products they are currently using provide to them. While you may not think to try and quantify value when you first put together your customer questionnaire, you will find that if you do, the pricing exercise becomes much, much easier.

When discussing value in the context of pricing, it is good to try and remember that there are two ways to look at value created or received. One is to look at it from the eyes of the company. From the company's perspective, there is internal value creation from the cost of the product to the selling price. Additional value is created, and is typically passed to the customer as shown in *Figure 9.19*.

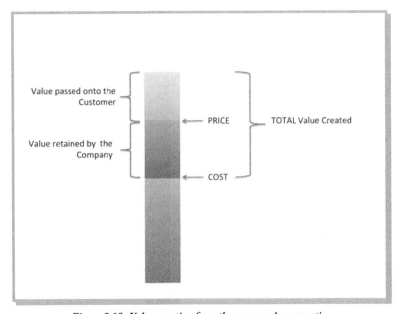

*Figure 9.19: Value creation from the company's perspective*

Of course, the customer rarely knows much, if anything, about your cost – they only see the price. So, their perspective about how much value is created is totally dependent on the amount of benefit they believe they will receive versus the price they will have to pay. As Warren Buffett once said, "*Price is what you pay. Value is what you get.*"

If their expected benefit falls anywhere below the price point, they will conclude that your product is *not worth it*. But once the value rises above the price point, they will deem that your product is clearly worth it, and could be considered a real bargain if that point is significantly above your price point:

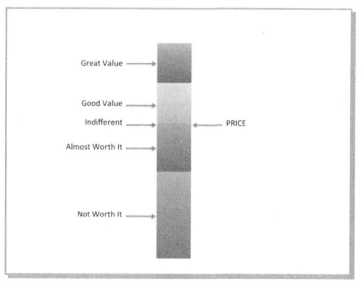

**Figure 9.20: Value creation from the customer perspective**

When looking to determine a pricing strategy based on value for your offering, it is also an important consideration to remember that the maximum price that you can charge for your product is the cost of the next best alternative, plus the incremental value your product or offering creates.

Looking at it on a formulaic basis:

*Maximum Price = Price of next best alternative + value your offering creates - value the next best alternative creates*

You can see that if you do not understand the value your offering creates and the value the competitive products create, you limit your ability to set a price that returns the maximum financial results to your organization. Of course, placing your product at the maximum price does not guarantee you will get the sale. It only ensures that you are priced at relative parity with your competition. If you wish to increase your chances over the competition, you need to determine both the maximum price as well as the optimum price.

Then the question becomes, "How do I set my optimum price?" To do so, you must have a much deeper understanding of the customer and what the customer values. If the customer values reducing installed cost of your type of product, you would need to know how much savings you can provide to the customer through reduction of procured price, as well as reduction in hours to install. As you can see, using the information we have gleaned in the VoC sessions can go far in helping us to set our optimum price and extract as much value (revenue) in return from the customer's engagement.

Your optimal price will maximize your revenue, while providing your customers with more "value" over the total life of the product. In essence, we need to understand both the value (the benefits your product brings) as well as the total cost of ownership for your product versus the rest of the market. To begin to gain insight into these areas, start by asking these questions:

> ➤ How differentiated is your offering?

> ➤ How sustainable is that differentiation?

> ➤ How much value does this differentiation deliver to customers?

> ➤ How would the customer describe the value your product brings? At a minimum, can they describe the value on the differentiation your product brings?

> ➤ How would they equate that value, or the value of the differentiation, to a monetary figure?

> ➤ What is the best pricing method to capture value (initial purchase price, price and maintenance, subscription, and many more)?

> ➤ What are your competitors likely to do relative to various price points? Will they try and undercut your price? Will they opt for premium pricing?

> ➤ Does the customer have the necessary capital available to purchase your offering?

> ➤ Do you have the ability to charge different price points to the differing market segments you serve?

You will probably not receive clear and consistent feedback from these questions that will drive you to an exact number. You will, however, develop more insights into the value of your product, and you can use this as well as the price of the competition and your costs to help drive to an optimal price.

Again, I would caution you against using cost-based pricing. In my experience, cost-based pricing leads to one of two things. Either you end up leaving money on the table that you did not need to, or you end up trying to compete in an industry where you do not have the cost structure or processes to be successful. In the first, you shortchange yourself. In the second, not enough customers buy your goods or services and you either exit the market, or you are pushed to fire-sale your products to meet the market price at a lower-than-optimal margin level. Better you know what the market price is before entering the market and investing your capital.

If you are able to set an optimum price for your products, you are better able to arm your sales team with the necessary sales collateral and differentiation story, so as to prove the incremental value to your customers and extract maximum revenue.

I believe it is often helpful to try and plot a number of the various considerations that go into your pricing analysis into a simple chart. Following is such a chart I have used in the past to help me visualize where various pricing levels would place my product with respect to customer value, gross margin targets, competition, and many more.

In *Figure 9.21* you can see I have plotted my current products price, a number of competitive products and their prices, the "value" price I could set based on my customer feedback for differing functionality, and the price for a customer to use a substitute product that is not a direct competitive product. The substitute product might even be a product you provide that the customer is attempting to force into his current application (see *Chapter 3, Laying the Groundwork* for a discussion on substitute products), as well as margin % and margin $ at the various pricing points. While it is not advisable to use cost-plus pricing, it is imperative you understand your **Margin $** and **Margin %** for your proposed product and pricing levels before you engage with your senior management:

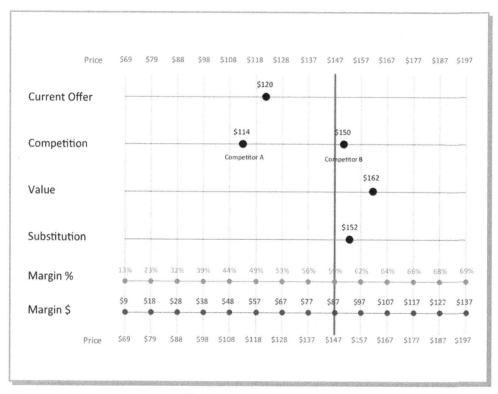

***Figure 9.21: Pricing analysis***

In the example shown in *Figure 9.21*, you will see that I have plotted a current product we are selling at $120 plus two competitive offerings as well as a substitute product, which has a higher price than the current products in the market. Based on the VoC we have done, we determined that the new product we will release provides $162 worth of benefits to our customers. In this example, if I were to choose a price for our new offering, I might select a price of $147. This would allow me to pass on $15 of incremental value to the customer ($162 - $147), while slightly undercutting competitor B. As a double-check, I can also see that this pricing level would deliver a 59% gross margin and $87 margin to the business for every unit sold. If this meets the internal hurdles for a new product, this may be a good price for our new product.

# Articulating the value

In the previous section, we talked about how value is a main component in our pricing analysis. In this section, we will also discuss how one can take the value that we have built into our product and communicate it to the rest of the customer base to help us market and sell our product.

Unfortunately, according to a Forrester study, only 15% of sales people are able to articulate their offerings in terms of solving a problem for their customers. This is very disappointing when one realizes that customers do not buy products, they buy outcomes. If they do not understand the value your product offers in solving their problem, the chances they will buy your product are very slim indeed.

Today's customers have access to more information than ever before about your goods and services. No longer can the salesperson simply expect to set an appointment and then "show up and throw up" with an expectation that a certain percentage of customers will buy their product. In today's world, you will be lucky to even get an appointment with a customer who does not understand the potential value your offering can provide. To stand out from the competition, your sales team needs to be able to communicate the business value of your products and services at every customer touchpoint.

Developing a value proposition for your new product can be very simple or very complex. Much is dependent on how well you have determined the needs of your customers and segments through your VoC interviews. While a complex value proposition may be beyond the level of this text, I have found the following method to be very useful in articulating your value to your targeted segments.

First, one must understand that features or benefits do not mean the same thing as value. Features are characteristics that your product does or has. As an example, having proximity sensors in your car is a feature. Benefits are how the features in a product can help improve your life or work. In our example, the benefit of having proximity sensors is that you can avoid having a minor accident or scrape. The value is the economic benefit or consequences to the user of the product. In our case, the proximity sensor value is the savings of the potential repair costs to your car by avoiding brushing a parked car in a parking lot. You can see how one feeds the other. Having the feature allows a customer to enjoy the benefit that drives the economic consequences of having the feature.

When we discuss value, we must keep in mind that value exists in the context of the competition even if the competition is for the customer to do "nothing." We must also be careful not to confuse value with the price. Certainly, understanding customer value is what should drive our pricing discussion, but value is ultimately defined by the user and is their incentive of whether to buy or not.

Based on this, it is helpful to understand what makes up value in the customer's eyes. One must understand the following three key points:

- ➤ Value is customer-specific
- ➤ Value is ultimately measured in currency
- ➤ Value is relative to the next best alternative

Looking at our definition, you can see that value certainly can be derived from product features, but to truly realize the value your product brings you should try and understand the total lifetime value of your product and look beyond the features that are on the product brochure. To define value, look at things such as benefits to the customer, process improvements, new capabilities your product brings to the user, cost avoidance and savings the customer can enjoy by having your product, additional services provided, risks that are reduced, and many more.

Once you have an understanding of these items, it is often beneficial to put your value into a statement that helps your customers and your company understand the value you deliver. To do this, you will need to have a clear definition of the following:

➤ Who are the target customers?

➤ What products or services are we offering?

➤ What is the perceived customer benefit?

➤ What is the perceived customer value?

➤ What are we planning to charge?

➤ What and who are the competitors, and what are our sources of differentiation?

➤ What are the barriers to a customer purchasing our product?

Having these things at hand, once can create a *value proposition* that is beneficial both for the company to understand how a product is positioned, but also to help drive sales and marketing material that will help the customer understand your value, and therefore create more sales.

A value proposition can be thought of as a specific promise to a targeted segment or customer of the unique value we offer at a specific price, as shown in *Figure 9.22*.

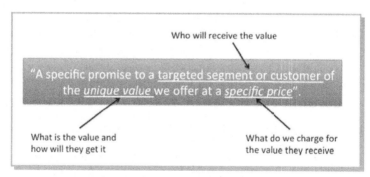

*Figure 9.22: Value proposition definition*

A good value proposition should have the following elements:

➤ Addresses the full spectrum of customers' needs in a priority-driven way.

 **Make a note**
These needs are *not* product features.

➤ How your product or service solves/improves problems.

➤ What benefits customers can expect.

➤ Provides a clear method for the customer to distinguish your offering from the competition.

➤ Must be tailored to each offering and adapted to the specific customer, segment, competitive situation, and individual circumstances. Value propositions are rarely one-size-fits-all scenarios.

➤ Gives the customer a clear idea of the price they are paying for the value and benefit they will receive, and the belief of the customer that the value will exceed the cost paid.

While it will not work for every circumstance, I find the following value proposition formula in *Figure 9.23* helpful to begin the process of forcing oneself to articulate a value proposition that will resonate with the customer. While this is a good way to frame your value proposition initially, often a value proposition can be reduced down to something shorter that resonates more clearly with the customer. However, I believe you have a much higher probability of getting to that point if you understand all the elements shown in the value proposition formula in *Figure 9.23*:

For _____ (target customer or segment)...
that require_____(the problem we solve)...
(Your company's name)_____(the product or service)...
provides_____ (quantified benefit or benefits)...
unlike_____(the next best alternative offering).
We do this by _____(how we do it)...
as demonstrated by_____(proof points).

*Figure 9.23: Value proposition formula*

To give you an idea of how this would look once it is completed, I have assumed the role of Apple and filled out a value proposition that they might have constructed, if they'd done this exercise:

For: Graphic Designers

That require: Running multiple memory intensive applications concurrently

Apple's: MacBook Pro

Provides: a multitasking environment

Unlike: conventional laptops

We do this by : Multi-threaded processing and quad core processors

As demonstrated by: Customer testimonials, PC Week benchmark test, cpubenchmark.net benchmark test

*Figure 9.24: Hypothetical value proposition for Apple MacBook Pro*

As a way to close the value discussion, I think it is always important to realize that one must quantify value if you are to capture value. Use the following guidelines to help yourself quantify value in your customer engagements:

Value is:

- Customer or segment specific
- Measured in currency
- Always relative to the next best alternative

To create value for your customer you must:

- Help them increase their revenue, or
- Help them reduce their costs, or
- Help them improve their processes, or
- Help them realize some other financial benefit

To quantify value you must know the following:

- The customers current baseline
- The next best alternative the customer has available
- The maximum they are willing to pay for the benefit received

*Figure 9.25: Quantifying customer value*

# Summary

In this chapter, we were focused on a process to take the input we had received from our customers and turn them into successful products and launches. First, we started by discussing the various types of requirements we may have uncovered during our VoC process, and learned how to write them into a meaningful document to be delivered to the engineering team. As part of this, we discussed functional versus non-functional requirements, as well as delved into detail on what kind of characteristics our requirements should have. From there, we discussed the origins of QFD, the elements of QFD, and went through a detailed exercise on how an airplane seat manufacturer might use QFD to prioritize the most important customer requirements, design requirements that will fulfill those customer requirements, the competitive landscape, and a design score that tells us which design requirements will yield the highest level of customer satisfaction.

Once the design specification was set, we turned our attention to marketing the new products. We discussed the various types of pricing, explored how value is such an integral part of pricing, and how the value quantification must become part of your VoC process. Leveraging the pricing and value discussion, we also explored ways to create a value proposition so we could bring the customer requirements full circle and explain to the market the value we have built into our product based on the feedback we received from them.

# > Epilogue

It is my hope that, as a result of reading this book, you will have gained a better understanding of VoC and how you can use the various tools and methods I've outlined to drive innovation and product success. By now, you should have a good understanding of your current position in the market and the various ways to get customer input. Hopefully, you've also developed the knowledge of how to create a culture of VoC in your organization, select customers to interview, create the interview team, conduct the interviews, and process the input you've received. With this, you should have the knowledge to develop the necessary internal documents to share with your development team to create the next great product breakthrough.

While the information presented in these chapters outlines many tools and processes that you can deploy to help your product innovation, the underlying message with all the areas discussed in the book begins with the customer. Without the customer, and your understanding of their needs, you will never have a successful product, no matter how great you believe your product is.

I hope you have enjoyed this book. If you would like additional information and access to some of the tools and spreadsheets I've used in this book, visit www.5pmarketing.com and select downloads from the top-level menu. You can also use this site to contact me should you have a need for consulting services or require VoC training for yourself or your organization.

Enjoy your journey in learning more about your customers' needs and creating great products!

Made in the USA
Middletown, DE
17 November 2021